Lear

Why are some people aggressive and others gentle? Why are some groups of people aggressive toward other groups but never toward members of their own group? Why are aggression and violence totally nonexistent in some cultures?

The answer lies primarily in child-rearing, particularly in the treatment of infants, according to these essays by E. Richard Sorenson, Patricia Draper, Jean L. Briggs, Robert Knox Dentan, Catherine H. Berndt, Robert I. Levy, and Colin M. Turnbull. Whether describing the !Kung of the Kalahari Desert, the Inuit of the Canadian Arctic, the Fore of New Guinea, the Semai of Malaysia, or the aborigines of Australia, the articles reinforce a central theme: that non-aggression rests on a foundation of loving maternal care. In each non-aggressive society, infants' basic needs are continuously satisfied without obstacle, and young children learn without punishment to cope with angers, fears, and hostilities.

The view that man is innately a violent and aggressive animal has gained wide attention in recent years through the controversial writings of Konrad Lorenz, Robert Ardrey, Desmond Morris, and others. In *Learning Non-Aggression,* Montagu and his contributors give us strong evidence "that the peaceful component in human nature is as strong as the aggressive impulses and that it only awaits the proper set of cultural conditions to flower into a way of life for people everywhere."—Marvin Harris, Columbia University.

"Qualified experts spell out, interestingly and usefully, how non-aggression is *culturally taught* in seven nonliterate societies. An authoritative work."—Weston LaBarre, James B. Duke Professor of Anthropology Emeritus, Duke University.

Ashley Montagu is the author of more than forty books and editor of eighteen others, including *Man's Most Dangerous Myth: The Fallacy of Race* (GB 414), *Man and Aggression* (GB 250), *The Natural Superiority of Women, Race and IQ* (GB 425), and *The Nature of Human Aggression* (GB 535).

The jacket design was inspired by Colin Turnbull's evocative essay demonstrating the effect of gentle child-rearing on adult non-aggressive behavior (pp. 164-166).

Learning Non-Aggression

LEARNING
NON-AGGRESSION

The Experience of Non-Literate Societies

EDITED BY

Ashley Montagu

OXFORD UNIVERSITY PRESS
Oxford　　London　　New York

OXFORD UNIVERSITY PRESS
Oxford London Glasgow
New York Toronto Melbourne Wellington
Ibadan Nairobi Dar es Salaam Cape Town
Kuala Lumpur Singapore Jakarta Hong Kong Tokyo
Delhi Bombay Calcutta Madras Karachi

Copyright © 1978 by Ashley Montagu

First published by Oxford University Press, New York, 1978

First issued as an Oxford University Press paperback, 1978

Library of Congress Cataloging in Publication Data:
Main entry under title:

Learning non-aggression.

  Bibliography: p.
  1. Aggressiveness (Psychology) 2. Personality and
culture. 3. Ethnopsychology. I. Montagu, Ashley,
1905-
BF575.A3L4   301.6'4   77-11675
ISBN 0-19-502342-0
ISBN 0-19-502343-9 pbk.

Printed in the United States of America

Contributors

Catherine H. Berndt
UNIVERSITY OF WESTERN AUSTRALIA

Jean L. Briggs
MEMORIAL UNIVERSITY OF NEWFOUNDLAND

Robert Knox Dentan
STATE UNIVERSITY OF NEW YORK AT BUFFALO

Patricia Draper
UNIVERSITY OF NEW MEXICO

Robert I. Levy
UNIVERSITY OF CALIFORNIA AT SAN DIEGO

Ashley Montagu
PRINCETON, NEW JERSEY

E. Richard Sorenson
SMITHSONIAN INSTITUTION

Colin M. Turnbull
GEORGE WASHINGTON UNIVERSITY

Dedicated to the Memory

of

Frank Speck

**PROFESSOR OF ANTHROPOLOGY
AT THE UNIVERSITY OF PENNSYLVANIA**

Contents

Learning Non-Aggression

Introduction

Much has been said and written about aggression, but very little about non-aggression or gentleness. What little has been said on the subject has seldom been based on the findings of research, except for a few studies by psychologists and anthropologists working in the field. In recent years a number of writers have revived the argument that humans are universally aggressive, that they are, indeed, instinctively so. Their argument has elicited a considerable amount of interest and support from the reading public, and also from a number of scientists. It has also evoked a good deal of criticism from many students of animal and human behavior.

Since the "innate aggressionists," as I have called those who, like Konrad Lorenz, Niko Tinbergen, Robert Ardrey, Desmond Morris, Anthony Storr, and others,[1] consider aggression to be universal and innate, they write as if all human societies conform to the view they have imposed upon them, that is to say, that all human societies are aggressive. This simply happens to be untrue.

Many human societies cannot be characterized as aggressive. And there are many individuals in aggressive societies who are unaggressive and opposed to any form of aggressive behavior. Many societies that appear to be aggressive are, in fact, composed of individuals who for the most part are not usually aggressive. Most people in civilized societies get involved in wars not because they feel aggressive toward the socially defined "enemy," but because their leaders—who themselves are seldom motivated by aggressive feelings—consider it necessary to make war. Such considerations have nothing whatever to do with feelings, universals or instincts, but usually mainly with political constraints.

When reference is made to aggressive societies we have to be quite clear whether the reference is to intragroup or intergroup aggression. There are societies in which intergroup aggression is high but in which intragroup aggression is low, as among a number of New Guinea peoples.[2] There are some societies in which aggression is high both within the group and between groups, as among the Yanomamö.[3] There are societies in which both inter- and intragroup aggression is low, as among the Toda of Southern India,[4] and there are some societies in which both inter- and intragroup aggression are nonexistent, as among the Tasaday of Mindanao, in the Philippines.[5]

In view of all the talk about aggressive societies it seemed worthwhile to attempt to discover what light, if any, could be thrown upon those factors that make some societies more or less unaggressive as compared with others. Toward that end I have invited a number of anthropologists, all of whom have worked in the field, to discuss their findings relating to aggression and non-aggression in the nonliterate societies with which they are familiar.

I had hoped to include a discussion of the Tasaday. Unfortunately, all attempts to elicit some response to my invitation to contribute to this volume from those having an intimate knowledge of this fascinating group have met with failure. It is a pity, because the Tasaday are probably the most unaggressive people in the world. Also, up to the time of their discovery in 1966 by a Philippine hunter, the Tasaday were an exclusively foodgathering people. Dafal, their discoverer, taught them how to make some simple implements and to hunt small animals. The total population consisted of twenty-six individuals, of whom thirteen were children. The first whites began to visit them in 1971, and all who have come to know them have agreed that they are a most unaggressive loving people. John Nance, a journalist, who spent some seventy-three days over a period of three years, visiting with them, found the Tasaday to be "inspiring emblems of social peace and harmony, of, simply, love." "Their love," he writes, "was everywhere—for each other, for their forest, for us—for life." "They are altogether a loving people. They have no weapons, and no apparent aggressive impulses."[6]

Nevertheless, Nance found that "the children showed the egoism one might expect—arguing over a stick, crying for food, slapping at one another." Dr. Irenäus Eibl-Eibesfeldt, who briefly visited the Tasaday, remarked to Nance that he had observed "classic" aggressive behavior between toddlers—striking at one another or pretending to, tugging at the ends of a stick. The key question, therefore, for Nance was how the Tasaday managed aggression in their children so that they grew to be loving adults.[7]

The answer would appear to be that from an early age the Tasaday reward cooperative behavior and discourage aggressive conduct, while setting models in themselves for their children to imitate.

There are many societies that are notable for their unaggressiveness, among them are the Punan of Borneo, the Hadza of Tanzania, the Birhor of Southern India, the Todas of Southern India, the Veddahs of Ceylon, the Arapesh of New Guinea, the Australian aborigines, the Yamis of Orchid Island off Taiwan, the Semai of Malaya, the Tikopia of the Western Pacific, the Land Dayaks of Sarawak, the Lepchas of Sikkim, the Papago Indians, the Hopi, the Zuni, and the Pueblo peoples generally, the Tahitians, and the Ifaluk of the Pacific.

There are few societies in which some form of aggressive behavior, however slight, does not occur. The range of variation is striking, all the way from the wholly unaggressive Tasaday to the highly violent societies of the civilized world. The variability and absence of stereotypy suggest that violent behavior is largely learned. How else can one account for the marked differences in the expression of violence? The resort to instinct or genes will not bear critical examination.[8] The "nothing but" reductionism of the extreme hereditarians or the extreme environmentalists leads to nothing but a quagmire of confusion. The development of aggressive behavior in both animals and humans depends, during each phase of development, on the complex interaction between genes and environment, with social experience playing a crucial role.[9]

The evidence suggests that as a consequence of natural selection in the unique environments in which humans have spent the greater part of their evolutionary history they became polymorphously educable. Human beings can learn virtually anything. Among other things, they can learn to be virtually wholly unaggressive. The human genetic constitution is in no way to be regarded as the equivalent of the theological doctrine of predestination. Whatever humanity's potentialities for aggression may be, and we know that such potentialities exist, it is clear that their expression will largely depend upon the environmental stimulation they receive. If this is so, then there is every reason for optimism, for if we understand the conditions that produce aggressive behavior, there is some hope that by changing those conditions we may be able to control both its development and expression.

Individually and together the present group of studies make an original and important contribution to our understanding of the nature of the conditions that produce aggression in different societies, and how the expression of aggression may be controlled. The facts must be distinguished from the theories. In this book we are concerned with the facts, facts which hold a special interest for us, not only because they throw light on the validity of the theories, but also because they provide insights from which we, in the Western world, could learn much that would be to our advantage.

In discussions of aggression it is quite frequently the case that the term is never defined. It is taken for granted that everyone knows what aggression is. The fact is that there are so many different kinds of behavior that are called aggression it is always necessary to state unambiguously what kind of aggression one has in mind.[10] In the contributions to this volume reference is made to many different kinds of aggression. These may be resumed, rather than defined, under a general rubric, as behavior designed to inflict pain or injury on others. The "pain" or "injury" may be no more than the snatching of a stick or toy away from another or involve the infliction of bodily harm. Aggressivity, even if it is limited to no more than a feeling, is probably something that most human beings have experienced and expressed.

The question that interests us in this volume is how it comes about that some societies are so little aggressive compared with others? What are the conditions that make for aggressiveness both in the individual and in the society? How do some societies manage to control the expression of aggression? And, finally, under what conditions do the individuals in non-aggressive societies tend to become aggressive? Some answers to these questions will be found in the following pages.

Years ago Margaret Mead was the first anthropologist to inquire into the origins of aggressiveness in nonliterate societies. In her book, *Sex and Temperament in Three Primitive Societies,*[11] she pointed to the existence of a strong association between child-rearing practices and later personality development. The child who received a great deal of attention, whose every need was promptly met, as among the New Guinea Mountain Arapesh, became a gentle, cooperative, unaggressive adult. On the other hand, the child who received perfunctory, intermittent attention, as among the New Guinea Mundugomor, became a selfish, uncooperative, aggressive adult.

Later research among nonliterate and civilized peoples has substantially confirmed this relationship, and so do the studies presented in this volume.

Today we know that by far the larger proportion of child-batterers were themselves battered or neglected as children.[12] We know that those who have been emotionally deprived are likely to turn into aggressive adults. And we also know that those who have been adequately loved as children are likely to develop into loving, unaggressive adults.[13]

It would appear that while the potentialities for aggression exist in all human beings at birth, such potentialities will remain nothing more unless they are organized by experience to function as aggressive behavior. This is especially brought out in Dr. Sorenson's contribution on the New Guinea Fore.[14] Aggressive behavior is no more innately determined than is the behavior we call speech. Without innate potentialities for speech we would be unable to speak, no matter how rich the environment were in speech. Without an environment of speech we would not learn to speak,[15] for while the innate potentialities are there, we must be spoken to and live in an environment of speech if we are ever to speak. Humans are clearly, as I have said, polymorphously educable, capable of learning whatever it is possible to learn. This does not mean that they are born Lockean *tabulae rasae,* blank tablets upon which the environment inscribes its instructions for the development of behavior.

What the evidence indicates is that there are no fixed action patterns, no "instincts," that determine either the spontaneous appearance of aggression or its triggering by a particular stimulus. What may appear to be "triggered," "automatic," "fixed," or a "stereotyped" reaction to a stimulus may, in fact, be something quite different. Elements of learning may enter into the conditions that produce the behavior, which can only be discovered when we look for them. In practice this would mean the avoidance of those situations in the life of a child that would tend to produce aggressive behavior; and when such situations do occur perceiving the resulting behavior, not as we customarily do in the Western world, but as an example of exploratory physical play with sensual satisfaction accruing to the players, as among the Fore. Among them such behavior was always allowed to follow its natural course and rarely resulted in squabbles or fights. As Dr. Sorenson shows, aggression among the Fore is not met with counter-aggression, but with playfulness and laughter, in the fun of which the "aggressor" quickly joins.

One of the ways the individual often deals with situations that threaten to explode in anger or violence is simply to walk away from them. In some cases this may mean joining another band until things have resolved themselves. The Tasaday, who have no other band to join, simply take a walk. It has been suggested that the scolding, complaining, bickering, and speechifying that go on in Bushman society may be a means of keeping aggression down to tolerable levels. A similar suggestion has been made in connection with the same behavior among the Pygmies of the Ituri Forest of Central Africa, whose spouse-beating, squabbling, noise-making, may serve to keep the expression of aggressive behavior under control.

Such suggestions grow out of the popular "letting off steam" conception of human aggression. This is known as the hydraulic energy model because it likens aggression to the rising pressure of steam within a boiler. The way to prevent the steam from rising till it bursts the boiler is to let some of it out through relief valves, which will serve to keep the pressure down and under control.

The only trouble with this pretty model of aggressive "energy" is that it has no counterpart in the nervous system of any known organism. Energy models suffer from the defect that they tend to be identified with physical energies that are directed toward discharge in physical action, thus allegedly "reducing" the "pressure" and bringing the behavior to an end. Such models overlook the fact that it is usually through change in the stimulus situation that the behavior is brought to an end.[16]

The evidence we have overwhelmingly shows that the expression contributes not to its reduction but to its reinforcement.[17] Konrad Lorenz and the other innate aggressionists only serve to confuse the issue when they assert that "in prehistoric times intraspecific selection bred into man a measure of aggression for which in the social order of today he finds no adequate outlet."[18] Neither individuals nor societies require "outlets" for aggressive behavior.

From the evidence supplied by most nonliterate cultures it is quite clear that they not only intensely dislike but also very much fear the expression of violence, and are usually grateful to those who put an end to the threat of it. Far from seeking "outlets" for violence, the violence itself is often a calmly reasoned behavior rather than an emotional expression, designed to bring it to an end as soon as possible. It is the show of violence rather than the violence itself which, on such occasions, most matters, in much the sense implied in the ancient injunction, "Who desires peace, let him make ready for war."[19] The joy with which many nonliterate peoples have readily abandoned fighting, raiding, and warfare constitutes powerful evidence against the claim that aggression is enjoyed for its own sake.

As the contributions to this volume show, whatever genetic potentialities we may have for aggressive behavior, early conditioning in cooperative behavior and the discouragement of anything resembling aggressive behavior serve to make an individual, and a society, essentially unaggressive and cooperative. That being so, the lesson, I think, is clear.

NOTES

1. Konrad Lorenz, *On Aggression*. New York: Harcourt, Brace & World, 1966; Niko Tinbergen, "On War and Peace in Animals and Man," *Science, 160* (1968):1411–18; Robert Ardrey, *African Genesis*. New York: Atheneum, 1961; Robert Ardrey, *The Territorial Imperative*. New York: Atheneum, 1966; Robert Ardrey, *The Social Contract*. New York: Atheneum, 1970; Robert Ardrey, *The Hunting Hypothesis*. New York: Atheneum, 1976; Desmond Morris, *The Naked Ape*. New York: McGraw-Hill, 1967; Desmond Morris, *The Human Zoo*. New York: McGraw-Hill, 1969; Anthony Storr, *Human Aggression*. New York: Atheneum, 1968; Anthony Storr, *Human Destructiveness*. New York: Basic Books, 1972.
2. Ronald M. Berndt, *Excess and Restraint*. Chicago: University of Chicago Press, 1962.
3. Napoleon A. Chagnon, *Yanomamö: The Fierce People*. New York: Holt, Rinehart & Winston, 1968.
4. W. H. R. Rivers, *The Todas*. London: Macmillan, 1906.
5. John Nance, *The Gentle Tasaday*. New York: Harcourt Brace Jovanovich, 1975; Carlos A. Fernandez II and Frank Lynch, "The Tasaday: Cave-Dwelling Food Gatherers of South Cotabato, Mindanao," *Philippine Sociological Review, 20* (1972):275–330.
6. Nance, op. cit. p. 447.
7. Nance, op. cit. p. 118.
8. Ashley Montagu, *The Nature of Human Aggression*. New York: Oxford University Press, 1976.
9. Robert A. Hinde, *Biological Bases of Human Social Behavior*. New York: McGraw-Hill, 1974, pp. 249–52.
10. Montagu, op. cit. pp. 14–15.
11. Margaret Mead, *Sex and Temperament in Three Primitive Societies*. New York: Morrow, 1935.
12. C. H. Kempe and R. Helfer, *The Battered Child*. Chicago: University of Chicago Press, 1968.
13. Ashley Montagu, ed., *Culture and Human Development*. Englewood Cliffs, N.J.: Prentice-Hall, 1975; Ashley Montagu, *The Direction of Human Development*, rev. ed. New York: Hawthorn Books, 1970.
14. E. Richard Sorenson, *The Edge of the Forest: Land, Childhood and*

Change in New Guinea. Washington, D.C.: Smithsonian Institution Press, 1976.

15. For illustrative case histories see Ashley Montagu, *The Direction of Human Development.*

16. R. A. Hinde, "Energy Models of Motivation," *Symposia of the Society for Experimental Biology,* 14 (1960):119–230.

17. Leonard Berkowitz, *Aggression: A Social Psychological Analysis.* New York: McGraw-Hill, 1962; Albert Bandura, *Aggression: A Social Learning Analysis.* Englewood Cliffs, N.J.: Prentice-Hall, 1973.

18. Konrad Lorenz, *On Aggression.* New York: Harcourt, Brace & World, 1966, p. 244.

19. Vegetius, *Epitoma Rei Militari,* 385, 3, Prologue.

E. RICHARD SORENSON

Cooperation and Freedom among the Fore
of New Guinea

*A Non-Aggressive Expression of Human Adaptation
Which Altered as Settled Agriculture Emerged*

Somewhat over a decade ago I, like many others, began to think
about the suggestion, then in vogue, that aggression was a very
basic attribute of humankind—something built inextricably into
human character. The argument went that for a great preponderance of the time human beings have occupied the earth they have
been hunter-gatherers. This was said to have evolutionarily anchored aggressive attributes in our species because of the value of
such traits in the hunt. It was also argued by some that aggressiveness was a requirement for survival in still another sense: because it
aided defense of "territory."

Then I had a chance to view some of John Marshall's extensive
film record of the daily life activities of the Kalahari Desert Bushmen, one of the last hunting-gathering cultures on earth. What I
saw was not a fierce and aggressive people. Better descriptions
would be gentle, hospitable, generous, and cooperative. Recently
Marshall has called their way of life a "gentle crucible."[1] About
this same time a reading of Colin Turnbull's *The Forest People*
also made me wonder whether aggressive maintenance of territory
was the only workable way adaptively to manage living space.[2]

These observations occurred before I first went to New Guinea
to work among the South Fore people;[3] but I did not give them

much thought as I departed, for I had heard that the New Guinea Highlanders were a rather fierce and combative people. Such people, I thought, would not shed much light on the question of alternatives to aggressive life style.

Upon arrival in the Highlands I took up residence in two South Fore villages and traveled widely through the territory. I quickly discovered that the Fore were not so formidable as I had been led to believe. Indeed, even at first, they seemed less aggressive, less competitive, and less contentious than people in my own culture. I recognized that my view might have been influenced by the hospitable reception they gave me and their obvious interest in the way of life I represented. Still, I was impressed by their independent cheerfulness, and eventually I came to see how remarkably in tune with one another they really were in their traditional shifting hamlets.

The Fore were hunter-*gardeners,* having already moved away from the hunting-gathering way of life. I was puzzled at first by what appeared to be a high degree of individual freedom blending with and supporting a close cooperative rapport. We Westerners, with our own culturally influenced patterns of thought and language, usually think of these as somewhat antithetical traits. Among the Fore they reinforced, not diminished, each other. This raised epistemological questions having to do with using the language of one culture as the means of inquiring into another. So I began to rely on film as a tool for gathering data on behavior patterns. The note pad was not sufficient.

The cannibalism of which I had been told turned out to be familial: the Fore only ate their dead close relatives out of love and respect, not fierceness. Sorcery tended to crop up to the north where the traditional pioneer life was giving way to a more settled and circumscribed gardening existence. It was emerging as a means of defending one's "turf" without having to be directly aggressive. In these same regions of increasing land pressure, intervillage "warfare" had also begun to emerge; but it was episodic, disorganized, and disliked. Even in the most congested regions the Fore tended to avoid conflict when possible, often by moving.

This "northern" way of life was in contrast to the regions in the south where the basic pioneer conditions still persisted. In these isolated regions newcomers were more welcome, conflict was uncommon, and a rather general social harmony prevailed.

It took a while before I became aware that the way of life I had stumbled into could be distinguished from better known types of swiddening society by 1) the socioecological conditions governing it and 2) the digressive explorative human organization it produced. Not simply shifting cultivators moving about within a general home territory, the pioneer Fore followed the retreating edge of virgin forest lands, continually diverging and expanding into a vast untapped region. They searched out new garden sites, tilled them while they lasted, and then searched anew. Diverging ever away from lands peopled and used, they had a self-contained life with its own special ways. Their distinct type of human organization was based on exploratory freedom, a personalized cooperative rapport, and open frontiers.

The same basic ecological and demographic conditions underlying this way of life would also have encompassed the world broadly before agriculture set its dominant imprint: they are the conditions which would precede the conversion of wild lands to regions of agriculture—thus the name, protoagricultural. It was a way of life which could remain stable as long as its ecological and demographic prerequisites persisted. In this respect the Fore region and its surroundings proved a setting in which some aspects of the early shift to agriculture in the world could be studied. Furthermore, the protoagricultural beginnings were giving way to more settled agricultural practice in some regions, so what also presented itself was a kind of transformation which may have occurred extensively during the emergence of settled agricultural practice on our planet.

The Fore protoagricultural communities were quite different from anything I had previously encountered. There were no chiefs, patriarchs, priests, medicine men, or the like. Moving about at will and being with whom they liked, even the very young enjoyed a striking personal freedom. Women were less mobile than men, being tied in by marriage agreements; but even they could always return to their home regions when things weren't going well.

Infants rarely cried, and they played confidently with knives, axes, and fire. Older children typically enjoyed deferring to the interests and desires of the younger; sibling rivalry was virtually undetectable. A responsive "sixth sense" seemed to attune the hamlet mates to each other's interests and needs. They were not likely to directly ask, inveigle, bargain, or speak out for what they needed or wanted. More often subtle, even fleeting expressions of interest, desire, and discomfort were quickly read and helpfully acted on by one's associates. A spontaneous urge to share food, affection, work, trust, and pleasure characterized the daily life. Aggression and conflict within communities was unusual and the subject of considerable comment when it occurred. Sense of tribe, family, or homeland was vague; there were no permanent residential or gardening sites and no traditional lands. It was an open, freely shifting life in which one typically moved with those with whom he got along well. Group segmentation to follow new opportunity was the standard practice and accepted as natural. I was impressed by how quickly novel ideas and practices entered into these groups. Ways of speaking, ways of counting, and even basic beliefs were open to rapid modification.

This basic protoagricultural situation had begun to change to the north and west. There population density had increased, and ecological change had reduced the availability of easily gardenable new land. Fighting had begun to break out, and community organization was becoming more tightly defined. Far to the west, in the Baliem Valley, the "Gardens of War"[4] of the Dani seemed to represent one extreme in this socioecological development; the "gardens of opportunity" of the Fore were the other. Obviously to shift from one to the other entailed alteration of temperament and life style.

To a degree we may examine this alteration by examining the Fore. Previously hunting-gathering, now protoagricultural, some moving toward settled agriculture, the Fore gardened, hunted, and gathered. Like hunter-gatherers they sought sustenance across an extended range, first in one locale and then in another, following opportunities provided by a providential nature. But, as horticulturalists, they concentrated effort and attention more narrowly on selected sites of production, on their shifting gardens. They were both seekers and producers. A pioneer people in a pioneer land, they ranged freely into a vast territory, but they had begun to plant to live.

Horticultural needs focus human interest and daily life in one way, hunting-gathering in another. Relying on horticulture necessitates a new pattern of human organization. A gardener does not search for his food across an extended range; he concentrates effort and attention on manipulating small, selected sites of food production. Territorial focus becomes narrower, and economic behavior is altered accordingly. Social behavior is exercised in a daily arena with different requirements.

Eventually, however, the protoagricultural innovation spawns population growth and can alter the ecology. Once "limitless" lands begin to fill up, their virgin richness is depleted. The ecological and demographic conditions which permitted the protoagricultural development erode. A new stage is set—one requiring a more acute sense of "territory." Land opportunities become circumscribed. Agriculture has to settle, and the settled lands have to be defended.

For a way of life to persist it must include practices by which its patterns of adaptation can be passed on to each new generation. Using motion picture film and a research film method I worked out, I sampled daily life behavior of growing children and then isolated and studied the patterns of behavior in relation to the protoagricultural way of life. Capturing data unnoticed and unanticipated at the time of filming, the research film records made it possible to discover culturally specific patterns of behavior by repeated reexamination at different times, at different speeds, and under different circumstances. Unlike the written word, the visual data provided by the films made it possible to discover and isolate subtle patterns and fleeting nuances of manner, mood, and human relation, and it made it possible to assemble similar kinds of events to more easily search for common features.

The core discovery was that young infants remained in almost continual bodily contact with their mother, her housemates, or her gardening associates. At first, mothers' laps were the center of activity, and infants occupied themselves there by nursing, sleeping, and playing with their own bodies or those of their caretakers.

They were not put aside for the sake of other activities, as when food was being prepared or heavy loads were being carried. Remaining in close, uninterrupted physical contact with those around them, their basic needs, such as rest, nourishment, stimulation, and security, were continuously satisfied without obstacle (Fig. 1).

An ever available possibility of exchanging meaning through touch was open to all Fore babies; even before they could talk, they were communicating needs, desires, and feelings to a number of responsive caretakers by touch and physical movement. This constant "language" of contact readily facilitated satisfaction of the infant's needs and desires and made the harsher devices of rule and regimen unnecessary. Infant frustration and disruptive protest, traits common in Western culture, were rarely seen. Fore mothers dealt with breast biting and other types of "accidental" aggression through distraction by affection, a possibility which seemed to stem from close physical attunement.

Responding actively to pervasive (but not coercive) tactile interplay, infants and toddlers soon recognized and accepted as natural the affectionate responses they constantly received. Contributing to the communicative ambience of this tactile situation was a playful eliciting of attention which was continually extended to infants and toddlers by older children.

Communication through touch was well suited to expressing and requiting the child's major concerns: nourishment, security, comfort, and stimulation, and it developed readily.

Although speech also emerged in due course, a basic pattern of human relation was established during the prespeech period which underlay and shaped the Fore life style. This "sociosensual" pattern provided for a quite intimate rapport with those around, and it seemed to lay the foundation for that sixth sense which bound groups together through spontaneous, responsive sharing of food, materials of life, and pleasure. In this sense, the cooperative livelihood, consensual human relations, and the egalitarian social order all emerged from the basic initial condition of tactile relation. The rather lavish degree of physical contact beginning at birth may have been crucial in initiating this basic Fore pattern of social and behavioral development. The spinning out of the effects of this type of early experiential input runs like a unifying thread through Fore

childhood, ultimately tying it to their protoagricultural way of life. A second crucial thread running from infancy through childhood was the unrestricted manner in which exploratory activity and pursuit of interest were left to the initiative of the child. As the infant's awareness increased, his interests broadened to the things his mother and other caretakers did and to the objects and materials they used (Fig. 2). Then these youngsters began crawling out to explore things nearby that attracted their attention. By the time they were toddling their interests continually took them on short sorties to nearby objects and persons. As soon as they could walk well, the excursions extended to the entire hamlet and its gardens, and then beyond with other children. Developing without interference or supervision, this personal exploratory quest freely touched on whatever was around, even axes, knives, machetes, and fire (Fig. 3).

Initially astonished by the ability of young children to manage so independently without being hurt, I eventually began to see how this capability also emerged from the infants' milieu of close human physical proximity and tactile interaction. Touch and bodily contact lent themselves naturally to satisfying the basic needs of the

---

Figure 1.   The most salient feature of early Fore childhood was the degree to which infants were kept with the mother or one of her close associates. They were rarely put down or out of actual physical contact with an habitual associate. There was always someone to hold or carry them. Usually it was the mother who held and carried the small infant; but as he grew older she shared this activity with other individuals of her social circle. Older children, in particular, participated in the holding and carrying of the young child. Small babies were sometimes carried in net bags padded with bark and leaves against the backs of their mothers almost as *in utero,* but they were also frequently carried under their mother's arms. As the infants grew they were also carried on their mother's hips. Older children who participated in the care and handling of toddlers frequently carried them on their hips, but they more often carried them on their backs, which adults did not. When the toddlers were not being carried, they were kept on the laps of their mothers or other caretakers. They were not put aside for sleeping or while their caretakers were otherwise engaged.

Figure 2. From the vantage point of close physical contact with his caretakers, the young child viewed the world around him and began to investigate and explore the materials and objects at hand. Most often these were the same things that were of interest and concern to his caretakers. Thus the young child was in contact with activities and materials of importance to his socioeconomic welfare at quite an early age.

Figure 3. A generally practiced deference to the desires of the young in the choice of play objects permitted them to investigate and handle knives and other potentially harmful objects frequently. They were expected to make use of the tools and materials which belonged to their adult associates and were indulged in this expectation. As a result, use of knives was common, particularly for exploratory play.

babies and provided the basis for an early kind of communicative experience based on touch. In continual physical touch with people engaged in daily pursuits, infants and toddlers began to learn the forms of behavior and response characteristic of Fore life. Muscle tone, movement, and mood were components of this learning process; formal instruction was not. Surrounded by continuous and extensive opportunities for spontaneous, unforced kinesthetic experience, infants and toddlers began to inquire and explore outward, following their own initiative and inclination, to objects and activities nearby which had attracted their attention. Competence with the tools of life developed quickly, and by the time they were able to walk, Fore youngsters could safely handle axes, knives, fire, and so on.

The early pattern of exploratory activity included frequent return to one of the "mothers." Serving as a home base, the bastion of security, a woman might occasionally give the youngster a nod of encouragement, if he glanced in her direction with uncertainty. Yet rarely did anyone attempt to control or direct, nor did they participate in a child's quests or jaunts.

At first I found it quite remarkable that toddlers did not recklessly thrust themselves into unappreciated dangers, the way our own children tend to do. Eventually I came to see that they had no reason to do so. From their earliest days, they enjoyed a benevolent sanctuary from which the world could be confidently viewed, tested, and appreciated. These human bases were neither demanding nor restrictive, so there was no need to escape or evade them in the manner so frequently seen in Western culture. Confidently, not furtively, the youngsters were able to extend their inquiry, widening their understanding as they chose. There was no need to play tricks or deceive in order to pursue life. Nor did they have to act out impulsively to break through subliminal fears induced by punishment or parental anxiety. Such children could safely move out on their own, unsupervised and unrestricted.

Beginning as physical attunement with caretakers, learning was next pursued through sociosensual exploratory attunement with age-mates. From this emerged the consensual cooperative approach to obtaining food, shelter, and pleasure which characterized the Fore life and the voluntary associations of adults who cooperated and segmented to exploit the virgin lands. In this way the nondirective Fore approach to child handling and rearing supported their protoagricultural existence by molding an unrepressed explorative personality able to segment and diverge to exploit the surrounding virgin ecological situation.

The Fore style of innovation was expressed neither compulsively nor anxiously. Not based on efforts to be different or better, novelty only became interesting and exciting when experienced as "play" among peers. When interest in something novel did not spark some degree of consensus appreciation, it was not likely to persist. Fore economic pursuit mirrored their approach to novelty. Both were cooperative and consensual; neither was aggressive or competitive.

Undoubtedly the lack of frustration during infancy and childhood was a key factor in the development of their cooperative and free protoagricultural character. Because the infants' basic physical and emotional requirements were quickly and readily fulfilled, they did not have to elaborate abstract mental constructions of schedule and human relation in order to feel secure, as do children in households organized by concepts of rule, schedule, and behavioral ideal. There was no need to develop and internalize abstract concepts of order and regularity in order to relate to the sources of sustenance and comfort. This obviated deep emotional commitment to security-associated abstract behavioral ideals. Neither well-being nor peace of mind required them. Without such notions there would not be much interest in manipulating people or altering surroundings to fit an emotionally embedded "scheme of life." This foundation for aggression or conflict at least would be absent.

With a basic behavioral program patterned by persistent benevolent early handling, Fore social dynamics proceeded rather flexibly toward a sense of personal identity not so dependent on name, place, position, or status. In the absence of commitment to security-associated abstract concepts, challenges to such beliefs or practices were not threatening. This left the Fore relatively free to think and behave in new ways. The resultant cognitive and behavioral flexibility facilitated protoagricultural adaptation.

This obviously has distinct implications for the understanding of the nature of aggression. The culturally specific child handling and rearing practices did not seat habits of withdrawal or "lashing out." "Getting even" and similar destructive impulses directed at family, loved ones, or way of life would not become anchored in the Fore behavioral repertoire. Such common problems in the West as "generation gap," sibling rivalry, social domineering, adolescent rebellion, and similar aggressive stances would not emerge. There were experimental and accidental aggressive acts by the very young. These were, however, considered a natural consequence of an immaturity which did not yet fully grasp the impact of such actions; they were regarded as amusing. No attempt was made to chastise or punish; nor was anger or marked displeasure usually shown. Instead the typical reaction of older children and adults who were the subject of aggressive or hostile actions by the young was interested affectionate amusement (Fig. 4). If the attack became painful, the subject of it would usually move away or try to divert or distract the young child by affectionate playfulness or by engaging him in other interests. When such "aggression" was directed toward young age-mates, it was discouraged, but, again, not by reproach or punishment but rather by diversionary playful activity or amusement.

The young children's experimental and accidental aggressive behavior did not persist; their nascent or accidental aggressive motions failed to find a place in the daily life style. Anger, squabbling, and fighting did not become natural to their lives. Momentary expressions of anger, as might occur during "accidents" in rough play, were quickly dissipated (Fig. 5). Conflict over "things" was typically sidetracked by behavioral habits of cooperative deference or attunement.

Anchored in the protoagricultural gestalt this non-aggressive social system began to break down as settled agriculture emerged. The weakness of the protoagricultural Fore type of psychosocial development was that only those who have grown up together were closely attuned to one another. It was not so easy to extend this rapport to strangers. It required growing up together in the sociosensual and consensual harmony of the protoagricultural hamlets. Without it the foundation for rapport was not so firm.

So the open, receptive, unaggressive character produced in the Fore protoagricultural situation was fated for trouble as the lands began to fill up. As different groups of Fore incursive gardeners converged on the few remaining stands of virgin forest, a time of troubles began to descend. The gardens of opportunity began to turn into gardens of war.

Under normal conditions a typical Fore reaction to interpersonal or intergroup difficulty was to go elsewhere, even to distant lands. However, as the lands began to fill up, this became less and less

Figure 4. When older children were the subject of attack by young children, they typically received it with amusement and affection. If the attack became painful, they sometimes moved away, but more often, they tried to divert the young child from his aggressive intents by affectionate playfulness or engaging him in other interests. The older children usually regarded such incidents as an amusing diversion rather than as an annoyance. They did not chastise or reproach the young child, nor were attempts made to discourage such behavior. Here, a toddler picks up a stick and throws it at a young girl who, laughing, picks up the stick and throws it away, while her associate of about the same age beckons the toddler with the standard Fore gesture of affectionate invitation. The toddler, seduced by this gesture, moves to her to be picked up.

Figure 5. By the time Fore boys were about eight years old, fighting among associates was unlikely to develop, even out of a moment of anger, as might be triggered during rough play. A mechanism for side-tracking anger is shown here. The boy on the bottom shows a momentary trace of anger (b, c, d); he then goes limp (e) for a few seconds, after which he resumes his activity with the previous friendly elan. Elapsed time from the first frame is in seconds as follows: 0.0, 8.8, 9.4, 10.5, 13.3, 15.5, 16.3, 18.7, 20.8, 21.8, 23.0.

practicable. In the more densely settled regions the Fore began to stand their ground. Stances of bellicosity and outrage developed. There would be raids on the gardens and even the hamlets of the "transgressor," and then reprisal murders.

This kind of warfare was usually small scale, and casualties were few. Fighting alliances were temporary and informal. Communities rarely acted as unified political units. Even in a small hamlet it was unusual for all the men to participate in a raid or battle. Fighting and raiding were usually by a few directly aggrieved close associates who felt personally wronged. Their hostility was typically aimed against particular individuals or small groups of associates in other nearby hamlets. Acts which impaired the value of someone's personal effort or property usually were the precipitating causes (e.g., breaking or weakening a fence, damaging a garden, killing a pig, or engaging in sexual liaison with another's wife).

The rather undefinable character of the warfare was a consequence of the informal Fore type of sociopolitical organization. Although most of one's close associates were neighbors, it was not uncommon for the respective members of a hamlet to have many out-of-hamlet associates of different degrees of camaraderie in different places because of the protoagricultural dispersion process. Members of some hamlets could trace their affiliations not only to other hamlets in their own region, but also to other population clusters afar. This created a situation in which there were individuals who would not join their hamlet-mates during fighting because of their close associations with individuals in the "enemy" hamlets. These "neutrals" could move freely across the lines of hostility, even during times of battle.

In other Highland regions, where the protoagricultural era had come to an end and land pressure was severe, the warfare became more common, better organized, and more institutionalized. More distinct sociopolitical units began to form; larger bands of combatants began to take to the field. The likelihood of direct attack on hamlets increased; those who had not yet joined the conflict had to fight or flee. Hamlet populations became more united in matters of conflict and warfare. Sorcery and threat of sorcery unified them. There began to be common enemies who could be identified by where they lived.

Three ecologically and demographically influenced phases can be associated with the development of warfare among the Fore:

Phase 1: *Abundant surrounding virgin land.* Small, isolated groups of protoagriculturalists made up of close and trusted associates diverged unhampered into the uninhabited surrounding forest lands. Fighting was rare.

Phase 2: *The beginnings of competition for land.* Previously diverging, somewhat alien peoples began converging on the same remaining stands of virgin forest. There were increasingly frequent episodes of confusion, anger and fighting. Conflict characteristically involved small raiding bands bent on redressing specific immediate grievances. There was an increase in migration to avoid conflict.

Phase 3: *The increasing rarity of new-forest land.* Contiguous free segmentation was no longer feasible. An increase in sorcery, suspicion, and accusation narrowed social horizons. Untrusted persons were excluded from residential areas. Interhamlet attacks began to occur. Defined sociopolitical groupings began to develop. Alien groups joined in alliance to drive mutually objectionable impinging peoples away. More severe dispersion of populations occurred as migrations took segmenting groups to distant new lands across intervening groups and lands.

This process was interrupted by the arrival of Australian government officers. The immediate effect was pacification. Fighting ceased almost spontaneously throughout the entire region. 'Most Fore groups did not wait to be told to cease fighting by the new administration but stopped on their own almost as if they had been awaiting an excuse to give it up. A few maintained a warlike stance a bit longer than the others but without serious raiding. The Fore said among themselves that the *kiap* (government officer) was coming, so it was time to stop the fighting. They looked to his arrival as the beginning of a new era rather than as an invasion. Disputes that could not be settled by the Fore themselves were eagerly and quickly put into the hands of the patrol officers for arbitration. An anti-fighting ethic quickly spread through the region. The aggressive posturing, which once accompanied assertions of rights and defense, faded away; talk of manliness in association with fighting prowess soon ceased.

The receptive Fore reaction to Western presence seemed, at least in part, to be the result of the historical timing of the Australian arrival. Warfare had become a serious and disagreeable problem. Indigenous political and social mechanisms for handling it had only begun to evolve. The arrival of the patrol officers permitted an immediate solution, and in good part because of this, the Australian arrival was considered millenarian.

The Fore culture represents one of many flowerings of human possibility allowed by the uniquely complex human neurophysiological apparatus, and it tells us something about an important aspect of the socioecological evolution of the world—the bridge between hunting-gathering and settled agriculture. It also tells us that aggression is a culturally programmed trait which is not necessarily always adaptive or even expressed.

However, it would be a mistake to assume that the Fore type of human organization would *necessarily* emerge in any protoagricultural situation. One example does not make a generality.

The progression from hunting-gathering to protoagriculture to settled agriculture as it evolved in the New Guinea Highlands is an interesting expression of human organization that emerged in response to a particular set of historical, ecological, cultural, and economic conditions.

Until we know more about the broader range of behavioral patterning possibilities of the human being, it will not be possible fully to assess the question of the nature of human aggression. Nor can we fully evaluate the adaptive role it has played or may play in human affairs. Even the word "aggression" reflects the cognitive organization of our Western culture. There is, therefore, the rather difficult epistemological question of how to apply it crossculturally. It would be helpful to have more data on non-Western patternings of human behavior which could be related to the Western concept of aggression.

NOTES

1. John Marshall's concern with the human formative conditions of the Pleistocene has recently led him to the concept of this hunting-

gathering period as a "gentle crucible" (J. Marshall, Personal communication, March 2, 1977).

2. Colin Turnbull, *The Forest People: A Study of the Pygmies of the Congo*. New York: Simon and Schuster, 1961.
3. E. R. Sorenson, *The Edge of the Forest: Land, Childhood, and Change in a New Guinea Protoagricultural Society*. Washington, D.C.: Smithsonian Institution Press, 1976.
4. R. Gardner and K. G. Heider, *Gardens of War: Life and Death in the New Guinea Stone Age*. New York: Random House, 1969.

PATRICIA DRAPER

The Learning Environment for Aggression and Anti-Social Behavior among the !Kung

The !Kung, a hunter-gatherer people of the Kalahari Desert, are of interest to this collection of writings on the teaching of non-aggression for a variety of reasons. They have been described as a "harmless people" by Thomas (1958) in a book-length account of the social life and cultural values of !Kung who lived in South West Africa. An opposite characterization of !Kung emerges from an unpublished study by Richard Lee. This study, based on interviews and examination of genealogical records collected in the field, reports on incidents of homicide among !Kung. The murder rate, according to Lee, is rather frequent for a people purported to be harmless and unaggressive. Still other writers, dealing more generally with factors common to hunter-gathering and band-level peoples (Service, 1966; Hoebel, 1954, 1958; Lee and DeVore, eds., 1968) have pointed out that hunting and gathering groups possess few formal mechanisms for dealing with social conflict. Such peoples typically rely on informal mechanisms of social control such as gossip, ridicule, sorcery, shunning, ostracism, and public debating which lead to the formation of concensus. In discussing the problem of social control in such societies, anthropologists show how conflicts are resolved circuitously and in a lengthy fashion. They point out that the aim of conflict resolution is not to place blame or necessarily to punish an offender, but rather to restore amicable relations among individuals.

The !Kung, therefore, are a provocative case study; a controversy exists as to whether they are harmless or, in fact, murderous. In addition, since the !Kung are by now well studied, one can use specific information about !Kung behavior to examine general propositions about social control and interpersonal conflict in hunting and gathering societies generally.

This paper will address the question of interpersonal conflict and aggression among !Kung, with particular emphasis on the learning environment of children and how it relates to the learning of aggressive behavior. Of concern here will be parental attitudes toward children's behavior and techniques for dealing with conflict. In the !Kung case there are many factors such as settlement pattern, economy, and the value of sharing which are less obviously related to values about child-rearing but which have substantial impact on the social and emotional climate in which children are reared. This paper will describe, therefore, not only some aspects of child socialization that bear on the teaching of non-aggression, but also these other dimensions of social organization which are relevant to the ability of !Kung to discourage interpersonal aggression and to encourage group cooperation. I will leave a discussion of the issue, "Are the !Kung unaggressive, aggressive, harmless, or murderous?" to the concluding section of this paper.

Before proceeding directly to the topic, there are a few caveats which should be laid before the reader. These concern the problems which an anthropologist faces in presenting and interpreting information.

When anthropologists describe the exotic peoples with whom they have lived and studied, they often organize their analyses around themes or preoccupations which are themselves central to the people's cultural life. This procedure can be a convenient and culturally sensitive vehicle for exposition; the pivotal institution or set of values becomes the basis for showing connections among superficially discrete and independent cultural processes. A disadvantage of this approach is that it necessarily underplays other customs which could legitimately achieve equal prominence given a different starting point in the ethnographic analysis. There are many examples of the "central cultural theme" approach. A few of the best known are Malinowski's portrayal of reciprocity and exchange among the Trobriand Islanders (Malinowski, 1920, 1922), Chagnon's treatment of aggression and ritualized conflict in both film and written documents (Asch and Chagnon, 1970; Chagnon, 1977), and, of course, Ruth Benedict's *Patterns of Culture* (Benedict, 1934).

The opposite approach, in which an anthropologist describes a culture by topic, treating different cultural systems in turn (e. g., religion, economics, socialization, and so forth), is currently out of fashion. For all the merits of this more exhaustive and balanced strategy, it can render the rough, crannied texture of social life into a flat, but admittedly easy to absorb, porridge.

In writing an essay on aggression in !Kung life, one encounters some of the problems outlined above. Aggression, conflict, and violence—none of these are culturally elaborated preoccupations. Nor could one argue that a central cultural theme is concerned with an opposite set of values—the enforcement of peace and the suppression of aggression. From this point of view, values about interpersonal aggression do not qualify as an especially auspicious position from which to view the cultural terrain. Nevertheless, the !Kung are a people who devalue aggression; they have explicit values against assaulting, losing control, and seeking to intimidate another person by sheer force of personality. Furthermore, on a daily basis and over months of fieldwork one finds that overt physical acts by one person against another are extremely rare. In two years I personally observed three instances in which people lost control and exchanged blows: two twelve-year-old girls who wrestled and fought with fists; two women who scratched and kicked each other over a man (the husband of one of the women); and two men who violently shoved each other back and forth, shouted and separated to gather weapons, only to be dissuaded by other people from their respective camps. In a fourth case I saw two women who had fought the night before. Lorna Marshall, an anthropologist with much experience among the !Kung, makes a similar report:

During seventeen and a half months of fieldwork with the Nyae Nyae !Kung . . . , I personally saw only four flare-ups of discord and heard about three others which occurred in neighboring bands during that period. All were resolved before they became serious quarrels. [Marshall, 1976, pp. 311–12]

If the !Kung succeed in avoiding direct physical confrontation in most instances, they clearly experience the same emotions which, in other societies, would lead more quickly to hostile acts. The !Kung harbor hatreds, jealousies, resentments, suspicions—the full panoply of negative emotions. In fact, their oral traditions are remarkably violent and fratricidal for a people who, on the surface, maintain the appearance of simple communal harmony (Biesele, 1972 a and b, 1975, 1976). The difference between the !Kung and other peoples is that the circumstances of their life are such that they must dampen their passions to manageable levels or, that failing, separate themselves from the people whose society they cannot tolerate. Interestingly, the !Kung themselves take on an edgy irascibility when their life style changes away from that which one sees in small mobile groups living in the bush and depending on foraging and hunting for subsistence (Lee, 1972a). The discussion in this paper will concern a group of about 120 bush-living !Kung whom I studied in 1968 and 1969. At that time they were living along the international border between Botswana and South West Africa near the !Kung watering places known as ≠To//gana and /Du/da. For readers not acquainted with the growing literature on the !Kung, a brief ethnographic description will be useful.

The literature on the !Kung has increased steadily in the last twenty years. The earlier work of Lorna Marshall, John Marshall, and Elizabeth Marshall Thomas give a general background to !Kung social organization and economy, although the publications of the Marshall family primarily concern !Kung living in South West Africa in the Nyae Nyae area. Since the early 1960's, another group of researchers has entered the field of !Kung studies.[1] This group has worked in western Botswana with populations of !Kung who overlap with those studied by the Marshall family.

The !Kung live today mostly on the western edge of the Kalahari sand system in what is now southern Angola, Botswana, and South West Africa, and until recent times they subsisted by hunting and gathering. The great majority of !Kung-speaking people of today have abandoned their traditional foraging life style and are living in sedentary and semisquatter status in or near villages of Bantu pastoralists and European ranchers. A minority of !Kung, amounting to a few thousand people, are still living by traditional foraging techniques, and these are the people who are described in this paper.

The few remaining groups of still mobile !Kung subsist on wild vegetable foods and game meat. They are seminomadic, moving their camps at irregular intervals, from a few days to several weeks. They live in small groups, averaging about thirty-five people, but these bands vary from as few as fifteen to as many as sixty-five persons. The factors that affect group size are chiefly season and the availability of water. During the rainy season (October to March), group censuses are lower owing to the fact that water and bush foods are widely available in most regions of the desert. Smaller numbers of people in the form of two and three family groups spread out over the bush. As the dry season nears and the temporary watering places dry up, the people begin to regroup and fall back on the remaining water sources which continue throughout the dry season. As there are few such sources in the heart of the drought, as many as two or three different camps may be found within one to three miles of the same water hole.

The rules governing the composition of these bands are extremely flexible; it appears that there is no such thing as "band membership." Close relatives move together over much of the year, although individuals as well as segments of large kin groups frequently make temporary separations to visit other relatives and affines.

The material technology of the !Kung is simple. Men hunt with small bows and arrows and metal-pointed spears. Women do the bulk of the gathering of wild foodstuffs and much of the food preparation. Their tools include a simple digging stick, a wooden mortar and pestle, and a heavy leather cape or kaross which doubles as an article of clothing as well as a carrying bag.

Child-Training and the Teaching of Non-Aggression

It is impossible to understand !Kung child socialization apart from the larger physical and social settings in which it takes place. For this reason a fuller discussion of these other features is provided to give a more comprehensive view of the lives of children. However, two factors, the public nature of family life and the omnipresence of adult supervision, are intimately related to the capacity of !Kung parents to control the learning environments of their children and in particular to discourage aggression. More detailed description of the physical setting of band life and the social use of space will appear in later portions of the paper.

A remarkable feature of camp life is the close physical and social interaction of adults and children. Children under the ages of six or seven years are rarely away from close supervision by adults.[2] The children living in the small bands have virtually no place where they can go to be by themselves. Once they step out of the camp, or even walk beyond earshot of camp, there is only the Kalahari bush stretching away for miles in every direction. From a child's vantage point the bush is not attractive; it is vast, undifferentiated, and unhumanized. Adults do not discourage older children from roaming out from camp, but these children seem to prefer staying at home.[3]

!Kung children, like children anywhere, will argue, tease, cry, lose their tempers, and strike out at each other. One can see the youngest toddler, with an angry face and clenched fists, straining from its mother's lap and trying to swat another child—or an adult for that matter. There are frustrations in this society for even the youngest age groups. The !Kung, however, have a special way of handling anger and physical assaults by one child against another. When two small children quarrel and begin to fight, adults don't punish them or lecture them; they separate them and physically carry each child off in an opposite direction. The adult tries to soothe and distract the child and to get him interested in other things. The strategy is to interrupt misbehavior before it gets out of hand. For older children, adults use the same interventionist technique. I was often surprised at the ability of adults to monitor the emotional states of children even when the children were far enough away that the conversations could not be heard. When play gets too rough or arguments too intense, an adult will call one of the ringleaders away. Alternatively, one or more adults simply drift over to join the children, and the mere presence of the adult puts a damper on the action.

This way of disciplining children has important consequences for aggressiveness in childhood and later in adulthood. Since parents do not use physical punishment, and since aggressive postures are avoided by adults and devalued by the society at large, children have relatively little opportunity to observe or imitate overtly aggressive behavior. Not only are aggressive models scarce, but the adult technique of interfering at the earliest stages of discord means that a child usually doesn't have the opportunity to learn the satisfaction of striking and humiliating another child. This situation, of course, is made possible by the fact that children and adults occupy the same close living space and by the fact that on any typical day there will be many adults in camp who are keeping an informal watch on the children.

When asked about physical assaults by children, !Kung will state that this is bad and dangerous—that children can actually harm each other. If an adult sees an older child mistreating a younger child, he will respond quickly and with a harsh scolding. On the other hand, adults are completely tolerant of a child's temper tantrums and of aggression directed by a child at an adult. I have seen a seven-year-old crying and furious, hurling sticks, nut shells, and eventually burning embers at her mother. The mother sat at her fire talking with the child's grandmother and her own sister-in-law. Bau (the mother) put up her arm occasionally to ward off the thrown objects but carried on her conversation nonchalantly. The other women remained unperturbed despite the hail of missiles. The daughter raged ten feet away, but Bau did not turn a hair. When the rocks and nut shells came close Bau remarked, "That child has no brains."

This example is not an isolated case but a common practice. Adults consistently ignore a child's angry outburst when it does not inflict harm. A child's frustration at such times is acute, but he learns that anger does not cause an adult to change his treatment of the child, and the display of anger does not get the adult's attention or sympathy. In these situations the reward to the child for hostile acts must be minimal. The child can rage until he is tired, but, in my observation, the tirade had little effect.

In the same way that the omnipresence of adult supervision protects children from mistreatment by each other, it also protects them from abuse by adults, particularly the child's own parents. As described above, children lose control and, particularly at the ages of about three to five years, they are capable of being persistently querulous and abusive toward their mothers. A common cause of the anger is the mother's decision to wean the child from the breast (breast feeding for three to four years is usual) or to wean the child from being carried on the back. In my experience, children found weaning from the back more traumatic than giving up the breast—perhaps because mothers were more inconsistent in discouraging carrying than in discouraging nursing. In some cases the two kinds of weaning occurred together and such children were especially distraught.

For these reasons and others I have seen several occasions when a child showed every sign of wishing to do real bodily damage to the mother. In such cases the mother remonstrates, ridicules, scolds, wards off the blows, and soon calls out to another woman or man sitting near her, "Hey! Come take this child away from me!" Someone responds by calmly and bodily carting the child away to another part of the camp, the mother now able to resume whatever activity the child had interrupted.

The ready accessibility of other people in the camp means that the mother is protected from being badgered by her child until she loses control of her own temper. This circumstance is unfortunately very common in our own society, with its nuclear family households and residence arrangments which confer what is probably an unhealthy degree of privacy on parents and children. In the !Kung case, parents are not likely to reach the point of abusing their children, but in the unlikely event that someone did abuse a child, other people would immediately step in.

For children who grow up in these isolated hunting and gathering bands, the socialization experience is continuous and consistent. As a result children have few opportunities to bully and fight with children of their own camps or to acquire antisocial habits of other types. The parents seem to rely implicitly on the constraint of continuous supervision of themselves and other like-minded adults to ensure conformity in their children. They do not rely on moral indoctrination about the right and wrong way to do things or to deal with other people.

Another factor which may minimize the aggressive interactions between children may be the age composition of the typical play group. The usual situation is one in which the children of a camp have only a few children available for play and these are normally not the same age or necessarily close in age. The lack of peers probably discourages not only physical assault but competitiveness generally. The older child learns that he must be subtle in his domination of younger children, and the younger child may appreciate that the difference in size and competence between himself and the older child is so great that most challenges are not worthwhile.

Economy and Ecology

The !Kung live in an extremely dry area but one in which, given their technological competence and their low fertility, a reliable food supply can be found. The wild game and vegetable foods, while fairly plentiful, are scattered unevenly over wide areas. In order to exploit this type of patchy environment the !Kung live and move in small mobile bands. The bands themselves are not stable units in and of themselves, although on occasion an entire band or camp will relocate to a new site. More often, however, individuals or one or more family groups will detach themselves from their co-residents and join up with another group which may be nearby or as many as thirty or forty miles distant. Given this hodgepodge of group mobility, dissolution, and coalescence, the flow of information over large distances is remarkably fast and accurate, despite the fact that the !Kung live at population densities which are among the lowest in the world—about one person per ten square miles.

The mobility of individuals and groups is, of course, adaptive under these circumstances, but because this degree of mobility renders food storage virtually impossible, the !Kung have no insurance against hard times. Whereas technologically more advanced peoples can look to filled grain bins or harvests ripening in the field, or to herds of domestic animals which may survive when crops fail, the !Kung have no stored surplus of a material sort. They cannot even look forward to periods of surfeit such as those enjoyed by hunters and gatherers whose ranges include migration routes of buffalo or caribou or the spawning runs of fish. !Kung can manage only if they keep moving and if they keep in contact with other groups similarly pursuing game and bush foods which appear randomly in both space and time.

The point here which has relevance to group solidarity and harmony is that the !Kung need each other. They are not unique in this respect, but the immediacy of this need on a day-to-day basis is unusual and not found to the same extent in most other cultures. For the !Kung, in this sense, the stored surplus is the group and the more distant groups scattered in the bush, with the social and economic insurance that they provide.

Under these circumstances one would expect to find cultural values against interpersonal aggression and in favor of regular sharing of temporary windfalls. This is exactly the case among the !Kung. They are extremely wary of persons known to have violent tempers or unpredictable behavior. Such people are openly criticized and censored and eventually shunned. In former times, before the national system of justice impinged on these remote hunter-gatherers, some of the infrequent homicides were in fact political assassinations of people who had proven to be incorrigible. To this day the !Kung fear irrational and hostile people; there are many reasons behind this, but at least two are central. A person who cannot control his behavior is dangerous to himself and his relatives. If people avoid living with such a person and those loyal to him, those persons lose both the resources of the group and the information available to the group. In addition, the !Kung, like most band-level peoples, lack institutionalized leadership roles and adjudicative processes. They have no means for bringing formal sanctions to bear on nonconformists.[4] Therefore truly antisocial behavior has a greater potential for disrupting the social fabric and the economic balance than is true for people in other types of societies.

Although the !Kung lack a system of formal sanctions against wrongdoing, it appears that they have compensated with a host of informal controls which normally work to keep people in line. They have a varied and subtle armamentarium suitable for squelching a variety of infractions; their repertoire is especially well-developed for dealing with arrogance, bragging, and attempts to manipulate others.

Pride and boastfulness are especially devalued; for example, when a young hunter returns from a hunt and announces to no one in particular, "I killed an eland!" he is greeted by indifference. No one pauses in his activities. If the young man persists, an older person will remark in a voice designed to carry across the camp clearing, "Why only one?"

The approved mode of revealing a successful hunt is more like this: the hunter returns at dusk and goes to his own fire to rest. Sometime later one or two other men will join him. In a circuitous way they ask him,

> "See anything in the bush today?"
> "No, there is hardly any game. I shot a little something, but who knows?"
> "Yes, one never knows."
> "Perhaps you will go out with me tomorrow morning and we will see if anything is dead."

Some men have told me that under similar circumstances, when they have accompanied another hunter, they have not learned what animal they were searching for until the original hunter led them to the place where the tracks could be recognized and followed.[5]

Personal success, excellence, achievement, or sheer luck must be handled delicately in this society, for the potential put-down is everywhere. The !Kung must have members of their society who are motivated to socially useful ends, but the individual must achieve these ends in an innocuous, nonassertive way. This process of leveling is, of course, consonant with the equalitarian ethos of band-level societies, generally, but there is more to it than this. Years and years of this type of conditioning produce a person who is highly sensitive to the evaluations of himself by other people. When an individual runs afoul of some norm and the sentiment of the camp is against him, he reacts in a way that seems extreme to a Western observer. Further, the way the wrongdoer reacts to the frustration of criticism suggests that the social norms are very well internalized by the individual. For example, a young woman, N!uhka, about seventeen years old and unmarried, had insulted her father. Seventeen years of age is late to be still unmarried in this society, and her father often talked with her and with relatives about eligible men. She was rebellious and uninterested in the older men who were named. (She was also having a good time flirting with the youths in camp who were her age-mates but judged too young to make good husbands.) In a flippant way she cursed her father. He reprimanded her and immediately other tongues took up a shocked chorus. (There is no privacy in these small bands.)

N!uhka was furious but also shamed by the public outcry. Her reaction took this form: she grabbed her blanket, stomped out of the camp off to a lone tree about seventy yards from the circle of huts. There she sat all day, in the shade of the tree, with a blanket over her head and completely covering her body. This was full-scale Bushman sulk. She was angry but did not further release her anger apart from this gesture of withdrawal. She kept her anger inside, incidentally at some personal cost, for that day the temperature in the shade was 105 degrees Fahrenheit—without a blanket.

In another case, Tsebe, an aunt of the same adolescent, took on the role of matchmaker for N!uhka with one of the young men also living with the band. To play matchmaker is not necessarily wrong, but in no accidental way, Tsebe arranged the marriage when N!uhka's father was absent and the young man's parents also were away visiting. When the new in-laws returned they were not only amazed but outraged that the marriage had been so swiftly engineered behind their backs.

The talk began; soon the whole camp was in on the discussion. Some took the parents' side and agreed that Tsebe had been high-handed. Others thought that the marriage itself was good, but that Tsebe should have waited for the couple's parents to return. No matter which interpretation, Tsebe received much criticism. She took to her bed and refused to eat. Two days later she made a few superficial cuts in her thigh and rubbed arrow poison into the wounds. She became quite sick and confessed that she had, in effect, attempted suicide. That evening and the following evening the people held a trance dance for her. All the medicine owners, the men who are capable of trance and healing in their trance state, worked on her. Everyone attended and joined in the singing and dancing on Tsebe's behalf. She recovered soon afterward, mainly because her suicide attempt had been essentially symbolic; only minuscule amounts of poison must have entered the wounds. In the days following a kind of reconciliation took place between the injured parties. More significantly, open talk against Tsebe and her behind-the-scenes manipulation had ceased.

In these examples there is a common and characteristic theme. When people are at odds and public opinion runs against one of the parties, the "wrongdoer" withdraws and turns the frustration and anger against the self. On the other hand, when arguments develop and there is no clear right and wrong side, the usual solution is for one of the parties to leave the group, moving off to another band where he and his sympathizers have friends and relatives. In time the disputes are not exactly forgotten, but they will be overlooked should the parties again find themselves camping together.

To say that the !Kung are unaggressive and capable of living harmoniously with their kind may or may not be true. That brawls and shouting matches are rare is true, both of adults and of children. The emotions which could fuel fights are clearly present; however, there are various reasons why most people contain their anger. The structure of camp life—the lack of privacy and the custom of camping with close relatives and affines—is such that loss of self-control will be recognized immediately. Other people will intervene before a person can act in a hot rage with possible serious injury to his enemy. Also, any other adult in camp is related to any would-be aggressor by dozens of overlapping ties of kinship and marriage. Once a person attacks his victim he is like a fly that attacks an insect already caught in a spider's web. Immediately both are caught. If the combatants forget the sticky web in the heat of their anger, the onlookers do not. Real anger frightens and sickens the !Kung, for it is so destructive of their web of relationships. They have no real means for coping with the aftermath of violent aggression.

Sharing

The expectation that valuable items, such as meat or material goods, will be circulated effectively limits much of the jealousy and envy which even temporary inequality of wealth can bring. Game meat must be shared with all consanguines and affines with whom a hunter is living. An excellent description of these rules is provided by Lorna Marshall (Marshall, 1961). The tensions which accompany the formal distribution of meat from a large kill are well known, both to the !Kung themselves and to the anthropologists who have worked with !Kung.[6] Many a young hunter will ask his father or an older male relative to distribute the meat from a kill he has made, because his heart quails at the prospect of facing his steely-eyed camp fellows. Every portion is watched by all as it is allocated to particular individuals. (Males and females are both allocated in the distribution.) During the proceedings people may openly abuse the distributor, saying such gracious things as, "Do you expect me to bother to stoop over and carry away such a miserable piece of carrion?"

Such comments are deflected by the toughened hides of seasoned hunters. They make caustic replies and proceed stoically, knowing that distributing meat is a thankless task. Not only are people often not satisfied with their portions, but they may feel that to complain is their role in the ritual. Although much bickering is routine, if a person feels that he has been severely slighted, it can be a serious matter, leading to arguments and eventually to the splitting of groups.

!Kung practice a formalized trade called "hxaro" with certain trading partners.[7] Although some "hxaroing" is carefully planned in advance and enacted in a formal, solemn way, much hxaro is done because the person who finds himself the owner of a particularly attractive item is simply worn down by the mutterings and taunts of his relatives. For example, when a woman wears a particularly attractive bead necklace, or a colorful piece of cloth, she does not receive compliments. She hears,

> "How is it that you are a person whose neck is nearly broken with the weight of all those necklaces and I am here with only sweat on my own neck? Hxaro me!"

The implication, of course, is that the owner should hand over the necklace. The one who asks would be gratified if she did "hxaro," but she would be taken aback that it was given on the first request.

The give and take of tangibles and intangibles goes on in the midst of a high level of bickering. Until one learns the cultural meaning of this continual verbal assault, the outsider wonders how the !Kung can stand to live with each other. Most of us who have worked with !Kung have our own stories to tell about how we learned to deal with the high velocity !Kung vituperation. People continually dun the Europeans and especially the European anthropologists since, unlike most Europeans, the anthropologists speak !Kung. In the early months of my own fieldwork I despaired of ever getting away from continual harassment. As my knowledge of !Kung increased, I learned that the !Kung are equally merciless in dunning each other. In time I learned the properly melodramatic disclaimers with which to reply to the dunning. I blush now when I recall some of my own oratory,

> "You expect *me,* one lonely European, a stranger in this territory, living away from my own kin, without even one spear or arrow or even a digging stick, and with no knowledge of the bush . . . you expect *me* to give *you* something to eat? You are a person whose hut is crammed full of good things to eat. Berries, billtong, sweet roots, stand shoulder high in your hut and you come to me saying you are hungry!"

Onlookers came to enjoy these exchanges as they did when they heard them in their own camps. Once these kind of speeches were delivered, then my visitor and I could go on to talk of other things. Europeans will talk idly about the weather or the state of the crops as conversational filler; the !Kung in part rely on dunning for the same purposes. But the dunning among themselves is not all idle form and no content. A person who does not continually recirculate what is given to him is marked, indeed.

Verbal aggression is commonplace among !Kung. In fact, the reason that goods are shared equitably and more or less continuously is that the have-nots are so vociferous in pressing their demands. Are these a people who live in communal harmony, happily sharing all among all? Not exactly, but the interpretation of meaning in any culture inevitably founders on these kinds of ambiguities. At one level of analysis, one can show that goods circulate, that there are no inequalities of wealth and that peaceable relations characterize dealings within and between bands. At another level, however, with some of the anthropologist's etic conceptual categories put aside, one sees that social action is an ongoing scrimmage—often amicable but sometimes carried on in bitter earnest.

Lorna Marshall (1976) has captured much of this ambiance with the precision of all her writing about !Kung. In describing the high level of bickering, she writes,

> All these ways of talking, I believe, aid the !Kung in maintaining their peaceful social relations. Getting things out in words keeps everyone in touch with what others are thinking and feeling, releases tensions, and prevents pressures from building up until they burst out in aggressive acts. [Marshall, 1976, p. 293]

> I consider that the incidence of quarrels is low among the !Kung, that they manage very well to avoid physical violence when tensions are high and anger flares, and that they also manage well to keep tension from reaching the point of breaking into open hostility. They avoid arousing envy, jealousy, and ill will and, to a notable extent, they cohere and achieve the comfort and security which they so desire in human relations. [Marshall, 1976, p. 312]

Deciding how to depict the emotional climate of group life is like deciding whether a glass is half empty or half full. Individuals do strive to avoid angering their co-residents, but they do so because the rules about behavior have teeth in them. Furthermore, as they live in close, intimate camps, the chances of committing various sins and getting away with them are practically negligible. The

!Kung, in their own way, are as constrained by their culture as we are by our own.

Settlement Pattern

It is much easier to understand why social norms are effective when one appreciates the spatial setting for camp life. The typical !Kung camp is an elliptical clearing in the bush, into which anywhere from thirty to sixty people settle for periods ranging from a week to several weeks. The way in which this space is utilized ensures that there is a minimum of privacy and a maximum of close interpersonal contact.[8] The people themselves are closely packed in this (arbitrarily) limited space and, in addition, the organization of the interior space increases the exposure of each person to every other person. For example, each individual nuclear family has its own hut, built by the women of grass and branches. The huts are located at the outer edges of the circular village space. The inside area is systematically cleared of grass, bushes, saplings, anything, in fact, which might provide shade or privacy or screen one part of the village from another part. In this way, neither the huts nor natural features of the vegetation serve to break up the inner space or to create micro-neighborhoods. Surprisingly, even the huts are not actually occupied in the usual sense. People do not live in their huts or go into them for rest or privacy. Instead, the huts are used for dry storage of food, skins, and tools. The huts are so closely spaced that people sitting at different hearths can hand items back and forth without getting up. Often people sitting around various fires will carry on long discussions without raising their voices above normal conversational levels.

Whereas the average Western European would find this close press oppressive, !Kung clearly thrive on it. The circular arrangement of inward-facing huts means, effectively, that forty or so people are living in one large room. As a result, the earliest and subtlest acts of an antisocial nature can be perceived immediately and corrective measures can be taken. If a person is angry, someone, if not everyone, will soon know about it. Given their propensity for living in such close quarters, it seems that the !Kung readiness to air grievances earlier rather than later is highly adaptive. When a person feels affronted, he or she can talk about it, usually at a time and in a way when practically everyone in camp will also hear the complaint. In this way a person's pique is publicized and in some measure vented. Other people become involved, and the weight of frustration does not lie with the individual alone.

In considering !Kung values and the social and economic constraints within which they operate, one needn't conclude that the !Kung are unusual because they avoid interpersonal conflict and achieve a degree of group harmony. Actual fights occur, and homicides have been known in the past. However, there are several factors which affect the expression of aggression in this society and in these respects the !Kung contrast markedly with other peoples. Physical aggression is not directly taught or subtly encouraged. Aggressive models are not readily available to inspire children or adults to violent display. Physical aggression and antisocial behavior are costly, given the social and economic interdependence of all people who live together. Furthermore, it is virtually impossible for a wrongdoer to escape detection. Unlike other societies in which an individual can brood in privacy or with the sympathy of a few supporters, among the !Kung an individual is always open to scrutiny and criticism. A person's complaint is rarely something that he or she can act on individually. Welcome or not, other people are always interposing themselves.

Are the !Kung aggressive or unaggressive? Are they more or less aggressive than certain other groups? Until the omnibus term, aggression, is refined and operationalized a comparison of !Kung and other people in aggressiveness will not be possible on an empirical and quantifiable basis. From my observation, the !Kung were extraordinarily successful in discouraging harmful and malicious behavior in young people. During the twelve months in which I lived with different camps in the ≠To//gana and /Du/da areas there were no conflicts between adults which led to serious injuries or homicides. Nor did such events occur among this population at camps at which I was not present.

Homicide and assault in recent times are no doubt discouraged by the fact that a government-appointed headman now lives in !Kung territory in western Botswana and by the fact that the South West African police now patrol the !Kung areas in adjacent parts of South West Africa. The !Kung realize that in the case of serious crime, word will spread and a wrongdoer will be hunted down by outside authorities. This no doubts acts as a restraint. Furthermore, in recent times the isolation of !Kung from other groups has decreased markedly. There are now many centers of Bantu occupation (and a few centers of European occupation) to which !Kung are attracted both by the change of paid work and by the opportunity of changing life style. In the past, such opportunities for individuals or family groups to opt out of !Kung society were not available. It is possible that serious crimes against persons were more frequent in the past in part due to the fact that deviants, outcasts, and fugitives had nowhere to go and still make a living. They had to be retained within the society and tolerated or eventually assassinated. Today the situation is different for two reasons. !Kung can leave the close pressures of the bush camps and move to Bantu or mixed !Kung-Bantu settlements where life is different. In addition the authority of external governments can now penetrate the remotest !Kung band, and punishment for criminal acts can be achieved.

NOTES

1. See Biesele, Draper, Harpending, Howell, Katz, Konner, Lee, Lee and DeVore, Shostak, Yellen.
2. See Draper, 1976, for a discussion of factors in child life among foraging !Kung.
3. Though children avoid the distant bush, age and sex influence the extent to which children use the bush near the camp site.
4. See Lee, 1972a, for a discussion of the role played by Bantu headmen in settling the disputes of sedentary !Kung.
5. Among the people of /Du/da it was common for a hunter to wound an animal one day, only to leave it, return to camp for the night, and to begin tracking the next day. There are several reasons for the delay. The poison on the arrow may require an overnight period to weaken or kill the animal. Also, the hunter reasons that the animal may travel several miles before it dies. The hunter realizes that he will need other men to help carry the meat back to camp.
6. See Lee, 1969, for a fine illustration of !Kung vituperation in context.

7. Polly Weisner, a graduate student in the Department of Anthropology, University of Michigan, has made an exhaustive study of hxaro among the !Kung of the /Tai/tai and !Kangwa areas in Botswana.
8. See Draper, 1973, for a more complete description of settlement pattern, density of occupation, and their relation to the concept of crowding.

BIBLIOGRAPHY

Asch, Timothy, and Napoleon A. Chagnon 1970 *The Feast.* (19mm film) National Audiovisual Center, Washington, D.C.
Benedict, Ruth 1934 *Patterns of Culture.* Boston: Houghton Mifflin.
Biesele, Megan 1972a "The Black-Backed Jackal and the Brown Hyena: A !Kung Bushman Folktale." *Botswana Notes and Records,* vol. 4.
——— 1972b "Hunting in Semi-Arid Areas: The Kalahari Bushman Today. *Botswana Notes and Records.* Special Edition No. 1 (Proceedings of the Conference on Sustained Production from Semi-Arid Areas).
——— 1975 "Folklore and Ritual of !Kung Hunter-Gatherers." Ph.D. Dissertation in Anthropology, Harvard University, Cambridge, Mass.
——— 1976 "Some Aspects of !Kung Folklore." *Kalahari Hunter-Gatherers,* Richard B. Lee and Irven DeVore, eds. Cambridge, Mass.: Harvard University Press.
Chagnon, Napoleon 1977 (*Yanomamo: The Fierce People,* 2nd ed. New York: Holt, Rinehart & Winston.
DeVore, Irven, and Melvin J. Konner 1974 "Infancy in Hunter-Gatherer Life: An Ethological Perspective." *Ethology and Psychiatry,* Norman F. White, ed. Toronto: University of Toronto Press.
Draper, Patricia 1973 "Crowding among Hunter-Gatherers: The !Kung Bushmen." *Science,* October, vol. 182, No. 4109, pp. 301–3.
——— 1975 "!Kung Women: Contrasts in Sex Role Egalitarianism in the Foraging and Sedentary Contexts." *Toward an Anthropology of Women,* Rayna Reiter, ed. New York: Monthly Review Press, pp. 77–109.
Draper, Patricia 1976 "Social and Economic Constraints on Child Life among the !Kung." *Kalahari Hunter-Gatherers,* Richard B. Lee

and Irven DeVore, eds. Cambridge, Mass.: Harvard University Press, pp. 199–217.

Harpending, Henry C., and Trevor Jenkins 1974 "!Kung Population Structure." *Genetic Distance*, James F. Crow, ed. New York: Plenum Publishing, pp. 137–65.

Harpending, Henry C. 1976 "Genetic and demographic variation in !Kung populations." *Kalahari Hunter-Gatherers*, Richard B. Lee and Irven DeVore, eds. Cambridge, Mass.: Harvard University Press, pp. 152–65.

Hoebel, E. Adamson 1954 *The Law of Primitive Man*. Cambridge, Mass.: Harvard University Press.

———— 1958 *Man in the Primitive World*, 2nd ed. New York: McGraw-Hill.

Howell, Nancy 1976 "The Population of the Dobe Area !Kung." *Kalahari Hunter-Gatherers*, Richard B. Lee and Irven DeVore, eds. Cambridge, Mass.: Harvard University Press, pp. 137–51.

Howell, Nancy 1973 "The Feasibility of Demographic Studies of Anthropological Populations." *Method and Theory in Anthropological Genetics*, Michael Crawford and Peter Workman, eds. Albuquerque, N.M.: University of New Mexico Press.

Katz, Richard 1976 "Education for Transcendence: Trance-curing with the Zhun/twasi." *Kalahari Hunter-Gatherers*, Richard B. Lee and Irven DeVore, eds. Cambridge, Mass.: Harvard University Press.

Konner, Melvin J. 1972 "Aspects of the Developmental Ethology of a Foraging People." *Ethological Studies of Child Behaviour*, N. G. Blurton Jones, ed. London: Cambridge University Press, pp. 285–304.

———— 1976 "Maternal Care, Infant Behavior and Development among the Zhun/twa (!Kung) Bushman." *Kalahari Hunter-Gatherers*, Richard B. Lee and Irven DeVore, eds. Cambridge, Mass.: Harvard University Press, pp. 218–45.

Lee, Richard B. 1968 "What Hunters Do for a Living, or, How to Make out on Scarce Resources." *Man the Hunter*, Richard B. Lee and Irven DeVore, eds. Chicago: Aldine Publishing, pp. 30–48.

———— 1969 "Eating Christmas in the Kalahari." *Natural History* 78 (December).

———— 1972a "Population Growth and the Beginnings of Sedentary Life among the !Kung Bushmen." *Population Growth: Anthropological Implications*, Brian Spooner, ed. Cambridge, Mass.: Massachusetts Institute of Technology Press.

———— 1972b "!Kung Spatial Organization: An Ecological and Historical Perspective." *Human Ecology,* vol. 1, pp. 125–47.

———— 1973 "Mongongo: The Ethnography of a Major Wild Food Resource." *Ecology of Food and Nutrition,* vol. 1, pp. 1–15.

Lee, Richard B., and Irven DeVore, eds. 1968 *Man the Hunter.* Chicago: Aldine Publishing.

———— 1976 *Kalahari Hunter-Gatherers.* Cambridge, Mass.: Harvard University Press.

Malinowski, B. 1920 "Kula: The Circulating Exchange of Valuables in the Archipelagoes of Eastern New Guinea." *Man,* no. 51, pp. 97–105.

———— 1922 *Argonauts of the Western Pacific.* London: Routledge and Kegan Paul.

Marshall, Lorna 1957 "The Kin Terminology System of the !Kung Bushmen." *Africa,* vol. 27, pp. 1–25.

———— 1959 "Marriage among !Kung Bushmen." *Africa,* vol. 29, pp. 335–65.

———— 1957 "N!ow." *Africa,* vol. 27, pp. 232–40.

———— 1960 "!Kung Bushman Bands." *Africa,* vol. 30, pp. 325–55.

———— 1961 "Sharing, Talking and Giving: The Relief of Social Tensions among the !Kung Bushmen." *Africa,* vol. 31, pp. 231–49.

———— 1962 "!Kung Bushman Religious Beliefs." *Africa,* vol. 32, pp. 221–52.

———— 1976 "Sharing, Talking, and Giving: Relief of Social Tensions among the !Kung." *Kalahari Hunter-Gatherers,* Richard B. Lee and Irven DeVore, eds. Cambridge, Mass.: Harvard University Press, pp. 350–71.

———— 1976 *The !Kung of Nyae Nyae,* Cambridge, Mass.: Harvard University Press.

Service, E. R. 1966 *The Hunters.* New York: Prentice-Hall.

Shostak, Marjorie J. 1976 "A Zhun/twa Woman's Memories of Childhood." *Kalahari Hunter-Gatherers,* Richard B. Lee and Irven DeVore, eds. Cambridge, Mass.: Harvard University Press, pp. 246–77.

Thomas, Elizabeth Marshall 1958 *The Harmless People,* New York: Random House.

Yellen, John E. 1971 Archaeological Investigations in Western Ngamiland, Botswana. *Botswana Notes and Records,* vol. 3.

———— 1976 "Settlement Pattern of the !Kung: An Archaeological Perspective." *Kalahari Hunter-Gatherers,* Richard B. Lee and Irven

DeVore, eds. Cambridge, Mass.: Harvard University Press, pp. 47–72.

Yellen, John E., and Richard B. Lee 1976 "The Dobe-/Du/da Environment: Considerations for a Hunting and Gathering Way of Life." *Kalahari Hunter-Gatherers,* Richard B. Lee and Irven DeVore, eds. Cambridge, Mass.: Harvard University Press, pp. 28–46.

JEAN L. BRIGGS

The Origins of Nonviolence:
Inuit Management of Aggression

Introduction

This paper[1] concerns the management of aggression in two Canadian Inuit[2] camps, that of the Utkuhikhalingmiut (Utku) in the central Arctic, and that of the Qipisamiut (Qipi) in the eastern Arctic. In it, I shall discuss one way in which the theory, values, behavioral models, and emotionally charged experiences which the Utku and Qipi have regarding aggression may combine to maintain the nonviolent pattern of behavior that is found in these two societies.

For purposes of this paper, I define *aggression* very broadly as an injurious act. The act may be physical, verbal, or merely imagined; it may be directed outward toward a person or object, or inward toward the self. If the act of aggression is physical, I label it *violence*.

Aggression is distinguished from *hostility:* an emotion which may provide the motivation for aggressive acts. I assume, however, that aggressive behavior may be a cultural idiom for the expression of feelings other than hostility. A careful analysis must determine whether a given aggressive act was in fact a vehicle for conscious or unconscious feelings of hostility, or whether it was, for example, a thoughtless—or perhaps a dutiful—imitation of an aggressive model, an idiomatic expression of affection, or a rational, dispassionate act of murder.

I should like to emphasize at the outset that I do not consider what follows to be a complete explanation of Inuit aggression management. For one thing, in addition to the few variables that I shall outline, others are certainly involved, and all of the variables are related to one another in multiple ways, not just in the ways that I describe here. For another thing, there are differences as well as similarities between Inuit groups with regard to interpersonal style—differences both between traditional camp groups in various parts of the Arctic and, nowadays, differences between camps and settlements. Therefore, the extent to which this analysis is applicable to Inuit in general is an empirical question. Nonetheless, the fact that it is possible to make generalizations which are applicable to both of the widely separated groups that are described here indicates, I think, that these statements are also relevant in large measure to other Inuit groups. The differences in aggression management between Utku and Qipi and, I think, also among other groups are variations on a common theme, a theme of strong disapproval and fear of hostility and of expressions of hostility. The most obvious differences lie in the extent to which the two groups actually control aggression and in the nature of the permissible aggressive forms. As compared with the Utku, the Qipi allow somewhat more open expression of hostility, as well as more aggressive expression of other emotions, such as affection, both nurturant and sexual. Nevertheless, the underlying values and fears, the ways in which they are learned, and the ways in which hostility is handled, in oneself and in others, are fundamentally similar in both groups. I therefore discuss them together and, on the whole, additively.

UTKU AND QIPI WORLDS

The physical and social situations of the Utku and Qipi are in some ways similar and in other ways different. At the time this study began, there were about thirty-five Utku and about fifty Qipi living in their traditional territories. Both groups live in isolated and seasonally nomadic camps about a hundred miles across open water from the nearest settlement, which means also from the nearest neighbors. This settlement is Gjoa Haven in the case of the Utku, Pangnirtung in the case of the Qipi. In both cases, these settlements provide the main link between the camp groups studied and the outside world, both Western and Inuit. Men of both groups travel into the settlements in small groups about once a month in winter, to trade furs for the store goods which they need in their camp life. Qipi trade in the summer, as well, and in all seasons have a much easier and faster trip to the settlement, equipped, as they are, with snowmobiles and powered boats. The Utku are cut off entirely by open water in the summer and autumn, and in other seasons travel by dog sled. For Utku, the round trip takes between four and twelve days, for Qipi an average of three days. Women and children from both groups occasionally go along on trading trips, but rarely more often than once a year and in some cases much less frequently than that.

These trading trips are almost the only contact the two groups have with the outside world, except for occasional visitors: settlement-dwelling Inuit who are out on hunting trips; officials from the settlement on "check-up" visits; and, in the case of the Utku, groups of sports fishermen who come and go during July and August. Individuals from both groups have been sent out to hospitals, and a few of the children in both groups have had a little schooling. On the whole, however, the outside world plays a minor role in camp life. Both groups live quite self-sufficiently, adjusting minimally to Western culture, except for the practice of Anglicanism and the incorporation of such material goods as are useful to life in a hunting camp.

In other important respects, the physical environments and living conditions of the two groups are very different. The Utku live in rolling open tundra at the mouth of a large river. In winter their shelters are iglus, in summer canvas tents. Their food is very largely fish, and their cash income, which is small, comes from trapping foxes during the winter months. The inventory of household goods is small, too—a convenience for people who travel by dog sled, by canoe, and on foot. Shortages of fuel, ammunition, and store food are not unusual experiences for the Utku in any season, and during the summer and autumn months, when they are cut off from Gjoa Haven, these shortages are, of course, chronic.

The Qipi, on the other hand, live at the base of bare, precipitous mountains. In summer they live in thin canvas tents like the Utku, but in winter they live in double-walled tents, insulated by a thick layer of dry Arctic heather between the two canvas walls. These tents can be heated up to 70° to 80°F. with three seal-oil lamps,[3] unlike the Utku iglus, which have to be cooled off to prevent melting when the indoor temperature rises above 30°. The Qipi have a more varied diet than the Utku, too. They hunt seal and harp seal, beluga, and caribou, as well as fish, birds, and eggs in season. Cash income comes from sealskins, and is ordinarily sufficient to provide expensive items such as tape recorders, phonographs, short-wave radios, and so on, in addition to the essentials: food, clothing, fuel, ammunition, snowmobiles, boats, and boat motors. The Utku know about the more affluent conditions in which the eastern peoples live, but they do not appear to feel deprived in their more austure environment. As one young Utku man remarked, "If I get twelve foxes this winter, I can buy everything I want."

Both the Utku and the Qipi live in bilateral kin groups. At the time my study of the Utku was begun, the core of the group consisted of two elderly brothers and their offspring of both sexes, including three married or widowed daughters and the families of the latter. The Qipi group consisted of one elderly man, three married daughters, and a married son. Both groups also contained a few other men, with their wives and children, who were related to the core group in various complicated ways. In both groups, everyone could specify kinship connections with everyone else in the group, but that did not mean that either camp considered itself to be a unified entity, except *vis-à-vis* outsiders. In relationships among themselves there were lines of division, which were reflected in tensions, in various, to my eye muted, forms of hostile expression, and also in the patterns of seasonal dispersal.

In both groups, winter is a season of coming together; in other seasons, people live in small scattered clusters, sometimes within sight of others but often, too, at much greater distances. In these seasons, the men meet one another quite frequently while out hunting or fishing, but the women and children seldom see those camped far away.

Among the Qipi, households tend to be nuclear whenever feasible, that is, when sufficient building material (wood, canvas) is available. Utku households also tend to be nuclear during the sum-

mer, but in the winter, joint iglus may be built by two lineally related families, perhaps for added warmth as well as for increased
sharing of food, work, and sociability.

Among the Utku, there are no acknowledged group leaders.
Each household head directs his own household but no others.
Among Qipi, however, as among other eastern Inuit, sons and
sons-in-law may continue to defer, in certain matters, to the wishes
of their fathers and fathers-in-law even after they marry and set
up their own households, especially if they live in the same camp.
In the case of the Qipi, the elder—the father of them all—is recognized as such an authority by everyone in the camp. He doesn't
exercise authority in everyday matters of whether or not to hunt
and where and what; but in long-range decisions, such as whether
to move to Pangnirtung or not, some people defer to his wishes.
No household head is sanctioned if he makes his own decisions in
such matters; deference is voluntary, but, phrased as loyalty, it is
nevertheless often there.

The Meanings of Aggression

My explanation for the maintenance of nonviolent behavior toward
human beings in Utku and Qipi societies focuses on the fusion of
affectionate with aggressive behavior in the socialization of children. In terms of Inuit theory of emotions, this fusion is paradoxi-
cal, since affection and aggression are conceived of as absolutely
antithetical; affectionate behavior is, by definition, not aggressive,
and vice versa. In what follows, I shall try to explain the paradox
and demonstrate its effects.[4]

Underlying my analysis are two assumptions: first, the truism
that behavior is channeled by ideas and values—specifically, in this
case, ideas about what human nature is like and values about what
it ought to be like and how people ought to be treated; and second,
the proposition—also widely, though not always explicitly, accepted—that these ideas and values must be supported by emotionally charged experiences to make the ideas seem true and the
values seem right. It is necessary, then, to define first the doctrines
and values that provide the philosophical rationale for nonviolent
behavior and then the experiences that reinforce the philosophy.

THE GOVERNING DOCTRINES

In both Qipi and Utku societies, two concepts and their associated values provide major support for nonviolence: *ihuma* and *naklik*. Ihuma covers roughly all of the functions that we think of as cerebral: mind, thought, memory, reason, sense, will. Naklik can be glossed as protective concern. These concepts govern the expression of aggression in several ways.

Ihuma. Ihuma is the criterion of humanness and maturity. Saying that a person has ihuma is equivalent to saying that he is a fully socialized, competently functioning Inuk. Inuit have ihuma; wild animals and dogs do not.[5]

A mature and good person is one who is governed by reason (ihuma) and who demonstrates this by consistently considerate, permissive, unaggressive behavior to everyone. In other words, reason is supposed to govern emotionality in general, and in specific, it is supposed to prevent a person from aggressing inappropriately. The possession of ihuma also defines the categories of living being against whom one may and may not legitimately aggress. Only those who have no ihuma—that is, dogs and animals—are appropriate targets; those who do have it—human beings—are thereby granted autonomy. Outside the limits of the role requirements to which people are expected to conform, possessors of ihuma ought not to be interfered with or violated in any way. The Utku, though not the Qipi, define interference much more rigorously than we do: one should not persuade another, not attempt to influence his opinions or actions, not criticize or suggest a different course of action, not even question motives. "Why?" is one of the rudest questions one can ask an Utku. In their view, a person other than one's natural subordinates should not be directly asked to do something, because he might feel awkward about refusing and thus would feel imposed on. Some of this attitude toward interference can be seen in the east, too, but in less extreme form. In both societies, a person who has ihuma demonstrates this fact by conforming voluntarily, by obeying his "leader" willingly when told to do a task. At the same time he will strongly resist, by passive withdrawal or polite circumvention, any encroachment on his legitimate areas of privacy and self-determination. The value placed on autonomy thus separates people to a degree and inhibits aggressive action.

The concept of ihuma, then, plays a threefold role in the control of violence: first, it provides a rationale for the value placed on autonomy or noninterference and defines who has the right to be regarded as autonomous;[6] second, it defines the force (namely, reason) that enables people to exercise self-control in respecting each other's autonomy; and third, it provides a sanction against loss of control by labeling such behavior "immature," "unreasonable."

Naklik. In other cultures, a high value placed on autonomy is not always correlated with peaceful behavior; on the contrary, people often defend their autonomy violently, even to the death. So why is it that in Inuit society autonomy is defended by withdrawal rather than by attack? A part of the answer is provided by the concept of naklik. Inuit theory and values concerning protective concern (naklik) parallel those concerning ihuma, and the two reinforce each other. Naklik is concern for another person's welfare; it is every kind of warm and generous behavior. Thus, when one asks for a definition, one is told that naklik is a desire to protect another person from hunger, cold, physical danger, or distress. However, the word may also have connotations of wanting to be with the person who is naklik'd and of missing that person when he is absent. In other words, it is not exactly like the Biblical "love," but has overtones of a more affective relationship.

As the possession of ihuma is the criterion of maturity, so naklik behavior is the criterion of goodness. Almost all negative qualities—and hostility and aggression in particular—are in opposition to naklik; people say, "So-and-so is angry; he doesn't feel naklik." It is the concept of naklik that defines what "reasonable" behavior is and clearly requires autonomous people to treat each other with circumspection and restraint and to defend their autonomy unaggressively.

The concepts of ihuma and naklik are related also in that capability for naklik behavior is derived from the possession of ihuma. The doctrine is that people who have ihuma feel naklik, and, conversely, not feeling naklik is a sign that ihuma is lacking or "spoiled."

Finally, it is, above all, possessors of ihuma—that is, human beings—to whom one ought to behave in a protective, naklik way. Toward dogs and other animals one need not be protective.

INTERMEDIATE CATEGORIES

So far, we have been speaking as if the categories of those with ihuma and those without, those who must be treated protectively and those who needn't be, were clearly bounded: humans on the one hand and animals on the other. But in fact, there are intermediate categories: children, whites, and idiots. These are thought to have some ihuma, but not very much. Predictably, the way these categories are treated is also intermediate between the ways in which adults and animals are treated.[7] I limit myself here to a discussion of children. Children, in the first place, do not have full autonomy. They are influenced, criticized, persuaded, and scolded; but, on the whole, they are not hit. More precisely, Utku children are not hit at all, and Qipi children are, ordinarily, not hit hard. Moreover, adults in both groups feel ambivalent about scolding. Utku feel it is not necessary; "teaching" should be enough, because, as a child acquires ihuma, he will remember. But they say that mothers (less often, fathers) get impatient and resort to scolding. Qipi hold the somewhat contradictory beliefs that scolding is proper and necessary, but that a good person never scolds. Again, mothers are thought to be more impatient and inclined to scold than fathers.

Children, then, are properly interfered with a great deal more than adults are; but on the other hand, they should not be physically abused. They should not be hit, and, of course, they should not be killed. Dogs, on the other hand, having no ihuma, cannot be taught (that is, told) how to behave; they have to be beaten, and Qipi, though not Utku, also kill them, as they do other animals. Utku prefer to abandon an unwanted dog and to let a sick and suffering dog die in its own time, and in explanation of their reluctance to kill they say: "Dogs are like people." In other words, physical aggression is acceptable only against creatures that have no ihuma. The fact that children occupy an intermediate position on this continuum is important, because it legitimates the playful disciplines—the fusion of affection with aggression—through which they learn to fear aggression.

The fact that children have only a little ihuma means that they are treated as intermediate categories not only with regard to autonomy, but also with regard to naklik, protectiveness. At first glance, this doesn't appear to be true. People say, "Nobody arouses more protective feelings than a little child"; and, instead of being treated with less naklik because they have less ihuma, they are treated with more naklik than anybody else, a fact that seems to contradict my argument and destroy the continuum I have set up between the treatment of creatures with ihuma and those without. If one looks closely at the way naklik toward children is expressed, however, it is apparent that, although children are not treated with the unadulterated aggressiveness with which animals are treated, neither are they always treated with the "pure," gentle form of naklik behavior that is the ideal in adult interactions. In other words, even though aggression in any form is theoretically opposed to affectionate behavior, affection for children may be expressed aggressively. This is most clearly seen among Qipi. The latter have a word, *ugiangu,* which describes affectionately aggressive behavior. When one asks Qipi what ugiangu means, one is told that it means to attack and kill, and in this sense it is used of dog fights. But it is also used of a bitch that kills her newborn pups in protecting them from aggressors, and, finally, it refers to the expression of intense affection through squeezing, biting, slapping, and other behaviors which are experienced by the child as painful. Utku, too, have a word, *kiilinngu,* which refers to an affectionately excited state, expressed, for example, in intense hugging and kissing of one's infant. Kiilinngu behavior, like most Utku emotional expression, is more restrained than the ugiangu behavior of the Qipi, and even so, it is not quite approved of—perhaps a little childish; nevertheless, it is understandable in their eyes as an expression of affection. Both kiilinngu and ugiangu assaults are restrained sufficiently so that they don't physically injure the child, and they are accompanied by affectionate smiles, laughs, and noises; but in both societies these affectionate assaults may be carried to the point where the child cries or withdraws or tries to appease the aggressive adult by hugging him or by offering a bit of food. Adults see that the child is upset; they interpret the reaction as fear of affection and comfort him tenderly. The relationship which Inuit see between this aggressive behavior and affectionate emotion is clearly shown by the explanation which one woman gave me for ugiangu behavior: "A hurt child is more lovable." I shall return to this explanation later.

There is a close parallel to this affectionate-aggressive treatment of children in the treatment of baby birds and other baby animals which, although not transitional with regard to ihuma, are borderline in another sense, being both animal and baby. This kind of borderline position, too, results in treatment in which affection and aggression are mixed. In this case, however, they are not blended— aggression is not labeled affection—but aggression and nurturance alternate. As animals, young creatures can be killed, but at the same time they are little and infantile and thus lovable. I shall describe at greater length below the mixture of tenderness and indifference with which pets are treated: on the one hand, stroked, cuddled, warmed, and fed; and on the other hand, teased, tormented, and killed. A similar alternation is seen in the hunting of young seagulls, which are still too young to fly. Qipi make special expeditions to bird cliffs in the spring to shoot these birds, and the women's shrieks of excitement when a baby gull is spotted are just like cries at sighting a school of beluga or any other much coveted game animal. When a gull is shot and flutters down to the water, however, the women watching its descent make affectionate clucking noises very like those with which they respond to an injured baby or to a baby that cries when it is affectionately aggressed against (ugiangu'd). I wonder if, in the case of the bird, as in that of the baby, the emotional logic is if a creature is hurt, it's more lovable.

VALIDATING EXPERIENCES

One might argue that the ambiguous treatment of transitional categories of being indicates conflict between violent and nonviolent tendencies or wishes and, therefore, an inherently unstable situation. But, paradoxically, I think it is precisely this ambiguous fusion of affection and aggression that produces a well-socialized naklik adult, one who can be relied on to behave violently only toward animals, creatures without ihuma.[8]

I think the fusion does this in three ways: (1) it provides the child with a benevolently aggressive model to imitate. The child learns both implicitly and explicitly that there is no other approved model; that is, hostile violence toward human beings is never approved. Learning to imitate a model of this sort is not a matter of merely copying it in a rote way, either "just because it's there" or to avoid disapproval of open hostility; the child learns motivations intrinsic to the model. In this case, he learns vividly and painfully what it means to be loved, to be aggressed against, to aggress, and to fear. Specifically (2) the labeling of aggression as affection legitimates the expression of aggression against children and creates a situation in which children can learn to fear. This fear in turn arouses protective feelings in the aggressing adult and pacificatory behavior in the frightened child. And (3) because it is affection that the child is taught to fear, an ambivalence about emotional closeness is created, which makes him afraid of losing loved ones by behaving violently—a possibility that is dramatized for him in a variety of ways, perhaps not least by encouraging both nurturant and destructive behavior toward the "borderline" category of creatures who are both infant and animal. In other words, he is given a nonviolent channel for the expression of hostility and strong motivations for limiting himself to that channel. I will discuss each of these motivations in turn.

THE PACIFIC EFFECTS OF FEAR

From what I have said about the doctrines concerning ihuma and naklik, it should be obvious why aggression needs to be smuggled in under the label of affection. The doctrine says that reasonable and good men do not aggress against other men; their ihuma makes them feel loving, not hostile. But if aggression can be explained as the expression of a properly naklik feeling of affection, that legitimates or, at least, excuses it.

Perhaps less obvious is the importance of providing a channel through which children can learn to fear (*ilira*) people. In order to explain the significance of ilira as a keeper of the peace, I shall have to digress to explain what the feeling is and Inuit theory and attitudes concerning it. Ilira is a fear of unkindness or of being scolded. It is, logically enough, felt only by creatures who are subject to being scolded or treated unkindly—that is, dogs and humans—and only toward those who are potentially more powerful than oneself. Children feel ilira toward those older than themselves; adults do not feel ilira toward children but feel it toward other adults. Ilira is one of the major emotional sanctions supporting Inuit values in general and the naklik value in particular; and, like naklik, it is associated with ihuma in several ways. First, only creatures who have ihuma are capable of feeling ilira;[9] and second, only creatures who have ihuma are capable of inspiring ilira feelings in others. Moreover, children, because they have less ihuma than adults, are said to feel ilira differently. Small children feel it only when they are actually scolded, whereas adults may feel it also in anticipation of being scolded or when somebody of whom they feel protective (naklik) is, or is going to be, scolded.

Inuit attitudes toward ilira are contradictory, or seem so in our terms. On the one hand, ilira is an undesirable feeling, both because the fear is uncomfortable for the person who feels it and because one person's fear makes others afraid of him. I think the logic here is the same as the logic that governs attitudes toward fear of physical injury, namely, that if a person fears attack from another, he will attack that other first, to forestall him. Therefore, a frightened person is a frightening one.

The cure for this uncomfortable situation is to reassure the frightened (ilira) person by being affectionate (naklik) to him. If I am kind to a person who fears me, he will stop being afraid of me—that is, will stop wanting to threaten me—and peace will be restored. As one Qipi man expressed it, "A happy person doesn't fight." This logic is an important source of naklik behavior; both Utku and Qipi are often at pains to reassure one another in this way. Another motive for reassuring a frightened person, of course, is that one wants to see oneself as a good person, and by definition a good person is a protective, affectionate one. If I am good, how could I possibly want to frighten anyone? So again, I will try to prevent others from fearing me.

This set of attitudes toward ilira and its treatment accounts very well for some of the facts of Inuit behavior; but fear has two faces. While on the one hand, it breeds aggressive behavior, on the other hand, it inhibits it; thus ilira is a desirable feeling, too. A person who feels ilira is a socialized person, and vice versa: "A person who does not feel ilira will impose himself on others"; he will intrude on their autonomy, be demanding, and may attack or even kill, because "he feels strong." People speak approvingly of a child who feels ilira toward his parents, because they see this fear as a motive for obeying parental dictates. Similarly, they say disapprovingly of a disobedient child, "He doesn't feel ilira." Yet, in the same conversation, if questioned, a parent will deny that he wants his child to feel ilira of *him* (or her).

Both Utku and Qipi are quite right in thinking that ilira feelings motivate their children to be unobtrusive and docile—and from a very young age, too; even a five-year-old is extraordinarily quiet and obedient in public. They also think, and I agree, that ilira feelings motivate children to try to appease those who make them feel ilira, just as adults do. Utku (I don't know about Qipi) say that this appeasing behavior—a hug, or an offer of a bit of food or a toy—is not genuine naklik behavior; children don't really feel protective until they develop ihuma. It is a false protectiveness, which they call *manigguuti,* but it resembles naklik, it may well be one of the precursors of naklik, and it has the same effect of eliciting protective, warm behavior from others.[10]

So, in at least two ways, ilira fears motivate protective (naklik) behavior: (1) if someone is afraid of me, I'll behave protectively toward him; and (2) if I am afraid of another person, I'll behave protectively toward him—and, of course, he will treat me protectively, too, because he sees that I fear him, and because I've reassured him that *he* has nothing to fear. So the circle is (ideally) complete.

But how are the fears that motivate all this protective behavior created, if everybody is so determined to prevent everybody else from feeling afraid? The answer, I think, is: largely in benevolent aggression situations. So far, I have described just one of the several forms taken by such aggression, namely, the physically intense expression of affection that is called ugiangu by Qipi and kiilinngu by Utku. It is clear that children often feel injured when attacked in an ugiangu manner, despite the accompanying tender gestures and also despite verbal interpretations which must help them to understand the underlying affection: "Mmmm, doesn't that [bite] taste good?" "Wasn't that [slap] fun?" The faces of small Qipi children are often a study as they waver between laughter and tears, reacting now to the pain of the bite or the slap and again to the warm smile and hug of the attacker.[11] When the child is defeated by the pain, both Utku and Qipi say, "My child is afraid of my [intense] affection," and Utku add, "Therefore he tries to pacify (manigguuti) me." Parents in both societies, of course, respond to their child's fear by laughing warmly, kissing the child, and speaking to him tenderly—in other words, they naklik him, reassure him.

Another form of benevolent aggression which produces fear (ilira) is teasing. The motives for teasing are various and complex. Some teasing is, like ugiangu, an expression of intense affection; often, too, it is a deliberate attempt to implant ilira, as a way of keeping children from being demanding; at other times (or at the same time) it helps a child to cope with crises in his life; tests how far he has succeeded in developing emotional control; reassures him that he is a well-liked member of the group; and elicits funny or charming behavior, which is entertaining to the teaser and the audience. It is safe to say that being teased is one of the most pervasive and powerful socializing experiences that Inuit children have.

One form of teasing which may be used with a child as young as a year (or even younger) is to frighten him by making horrid faces at him or by speaking to him very loudly, or in a throaty voice associated with scolding, until he cries, whereupon the audience and the tormentor will laugh, and either the latter or the child's mother will comfort him by offering food. In the cases I observed, the tormentor always tried to appease him, but the child refused comfort from anyone other than his mother. In a variant of this game, the tormentor holds out a piece of food or a toy to the child and sweetly coaxes him to take it. The mother enters into the game, too, encouraging her child to take the food, even holding him out toward the tormentor. But when the child reaches for the goody, the tormentor slaps him and speaks sharply, so that he withdraws and sometimes cries. This sequence is repeated until the child learns not to reach for the proffered object. In all cases, the mode is playful and the expressed aim is benevolent. Indeed, the ability to interact with children playfully and not in a serious, scolding manner, even in disciplinary contexts, is seen as a sign that the socializer is a good, naklik-ing person, well governed by ihuma. And just as with the intense expression of affection, this teasing is followed by reassurance, if the child seems upset.

So children learn to feel ilira as a result of being benevolently aggressed against, and in the same context they learn to behave in a conciliatory manner, toward both aggressors and the victims of aggression. This conciliatory behavior they learn, by imitation, to pattern on the protective (naklik) or false-protective (manigguuti) behavior that they see in adults.

One might argue that aggression need not be labeled benevolent or affectionate in order to produce this result. "Pure" aggressive— that is, hostilely aggressive—treatment from adults might equally well elicit conciliatory behavior from the child victim, since the latter is considerably weaker than the aggressor. If the aggressive behavior were really hostile, however, the child would probably learn to retaliate by aggressing angrily against those weaker than himself, instead of learning to treat weaker people protectively. In other words, he could easily learn strategic pacificatory behavior (manigguuti) from being treated hostilely, but it is more difficult to see how he could learn that kind of pacificatory behavior which is motivated by genuine concern for the other's welfare (naklik).

Furthermore, calling the aggression benevolent (naklik) legitimates it. Given the strong value placed on naklik behavior, it would be harder for an adult to aggress if he couldn't cover his tracks by calling the aggression "naklik." As it is, he can not only justify his behavior, he can positively enjoy his aggression, a fact which must help to perpetuate the pattern. My guess is that naklik aggression is enjoyed both for its own sake—as an outlet for hostility when needed—and also, paradoxically, as a means of making the aggressor feel loving. As my informant said, the sight of a child one has hurt reinforces protective feelings. This is perhaps even more true, if at some level one also has inadmissible hostile feelings toward the child, which, as we shall see in a moment, is quite likely. The reinforced protective feelings in turn perhaps make the adult more naklik toward the child than he otherwise would be.[12]

LEARNING AMBIVALENCE ABOUT AFFECTION

The other major way in which the fusion of affection and aggression produces a well-socialized naklik adult is by creating an ambivalence about emotional closeness—about loving and being loved— which makes a child afraid of losing his loved ones by behaving aggressively. This ambivalence is brought about, I think, in the following way. On the one hand, adults are frequently very warm and tender with children, without any aggressive overtones. The mother is sensitive and attentive to her infant's needs; and, throughout his first years, the child is the center of affectionate attention—cuddled, cooed at, and held by all close relatives of both sexes and all ages— which must certainly encourage emotional closeness to others.

Furthermore, affection, especially that of the mother, comes to be tremendously important in two ways. First, it is associated closely and consistently with food, not only in infancy, but throughout childhood and later life. The child can be sure of being fed only by people who love him, and food has critical importance as a symbol of affection. Second, the mother's affection serves as a refuge from outsiders who are less reliably warm. The world outside the home is full of people who may tease, or reject one by refusing food, or in other ways make one feel afraid. So far, in the hope of keeping this somewhat complex analysis clear, I have spoken as though all the child's fears were learned in the context of being benevolently aggressed against; but in fact, there are other fears in the child's life, too. Notable among these are fears of unkindness (ilira), which are engendered by the hostility of other children, and fears of physical injury (kappia, iqhi), which are felt particularly in relation to dogs and other animals. I have said that children tend to be nurturant toward younger children, and that is generally true of their relations with children much younger than themselves. However, relations with the immediately junior age group tend to alternate between nurturance and rejection; and when a babysitter runs away, leaving her smaller charge on the hillside, surrounded by loose dogs, which all children are taught, for their own safety, to fear, that small child can be very frightened, indeed. The cries of an abandoned child always bring succor, however, from the mother, from another sympathetic adult, or from an older (usually much older) child, who will return him to his mother. Mother, of course, kisses and cuddles, and feeds or nurses the frightened child back to peacefulness. Although she may also tease or scold on occasion, mother will always comfort, feed, and nurture; and she will always defend her child against outsiders. The mother-child relationship, then, is an extremely positive one, warm and trusting. In Qipisa, where feelings are expressed more freely than among Utku, even young adult men, roughhousing with their peers or enjoyably frightened in a game of ghosts, will cry, "Anaaaanaaaak! (Mother!)"—that is, Mother, help me!

On the other hand, there are three fears associated with affection, which complicate attitudes toward that emotion: (1) a fear of losing loved ones (which, in adults, is expressed partly in a fear of loving); (2) a fear of aggression—one's own and other people's—because (among other bad effects) it may cause loss; and (3) a fear of being loved, because affectionate people are sometimes aggressive.

The Fear of Losing Loved Ones. Fear of loss is inculcated in various ways. I think the first lesson that love can be lost is received in infancy. At first glance, this seems an astonishing statement to make, in view of the exceptionally tender care that Inuit infants receive. During the daytime, the needs of infants are very rarely frustrated. Utku babies are backpacked a great deal of the time, either by the mother or by a babysitter, who returns her charge to his mother at the first sign of distress or when he falls asleep. Because the mother is so close to her baby and in physical contact with him so much of the time, she can notice the slightest signs of restlessness and discomfort. She knows when he is waking up or going to sleep, when he is afraid, when he is about to wet, and when he is hungry. Except on the unusual occasions when she is doing something that cannot be interrupted—such as harnessing dogs, loading a sled, or trying to finish building an iglu before dark—she will attend to the baby's needs at once. If she is not able to nurse the baby immediately, she usually bounces him soothingly and speaks to him reassuringly, even though he is too young to understand. An indication of the mother's responsiveness is the fact that even though the baby wears no diapers, the mother rarely gets wet; she quickly removes the baby at the first sign that he is about to urinate.

Qipi infants, like Utku, are often backpacked, in order to transport them from one place to another, to keep them safe and under control while visiting, and to pacify them or put them to sleep when they are irritable and sleepy. However, Qipi babies are much less often backpacked while their mothers are working at home. Qipi winter tents are warmer than Utku iglus, and it is uncomfortably hot for a woman to wear her parka indoors; then, too, a baby is not in danger of freezing while lying in a tent heated to a temperature of 70° or 80°. Partly as a result of this physical separation of mother and baby, Qipi mothers tend to be a little less immediately responsive to their babies' needs. Nevertheless, they believe, as Utku mothers do, that babies should not be allowed to cry for any length of time, because "it will teach them to cry." If they are in the midst of a particularly dirty job, like scraping the blubber off a sealskin, they may allow other adults or older children to comfort the baby temporarily by patting, or cooing, or picking him up, but, ordinarily, they will stop work in a few minutes to feed him.

In both societies, however, this picture of maternal responsiveness applies much more to daytime than to nighttime behavior. Both Utku and Qipi sleep very deeply, and although an infant sleeps right beside his mother under her quilt, she often fails to hear him when he cries. Heavy sleep is not limited to mothers, either. Most Inuit of my acquaintance sleep extremely soundly, accustomed as they are to sleeping in the presence of other adults and children who are talking, playing, eating, crying, and so on. It often happens that all household members sleep through the baby's crying, and it is a wakeful neighbor who comes to rouse the mother. Thus, in spite of the extreme solicitude that characterizes Inuit infant care, babies do periodically experience the loss of nurturance right from birth.

The lesson that nurturance can be lost is also contained in a form of teasing, found in both societies, in which the mother pretends to withhold food; the breast is offered to the baby, but then he is made to search for it, while the mother laughingly moves it just out of reach. And when the baby is old enough to understand the gesture as a threat, the mother may offer her breast to another child, and even give the latter suck. Sometimes this is a way of encouraging her own child to nurse; at other times, it is a game she plays, which rouses her naklik feelings for the baby: a protesting baby, like a hurt one, is lovable.

Such teasing is rarely carried to the point of seriously upsetting the baby, but it is followed by other, more severe, experiences of rejection—both the hostile rejection of older children (especially in the Qipi case) and the teasing rejection of adults. Teasing, both that which is labeled ugiangu and that which is designed to inspire ilira feelings and to test progress in self-control, often impugns the child's self-worth. A Qipi mother, in an access of affection, may tease her child in this way long before he is able to understand: "Are you under the mistaken impression that you're lovable? Aren't you grateful that so-and-so loves you and wants to hold you, although you're such an ugly little thing?" I am not sure that Utku mothers begin such teasing as early as Qipi mothers do, but they, too, begin when the baby is only a year or two old; and in both societies it is carried on well into the age of understanding. At first, of course, the baby responds to the ambiance, or to the tone, which is tender, rather than to the verbal content; but in later games of this sort, mothers in both societies may assume a tone to match the words, and then the baby (or child) is not always sure whether to take the game seriously, judging by his solemn and attentive, or depressed, expression. When a mother kisses her one-year-old's foot and says in a tone of "playful disgust," "Ugh! It stinks!" baby and mother smile and laugh together. But when the same mother says to her three-year-old in a mock-rejecting tone, "You're not lovable, you're an old woman," the child cries. Such teasing is usually followed by explicit reassurance, especially when the child is small, but I wonder if a residue of self-doubt—doubt about one's lovability—nevertheless remains, contributing to the ilira fears that are engendered by this teasing. Evidence that this is so is provided by a central Inuit (Netsilik) man, who described what it is like to feel ilira: "When I am scolded, I shrivel away to nothing; I feel about so high [half an inch]. . . . One should never tell a child that he is bad, because he might believe it, and it would make him feel worthless. When I went to work for whites [as a young man, on the DEWline] and they cursed me out, I believed all the things they said, and I felt terrible." Small Qipi children, unlike Utku, are told they are "no good." This is usually said in a teasing context, rather than when scolding, but the child obviously believes it; his face falls, and he seems about to cry, until his tormentor tells him, reassuringly, "I was lying; I love you. Have some tea."

A quote from an Utku six-year-old illustrates both self-doubt and its association with fear of loss. She had been left with her grandfather and an aunt for several weeks while her parents and most other camp members were away on the autumn caribou hunt, and, more than once while they were gone, she asked me, "Am I good?" This child was normally the center of affectionate attention in the camp, not only from her parents, but from aunts, uncles, and grandfather. I think she felt affectionally starved and therefore uncertain of her worth when left with just two loving people, both of whom were accustomed to teasing her in the way described.

Self-doubt must also be generated in small children by the experience of being abandoned by hostile older children, which I have mentioned above, and by quarrels with peers. Small Qipi children are wont to take the teasing words of adults—"*you're* no good"—and fling them without humor at other children, when they are angry.

Utku, if not Qipi, children may also learn to doubt their lovability by contrasting their own hostile, demanding outbursts with their parents' unfailing patience and self-control. An Utku mother presents herself consistently as a "protector" against unknown and mostly imaginary dangers. She may say, "The lemming will get you if you do that; better come here so I can protect you." She is not likely to say, as I have heard Qipi mothers say, "I'll let the dogs' into the tent." She is gentle, patient, and sympathetic. The doctrines concerning ihuma make it unnecessary for her to insist on winning individual battles, as well as demeaning and childish for her to quarrel with her child. Instead, she presents the child with a very consistent picture of what his behavior should be, and she expects that ultimately, as his ihuma develops, he will increasingly conform. In cases where conflict is unavoidable, passive resistance—experienced by the child as rejection?—is one of her major weapons. I once heard an Utku child, who was struggling to learn control of hostility, cry out in a nightmare, "Mother, mother! . . . I'm bad, bad!" (Briggs, 1970:145). Hostility to the mother can't be expressed directly, both because it is not approved, and because (especially in the Utku case) she doesn't deserve it—she is always good. So it is turned inward, contributing to self-doubt and to ilira feelings.

The fear of losing loved ones is also reinforced by threats of adoption and abandonment and by the actual experience of loss. Many of the threats are made in a teasing context, but some are not. For example, a Qipi child who is being difficult in some way while his parents are packing to move to a new camp, may be told, "Stop that, or you'll be left behind!" People do appear and disappear frequently in a nomadic camp—a loved aunt or uncle, a playmate or a sibling, may move away for short or long periods; fathers also go away for extended hunting or trading trips. The child's attention is invariably called to these absences: "Where's so-and-so? All gone. . . ." He is asked if he misses the person, and any unusual crankiness during the period of absence is attributed to the child's loneliness. Sometimes, too, he is explicitly threatened—teasingly, of course—that the absent person will not come back: "Do you wrongly imagine that your father is going to bring you some candy? gum? something good to eat [i.e., love]? He's not. He's not coming back at all." Small children react to this teasing the way they do to the other "you're not lovable" teasing; they look distressed and are comforted.

Adoption, too, is a fact of life, which is both experienced in reality and dramatized through teasing. The rate of adoption among Inuit is high,[13] and there are several adopted children in both Utku and Qipi societies. As one of my eastern informants, herself adopted, said, "Moving from one family to another, losing someone you love, that's one of the biggest things [contributing to mental illness]." Finally, illness and death are a vivid part of an Inuit child's world in ways that would be inconceivable to a sheltered middle-class urban child.

The fear of loss and accompanying doubts about one's lovability can, I think, be seen in the possessiveness toward people that is characteristic of Utku and Qipi. Quite often, when teasingly threatened with the loss of his loved protector and nurturer, the small child's reaction is to cling to the person he is threatened with losing, or to shriek in protest and try to beat the threatener away with flailing arms—in other words, to intensify his dependent, possessive behavior. The protector, of course, rewards him by laughing and cuddling him. Indeed, the adult's own possessive feelings toward the child sometimes motivate this teasing that tells him he may lose her and that intensifies his clinging. One young Utku woman regularly played a game in which she teased her favorite two-year-old niece by pretending to leave the tent: "Bye bye, I'm going out now." Each time the little girl shrieked, *"No!"* and her aunt, laughing, pretended to accede to the child's demand and came back in, only to repeat the performance a few minutes later. Finally, of course, she really did leave, and the child calmed down, but not before the event of parting had been vividly dramatized and the child's possessive feelings roused to a high pitch.

I have shown how doubts about one's lovability come to be associated with the possibility of losing a loved person; and one can see doubt motivating the possessive remarks that older children and adults make: "So-and-so never comes to visit us any more." Or (said jokingly by a teen-aged eastern Inuit girl to her slightly younger sister, who was about to go and visit with a friend): "You don't like us." The sister's reply was reassuring: "Yes, I do, honest! I'll be back real soon."

The Fear of Aggression. One of the major ways in which loved ones may be lost, of course, is by aggressing against them, and so we come to the second negative theme in the ambivalence about affection: the fear of aggression. In the first place, as I have said, aggressive behavior is strongly and clearly defined as unloving and unlovable, and we have seen the creation of a frightening association between unlovability and loss. But this is not the only association that is established between aggression and loss. One can cause the emotional or physical withdrawal of loved ones not only by displeasing them but also by killing them. The connection between aggression, on the one hand, and injury and death, on the other, are explicitly made by adults in teaching children not to attack others physically. If a small child approaches a newborn, the latter's caretaker is sure to say in a tender voice, "Kiss him, don't hurt him," and any overenthusiastic exploration of the baby, or even an overly vigorous kiss, will again elicit the caution, "Don't hurt him." Similarly, if a child attacks an older person, the latter will respond with an exclamation of pain: "A-aaa!" And if the child uses a weapon in his attack—a stick, a knife, or a stone—he is likely to be lectured in a serious or, in the Utku case, in a hushed and solemn tone on the dangers of murder: "You could kill me; do you really want to kill me? And do you want the police to come and take you away?" The child is told that thunderstorms and darkness and everything else that he is known to fear are caused by his own hostility: "It got dark because you were angry." So he is made to feel that he is omnipotent and his suggestion all-powerful.

Utku children (I am not sure about Qipi children) are told that they can injure themselves as well as others through their uncontrolled behavior. An Utku mother will say in a sympathetic voice to her angrily crying three-year-old, "Don't cry; your eyes are bleeding," or, "Your tears will wet your feet, and they'll freeze."

Fear of aggression is also taught by warning unruly children that they will be attacked by animals, usually animals that the child is known to fear—indeed, taught to fear—such as dogs or lemmings.

All of these threats are given reality by everyday experiences with injury and death. A child's older brothers and his father are hunters; he knows that death can be caused by aggression. He plays with carcasses and fetuses, pretending to kill and butcher them, while making them "cry" with pain: "Maaaa-maaaa." He knows, too, that everyone around him fears aggression; he hears them talk about how frightening angry people are and about how, in the old days, Inuit used to murder one another in anger—or sometimes for no reason at all. And he sees that when someone is angry, others are likely to run away. The effects of aggression are also made real for him by his own painful experiences of being aggressed against. These will be discussed further in a moment, in connection with the third element in the ambivalence, the perils of being loved.

First, however, I want to suggest that, in addition to the foregoing, more or less straightforward, lessons that children learn concerning the dangerousness of aggression, they also learn in sub-

tler ways to fear aggression and to translate that fear into conciliatory (naklik or false naklik) behavior. In brief, these additional
fears may arise from the fact that aggression is not always condemned, it is sometimes encouraged; and the contexts in which
children are taught to enjoy aggression are, I think, easy for children to associate with those in which aggression is prohibited,
which makes the enjoyment, and, indeed, the aggression itself,
highly dangerous.

I have mentioned that baby animals and baby birds are conceptually borderline, being both infantile and animal, and that, as
such, they are both nurtured and killed. I have given examples of
this mixture of opposites in the behavior of adults toward these
creatures, but it is important to look also at the behavior of children
and how it is learned. On the one hand, children seek out and are
given young animals and birds as pets. They stake out birds' nests
as private property long before the young are hatched, and not
many days after they do hatch, children take them home, carefully
and tenderly, and are instructed, equally tenderly, by their mothers,
to "feed it; keep it safe; don't hurt it." When a child plays a little
roughly with his pet, his mother may repeat her warning: "Don't
hurt it." Puppies are also given to children as pets. Indeed, I was
told that being given a puppy signifies that one is a bona fide member of one's family. When it grows up, the dog will be an ordinary
member of the household's work team, and the adult male owner
of the team will have full jurisdiction over it; but the child-owner
names it, and, while it is a pup, he plays with it very much as
though it were a baby. He takes it to bed with him and cuddles it
under his quilts beside him in the same way that he cuddles his
baby sibling or cousin; he taps its penis to make it urinate, just as
his mother taps a baby's genitals; and girls, sometimes even small
boys, will backpack their puppies, as older children and mothers
backpack babies.

On the other hand, small children are taught, through teasing, to
fear moving fuzz—not excluding puppies and baby birds. They are
also expected (I haven't seen them taught) to fear and be revolted
(*quinak*) by newborns, including puppies and human babies. And
they are further taught that one way to cope with what you fear—
when it is animal—is to kill it. I said earlier that Inuit consider a

frightened person to be dangerous, because he might kill in self-defense, and it is in relation to small animals that babies begin to learn this way of handling fear.[14] I saw a one-year-old one day being given a first lesson. He was peering from a distance at a baby duckling that sat in a box nearby. His grandfather said, "Come and hold the duckling." The child didn't move, and his mother said, "He's afraid of it." "Really!" said the grandfather, in an amused tone, picked up a large stick and held it out to the child: "Kill it! Since you're afraid of it, kill it!" The grandfather himself, be it noted, an accomplished hunter, is afraid of lemmings, as are most other Inuit of my acquaintance, and chases them, as do others, with enormous enjoyment.

Fear is not the only motive for killing small animals, however. The child is also taught to kill for the fun of it—that is, for the pleasure of hunting, of getting "game." Indeed, in Qipi baby talk, the word *uquuuquu* (game) is often applied not only to caribou and seal, but also to baby birds, mosquitoes, and tomcod, none of which are eaten, but all of which are hunted for the pleasure of the chase. Most dramatic, and perhaps problematic, of all is the fact that the contradictory directives, nurture and kill, may be applied by the same socializer to the same object in consecutive minutes. Thus, while a two-year-old is playing with a pet bird, the same person who a few minutes ago said in a sweet, persuasive tone, "Don't hurt it! Be gentle!" may now hand a stick to the child and say in the same tender tone, "Kill it, it will be a catch [of game] for you!" The fact that children learn this complex lesson is demonstrated by an Utku child who gently stroked and fed a pet bird, then squeezed its heart out with her thumbnail; and by a Qipi girl who, looking at a lemming she and others had just cornered after hot pursuit, remarked tenderly that the poor thing was hungry, and tried to feed it a little grass before stepping on it and killing it. Children in both societies are also given newborn puppies to kill—not, in this case, their own pets, but newborns that the team owner decides are undesirable to keep. An Utku woman explained to me: "We adults would find it revolting (quinak) to kill puppies." The children do it with every appearance of pleasure: dashing them against boulders with squeals of excited laughter, dropping them off cliffs, or swinging them round and round by one leg and throwing them out to sea. Occasionally, a child will scream and cry in protest at the killing of a particular puppy or at the abandonment of a pet bird when the camp moves, in which case his mother may comment in an affectionately amused voice: "He feels naklik." And on the occasions I observed, a child's desire to save a puppy or a bird from death was honored; his naklik feelings were respected.

It seems to me that these kinds of experience with affection and aggression in relation to baby animals could teach children several lessons. In the first place, of course, children learn that it is not only legitimate to kill animals but also gratifying, enjoyable, in various ways: as a way of stilling fear, as a game (a hunt), and perhaps, on occasion, as an outlet for hostile feelings. (Dog-beating is an extremely common outlet for hostility and frustration among adults.) At the same time, the dangerousness of aggression, the ease with which one can injure that which one loves, could well be underscored for the child who learns that it is acceptable, and in fact fun, to kill pets—creatures whom one has loved and who are in many contexts conceptually associated with human babies. It seems to me possible for a child to create either or both of two links between the killing of a lovable animal and the killing of a lovable human. He could identify with the pet, in that both are borderline creatures—lovable, petted, played with (as a toy),[15] and aggressed against—and could fear being killed like the animal. This fear belongs to the dangers of being loved, the third aspect of the ambivalence about affection, to be discussed below. Secondly, he could identify with the killer and fear that he might do damage to a loved human object out of fear, or hostility, or even in play, just as he kills pets. The warnings that he receives not to hurt or kill the baby by hugging or playing with it too hard could feed both fears. As I have said, children play with puppies very much in the way they and others play with babies. But babies are not the only lovable, fearable, hatable humans. Mothers have all those qualities, too, and so, if the child can make a somewhat larger leap—from infantile lovable objects to adult lovable objects—his association of mothers, too, with killable objects and, hence, his fear of killing his own mother (created in the first place by direct warnings that his hostile pebble-throwing could kill her) could be intensified by the experience of killing baby animals.[16]

It is clear that these experiences with small animals contribute also in another way to the creation of the adult nonviolent behavior that we are trying to explain. Not only do they, probably, intensify the fears of aggression that are generated in so many ways; they also, very evidently, arouse nurturant, protective behavior in response to these fears. The simplest way in which they do this is by making a child want to protect a pet that is threatened by someone else. I have mentioned that in such circumstances—whether the threat is real or a tease—children do show protective behavior, and that their parents label it "naklik" or "siqnaaq" (overprotective), and, most important, often respect it and accede to the child's demand. The link with injury to humans is made by a game which adults and older children play with smaller children, in which the teaser pretends to injure a person the child loves—for example, by holding a hand over the head of the threatened person, as if about to pull the latter's hair and saying, "I'm going to hurt her. Shall I hurt her?" Usually in this case, too, the child protests, and the teaser playfully withdraws, commenting with affectionate amusement on the child's protectiveness and allowing the child to experience success in protecting the "victim."[17]

Protectiveness may also be elicited more indirectly. As we have seen, it is not only others who aggress against the animals the child loves, it is also, on occasion, the child himself. Consequently, it seems to me possible that a child might feel anxiety and remorse over his own aggressive behavior—and more, over his own enjoyment of aggressive behavior—toward that which he loves, particularly if he identifies the animal with a human, baby or adult; and this remorse could generate nurturant compensation. I have argued, in line with some psychoanalytic thinking, that remorse results from the child's aggression against loved humans (just as adults feel "a hurt baby is more lovable"). Now I am suggesting that in the case of the baby animal it is easier for the child to see the lethal effects of his aggression. In other words, vis-à-vis the animal, the human plot is dramatized for the child. I have, however, no direct evidence that this is so.

The Fear of Being Loved. The third negative element in the ambivalence about affection—the fear of being loved—is derived from the painful experience of being aggressed against in the name of love. The lesson that affection has a price seems implicit in the way both Utku and Qipi babies are treated from birth. In infancy, this price is physical discomfort, and it is greater for Qipi than for Utku infants. In both societies, as I have said, the language of affection is tender, consistent, and sensitive attention to the baby's needs. In both cases, however, babies are overfed. A mother worries about her newborn's resistance to cold and wind until he gets fat. Furthermore, a fat baby is considered much more lovable than a skinny one. Giving food is explicitly recognized as a major way of expressing affection; and withholding food, either from an adult or from a child, is seen as hostile—a symbolism which is related to anxiety about the availability of food in a hunting economy. In any case, whenever an infant shows a willingness to suck, he is considered to be hungry, even if it has only been a few minutes since his last feeding, and even if he vomits immediately after feeding. Since babies are never burped, it seems possible that the mother may sometimes be interpreting the baby's gas pains as hunger cramps. In other words, love is overprovided to the point of causing discomfort; and the cure offered for the discomfort is more love, more discomfort.

Qipi infants also experience the discomforts of love in a certain amount of rough handling or handling against their will. One thinks particularly of the aggressive (ugiangu) expression of intense affection, but babies are also sometimes handled in ungentle ways in the course of daily care. For example, in cleaning a baby's nose, a Qipi mother detaches the mucus from the nasal lining by circularly rubbing the flat of her hand hard against the baby's nose, then sucks out the mucus and spits it out. The baby usually cries. Other grooming activities, such as pulling scabs off sores and removing fluid from blisters, are also experienced by the baby as unpleasant, and these things are usually done while the infant is maximally relaxed, that is, while he is nursing. So again, affection and pain become associated.

Both Qipi and Utku children, but particularly Qipi, who are less regularly backpacked than their Utku counterparts, also sometimes experience being packed as a discomfort. It comes to have a double association: when children are tired, afraid, or sick, it means closeness and comfort, but when they would prefer to be independently active, it spells restraint.

Finally, the expression of affection by older siblings may be unpleasantly experienced by babies. If the baby is a favorite with one or both of his parents, his siblings may compete with one another for his attention, each showering kisses on him and insisting that "I love him the most." One may question, of course, whether such behavior represents pure affection. In any case, the baby, overwhelmed by the attack, is likely to resist and cry.[18]

In later childhood, the intense (ugiangu) expression of affection continues in Qipisa; moreover, in both societies, as I have mentioned, affection is expressed through ambiguous mock-rejecting teasing, which is also experienced as aggressive. Younger children cry, look sad, or become furious; older children sit with stony faces, hide, or run out.

One of the most dramatic manifestations of aggressively expressed affection is the inverted expression of affection toward favorite children, which is called *siqnaaq*. The word siqnaaq refers to the attack that a mother animal or bird makes on predators, in order to defend her young. A human who defends a weaker person—a child, for example—against the attacks of another is also said to siqnaaq. In these contexts, the word clearly means something like "protect." But the word also applies when someone attacks the person he is ostensibly protecting, notably a parent who mistreats his favorite child. The harsh treatment may consist of feeding and clothing the child poorly, scolding him frequently and severely, and never acceding to his wishes. The three justifications that are given for this behavior are clear evidence for the presence in adults of the ambivalence about affectionate dependence which we are discussing. The first two are evidently rationalizations, but no less revealing for that: (1) treating a child in a siqnaaq manner makes him strong and independent, so that he can take care of himself in the world and won't have to rely on others; (2) if somebody wants to hurt the child's father but doesn't dare to do so, they might hurt his favorite child instead; but if they don't know that the child is his favorite, then the latter will be safe; (3) if the child dies, his parents won't feel so badly—if they have been used to expressing affection to him, they will miss him more. Often, I am told, it is a child who has almost died who is treated this way. Quite apart from the parental ambivalence about affection which is expressed in this behavior and which the harshly treated child may perceive, the treatment itself must certainly lead him to question the value of being loved.

Reinforcing the experience of aggressively expressed affection are the threats that explicitly teach children that affection can be frightening: "Watch out, that [stranger] will kiss you!" or, "That [stranger] *loves* noisy children and will adopt you, if you're not quiet." Ilira training, too, may take the form of teasing, mock-affectionate invitations from outsiders: "Come sleep with me in my house; I love you." The child's reaction is to cling to mother, or—if older—to freeze in fear of the outsider's "affection." It should be emphasized that, in general, adoption threats are presented, not as rejections of the child, but as invitations, motivated by affection. It seems possible, also, as I have suggested, that small children may identify with the baby they are told not to hurt, when they are warned: "Don't kiss him so hard, you'll injure him."

Aggressive expression of affection is experienced in a sexual form by Qipi girls from age eight or nine on into adolescence. They are jokingly chased around the tent by men who, with loud cries of excitement, threaten to goose them. The older girls appear to enjoy this game, but those under twelve or so have mixed feelings. On the one hand, they "count coup" in their private, peer group conversations, but on the other hand, they avoid visiting the houses where they are most likely to be teased in this way, saying that they feel ilira. It is quite possible that ilira feelings remain in older girls, also, although they conceal it better. Young married women occasionally talk about how they feared sex when they were first married; and once I heard a middle-aged grandmother whisper to another unmarried woman who had just been chased in the manner described: "Were you scared?" This, despite the fact that the young woman who was pursued had laughed and shouted with apparent merriment.

In all these cases, the discomforts, real and imaginary, that the child experiences are represented to him as an integral part of the expression of affection—that is, they are an aspect of love itself. I think this is a fact of crucial importance. In some instances, the affectionately aggressive behaviors may in reality be motivated by hostility or by a mixture of hostility and affection; but, because they are perceived as benevolent by the attacker and are represented as such to the child, the latter is not alienated from people, as he probably would be if he were treated with open hostility. He is only made to doubt; he can never be quite sure how to interpret people's negative remarks. Even adults need reassurance on this score. I once heard an older Qipi woman in a loud good-humored voice tell a younger woman that she was bringing up her baby all wrong. Then she said warmly, "I'm not scolding you; I'm trying to teach you." The uncertainty about whether people are really hostile or "just joking" warmly, "just teaching," coupled with the real pleasure a child derives from being loved, intensifies the latter's dependence. It is noteworthy that, although it is easy to disconcert Inuit children—put in their terms, it is easy to make them feel ilira—it is also easy to reassure them. When threatened by one person, they seek security, not in solitude, but from another person. Orphans, on the other hand, and other children who are unhappily adopted and who do experience genuine hostility, are not so likely to seek comfort from another person when teased; instead, they may wind themselves around a supportive tent pole or wander off by themselves.

In sum, it seems to me likely that the aggressive expression of affection creates in both Utku and Qipi children an ambivalence about closeness to other people. On the one hand, a need and desire for closeness exists and is intensified by the fear of losing it; on the other hand, there is a fear and consequent dislike of closeness. This ambivalence is expressed by adults in a variety of ways. The wish for closeness and the fear of losing it are seen in the possessiveness that I have described, the need for exclusive relationships with one's spouse, one's children, and one's peers, as well as in a preoccupation, at all ages, with loneliness. Loneliness is an extremely common complaint in both societies. Utku say, "It is impossible to be happy when one is alone," and I am quite sure that Qipi feel the same way.

But the intense dependent needs which are expressed in possessiveness and loneliness hurt and are therefore to be avoided. One Utku expressed this feeling very clearly, with reference to his four daughters: "I love (naklik) Saarak and Kamik a little bit more than I love Raigili and Qayaq. I love them too much. When I am away on trips, hunting or trading, I want to see them. I sleep badly. When Kamik is away at school I miss her; it makes me feel uncomfortable. If I love a child too much I am concerned if she cries a lot; otherwise I don't mind. People don't like to feel uncomfortable. If one doesn't love too much it is good" (Briggs, 1970: 71–72). We have seen that the justifications given for the defensively harsh treatment of favorite children express the same negative feelings about loving. Utku also dislike *being* loved too much. It was the wife of the man just quoted who expressed it best: "My father . . . used to love me too much. But it's all right now; he has stopped loving me so much" (Briggs, 1970:71). In both societies, the extremely high value placed on autonomy, on noninterference, may also be explained in part as a way of counteracting or resisting dependent needs.

To bring the argument full circle—I see this ambivalence about affection playing a crucial role in the inhibition of violence by powerfully intensifying the fear of doing anything that might destroy the fragile relationships that are so important. For the members of these two societies, the fusion, in various ways, of affection and aggression both provides an approved channel for the expression of hostility and motivates them to stay within that channel. This fusion is supported in complex but coherent ways by the values and theories concerning interpersonal motivation that are held by these Inuit.

In conclusion, I should like to return to the caveat I began with and to elaborate it very briefly. What I have written here is by no means a complete analysis of Inuit aggression management. In particular, I regret that it has not been possible to discuss more systematically the importance of the playful mode of value socialization which is so characteristic of Inuit. I have described some of the ways in which the varieties of benign teasing create the complex motivations that underlie nonviolent behavior. But the way in which adults and children together play with aggression not only creates an emotional maze through which children must learn to thread their way; it also creates the strength to cope, and provides a means of renewing from day to day the certainty that one is able to cope, with that complexity. This aspect of the role of playfulness there is not space to discuss here.

NOTES

1. This paper is a greatly abbreviated and slightly rewritten version of a paper which was published in W. Muensterberger, editor, *The Psychoanalytic Study of Society,* volume 6, New York: International Universities Press, 1975, pp. 134–203. Readers interested in more ethnographic data on Inuit management of aggression, both ideal and real, are referred to the original paper.

The fieldwork on which this paper is based was supported by the Wenner-Gren Foundation; the Northern Co-ordination and Research Centre of the Department of Northern Affairs and National Resources (now the Northern Research Division of the Department of Indian and Northern Affairs) of the Canadian Government; the National Institute of Mental Health of the United States Government (Pre-doctoral Research Fellowship 5 FI MH-20, 701-02 BEH with Research Grant Attachment MH-07951-01) ; the Canada Council (award from Isaak Walton Killam bequest to the Department of Sociology and Anthropology of the Memorial University of Newfoundland); the Institute of Social and Economic Research of the Memorial University of Newfoundland; and the National Museum of Canada.

Between 1963 and 1965, seventeen months were spent with Utkuhikhalingmiut in Chantrey Inlet and approximately four months with their relatives in Gjoa Haven. An additional eight months were spent in Chantrey Inlet in 1968. During the next two or three years, most of the Utkuhikhalingmiut moved to Gjoa Haven, where they now winter, and I have visited them there three times: for one month in 1971, one month in the winter of 1971–72, and three months in 1972. This paper deals with life as it was lived in Chantrey Inlet, and the ethnographic present is used in referring to this earlier period. The study of the Qipisamiut was made in 1970 (two months), 1971 (eight months), 1974 (three months), and 1975 (three months).

The argument outlined in this paper was presented originally in a seminar at the Johns Hopkins University, December 1970, and a first version of the longer paper was presented to the Interdisciplinary Colloquium on Psychoanalytic Questions and Methods in Anthropological Fieldwork at the Fall Meeting of the American Psychoanalytic Association, New York, December 1971. Amendments and additions to the analysis were worked out in a series of seminars at the Universities of Tromsø and Bergen, Norway, during the spring of 1976.

At various stages in the preparation of this paper, colleagues and friends have contributed valuable comments and questions. I am especially grateful to the following: Marina Gorodeckis-Tarulis, Georg Henriksen, David Moyer, George and Alice Park, and Robert Stebbins, who, in an informal seminar, helped to formulate the argument; Minnie Freeman, Charles Hughes, Margaret Lantis, Elliott Leyton, Warner Muensterberger, Rebecca Qitsualik, Carol Ryser, Hugh Sampath, Charles Sarnoff, Ronald Schwartz, and Victoria Steinitz, who made useful criticisms of the first version of the paper and raised questions which I have discussed, however briefly, here; and, finally, Hanne Haavind and the other participants in my Norwegian seminars who helped me to rethink the whole.

2. *Inuit* (singular, *Inuk*) is the name that Eskimos give themselves in their own language (*Inuktitut*). Many Canadian Inuit now prefer that term to "Eskimo," a word derived from Algonquian, which originally had derogatory connotations. In this paper I will therefore follow present-day Canadian form and will use *Inuit* as plural noun and as adjective, and *Inuk* as the singular noun.

3. I refer to the traditional shallow half-moon-shaped Inuit lamp with a wick, varying in length from several inches to two feet, laid along the flat edge.

4. In psychoanalytic theory, too, the fusion of affection with aggression is problematic for the child, and the ability to develop, maintain, and cope with ambivalence toward the parent, who is loved and hated, or loved both nurturantly and destructively (incorporatively), is considered an essential achievement in the child's early emotional growth (e.g., Winnicott, 1965:16–17, 74–77). Though the ambivalences to be discussed here seem in part related to that described in the psychoanalytic literature, they are also partially different from the latter, both in cause and in content. Indeed, the whole situation as elaborated by Inuit is different to some extent. I shall not have space to discuss the differences explicitly in this short paper, but psychoanalytically oriented readers may like to keep comparisons in mind as they read.

5. But see note 7.

6. The reverse is also true, of course: the value placed on autonomy, which has its source in a variety of experiences, may also reinforce the value placed on reason. I do not wish to imply a one-way causal relationship here.

7. I have said that dogs are thought not to have ihuma. However, there are contexts in which dogs are spoken of as having it. I think this is a "contradiction" only to our way of thinking, and I take it as evidence that in the Inuit view dogs are also a transitional category: they have ihuma, and they don't have it—like children. In other ways, too, dogs are conceptually intermediate between animals and humans (Briggs, 1975:149).

8. I am, of course, describing the way the situation works when it works as it should. It has been pointed out to me that my description of the well-controlled Inuk does not accord with other ethnographic descriptions of impulsive and violent Inuit. Two things can be said in response. First, the very great majority of the Inuit I know are very well controlled indeed in the conduct of everyday life; but, secondly, the motivations underlying this control are so complex and the elements of the training that creates these motivations so mutually interdependent, that there is plenty of opportunity for something to go wrong in individual instances. I do not argue that Inuit socialization causes violent feelings to vanish. On the contrary, they are very much there. It is even possible to argue that they are intensified by the training I shall describe, which is a kind of playing with fire. And while intense feelings may be more greatly feared than moderate feelings, and thus better controlled under certain conditions, they may come out and be acted on in violent form if they are *too* intense, or if one of the controlling conditions is absent. Inuit themselves do not trust control to operate under all circumstances but recognize danger in a variety of conditions. As we shall presently see, they are afraid of people who have somehow not learned to fear (*ilira*) the displeasure of others; of people, such as drunks, who are not governed by the reasoning power that they label ihuma; and of people who are in an extremely intense emotional state, such as grief or fear of others' imagined hostility. And, indeed, when the demands for emotional control are very stringent, as they are in Inuit society, it is quite easy for hostile and paranoic imagination to run wild and for emotion to accumulate internally to boiling point. As one woman said to me: "A person who *never* loses his temper can kill if he ever does be-

come angry." I therefore see no contradiction between my analysis and the ethnography of others.

9. See note 7.

10. Manigguuti behavior is found in adults, too, where its aim is to pacify, to shame by superior example, or to obtain favors from a feared person.

11. The resemblance between this situation and the double bind described by Bateson (1956) is striking. There is a significant difference, however, in that the Inuit child is consistently taught how to interpret the apparently conflicting messages. He is told that the "I love you" message should always be given priority; and, whether he responds with laughter to that message or with tears to the apparently hostile message, he is rewarded by affection: encouragement or reassurance, as the case may be. In other words, "You see? I do love you." Thus, Bateson's third condition for the establishment of a double bind situation is not fulfilled; the child *is* able "to correct his discrimination of what order of message to respond to" (p. 176).

12. The Inuit perception that a hurt baby is more lovable calls to mind Winnicott's (1965:74–77) idea that the origin of concern lies in guilt over one's destructive wishes toward a person who is loved as well as hated, and the subsequent wish to make reparation to that person. I am suggesting here that the same dynamics may underlie the naklik behavior of Inuit. One could go even farther and suggest that possibly one reason for expressing affection in an aggressive mode may be that at some level adults really feel hostile toward babies, both because babies often are troublesome (and it is clear that Inuit mothers sometimes do feel them to be such), and because adults are ambivalent about feeling affectionate and resist the feeling. The latter ambivalence will be discussed further in the next section. (See particularly the description of *siqnaaq* on pages 82–83.) At the moment, it suffices to say that remorse on both these counts could well make the aggressor feel that a hurt baby is lovable. It should be noted that Winnicott was describing the origins of concern in children, whereas I am applying his reasoning to adults. It is the adult who makes reparation to the injured child by comforting (naklik-ing) him, rather than vice versa, as in Winnicott's argument. I rather doubt that the same emotional logic explains the earliest manigguuti behavior of a baby. The latter seems both to Inuit and to me to be primarily a response to the threat

presented by the adult's aggression, rather than to any threat inherent in the baby's own aggressive feelings, and this, too—the simple wish to disarm an aggressor and restore nurturant behavior toward himself—is certainly, as I have said, one of the important motivations underlying naklik behavior in both child and adult. But as the child begins more and more to develop ambivalences toward affection and toward aggression, the motivations just described, to the extent that they explain adult naklik behavior, must also begin to contribute to the reparations he himself makes to loving adults (see page 80).

13. Ann McElroy (1975:27) cites census figures for Pangnirtung and Frobisher Bay, which show that in Pangnirtung the rate of adoption between 1965 and 1969 was 20% of infants born, and in Frobisher Bay for the same period it was 42%. Between 1939 and 1943 in Frobisher Bay the figure was 27% and between 1954 and 1958 it was 31%. Although the rate seems to be increasing in Frobisher Bay, it is clear from the informal accounts of camp Inuit that the present trend merely continues a traditional pattern.

14. I do not exclude the possibility (even probability) that wishing to kill what one fears is a "human" reaction, a "natural" way of eliminating danger. But this way of coping can be either discouraged or encouraged, and it can be pointed out, or not, as a possibility in situations in which it has not spontaneously occurred to a child. The point here is that killing is both encouraged and pointed out to children as a possibility in their relationships with small animals, and discouraged in relationships with small humans, who, conceptually and behaviorally, are rather close to small animals.

15. See note 16.

16. Two possible counter-arguments to this reasoning occur to me. First, the fact that children enjoy killing newborn puppies, whereas adults are fearfully repelled (quinak), might mean that adults, but not children, make the link between the killing of baby animals and baby humans. Or it could mean that children make the link but haven't yet learned to feel distressed at the thought of killing a baby. There is other evidence that adults do link the killing of animals with the killing of humans, for example, the statement of an Iglulik shaman who is quoted by Birket-Smith (1959:166) as saying that "life's greatest danger . . . lies in the fact that man's food consists entirely of souls." In former times, attempts were made to counteract this danger by means of conciliatory taboos and ceremonies. In most Inuit groups, mourning rituals were performed

for important animals, just as they were for humans (Birket-Smith, 1959:166; Lantis, 1946:194). It is interesting in this connection to note the eastern Inuit belief that infants who are ill-treated or killed can take revenge, just as animals were thought to do.

It is clear that children associate humans and animals. I have described how they play with pet puppies as though the puppy were a baby, and they often play at being animals, too. Sometimes, as "hunters," they pretend to stalk, kill, and butcher each other; at other times, they pretend to be dogs or birds. But I have no direct evidence that they associate animal and human killing.

The second counter-argument is that possibly it is ethnocentric to imagine that the baby animal who is killed is the "same" one who was nurtured a minute ago. Just as a piece of wood or a bundle of grass can be a "baby" one minute and a "dog" or a "boat" the next minute in a child's fantasy, so might a puppy or a pet bird be a "baby" one minute and an "animal" the next—and perhaps "instruments," toys, do not have stable "essences" (a thought that I owe to an unfortunately nameless student with whom I talked at the University of Bergen, April 1976). This argument is, perhaps, supported by the fact that although, as I have said, children may protest the killing of an animal and so rescue it from death, nevertheless I have never seen a child mourn the death of a pet. Once it is dead, it is just thrown away. This attitude is taught by the adult who tries to persuade his child to abandon his pet when they move: "Shall we leave this one behind? You'll get another one."

On the other hand, babies and small children themselves are played with, for the most part, instrumentally and not companionably. That is, adults and older children do not enter into the play of small children, but rather use the children as toys for their own entertainment. The suggestion that instruments don't have essences might, then, equally well apply to children, which, if they perceive this, could intensify their sense of being in a dangerous position. But here I enter into the realm of pure speculation.

17. Cf. Briggs, 1970:173.

18. This experience sometimes leaves conscious traces. One eastern Inuit boy about six years old, whose older sisters had competed for him in this way, was once heard to say tenderly to his baby brother (in English), "You're not going to be spoiled like me." His mother, inquiring, discovered that he remembered unpleasantly the experience of being told by all of his sisters, "Nice baby, you're *my* baby. . . ." To be sure, in this case there is no way of knowing

whether the unpleasant affect was associated with the original experience or whether it is a reaction formation, owing to the fact that the child is now too old to be "spoiled."

19. With the exception of *ihuma* and *uquuuquu,* none of these terms constitute complete words in Inuktitut. Although in the text I have sometimes referred to them as "words," they are, properly speaking, only word-bases; they cannot stand alone (except that the base, *quinak,* can occur alone as an ejaculation). Because Inuktitut words are long and awkward to the Western eye, I thought it simpler to present just the bases.

GLOSSARY OF INUIT TERMS[19]

ihuma: mind, thought, memory, reason, sense, will, i.e., all cerebral functions. First mentioned on page 59 and discussed at length on pages 59–60.

ilira: fear of unkindness, fear of being scolded. First mentioned in note 8 and discussed more fully on page 64.

iqhi: fear of physical injury or death. First mentioned on page 69.

kappia: fear of physical injury or death. Utku use this word more commonly than iqhi. First mentioned on page 69.

kiilinngu: overexcited, tense; often refers to too intense, aggressive expression of affection (Utku). Defined on page 62.

manigguuti: false protective concern. Described on page 66 and in note 10.

naklik: protective concern or "love" in the Biblical sense. First mentioned on page 59 and discussed at length on pages 60–61.

Qipi: abbreviation of *Qipisamiut(aq)*—a person, or people, living in the place called Qipisa.

quinak: a frightened revulsion. First mentioned on page 77.

siqnaaq: defense of a loved one, with connotations of over-protectiveness. First mentioned in note 12 and discussed at length on pages 82–83.

ugiangu: aggressive expression of affection (Qipi). First mentioned and defined on page 62.

uquuuquu: Qipi baby talk for game (in the sense of animal to be hunted). First mentioned on page 78.

Utku: abbreviation of *Utkuhikhalingmiut(aq)*—a person, or people, living in the place called Utkuhikhalik or (in English) Chantrey Inlet.

BIBLIOGRAPHY

Bateson, Gregory 1956 "Toward a Theory of Schizophrenia." *Personality and Social Systems*. N. J. Smelser and W. T. Smelser, eds. New York: Wiley, 1963. Pp. 172–87.

Birket-Smith, Kaj 1959 *The Eskimos*. London: Methuen.

Briggs, Jean L. 1970 *Never in Anger: Portrait of an Eskimo Family*. Cambridge, Mass.: Harvard University Press.

—— 1975 "The Origins of Nonviolence: Aggression in Two Canadian Eskimo Groups." *Psychoanalytic Study of Society*, 6:134–203. W. Muensterberger, ed. New York: International Universities Press.

Lantis, Margaret 1946 *The Social Culture of the Nunivak Eskimo*. Philadelphia: American Philosophical Society.

McElroy, Ann P. 1975 "Continuity and Change in Baffin Island Inuit Family Organization." *Western Canadian Journal of Anthropology*, 5(2):15–40.

Winnicott, D. W. 1965 *The Maturational Processes and the Facilitating Environment*. London: Hogarth.

Notes on Childhood in a Nonviolent Context: The Semai Case

Background

Westerners have long been interested in the nonviolent way of life of the "Senoi" of West Malaysia. The Semai and Temiar are the most numerous Senoi peoples.

Kilton Stewart, then a graduate student in psychology at the University of London, made three brief field trips to the Temiar around 1936, accompanying H. D. Noone, the first anthropologist to do extensive work with the Senoi. Many years later Stewart published a series of articles on how Senoi attained "mental health" by manipulating their dreams. These articles attained some notoriety in America in the late 1960's. References to "Senoi dream therapy" occur in many popular books on dream analysis, and there are "Senoi dream clinics" in southern California. Semai do not treat their dreams in the way Stewart describes. I doubt the Temiar do either.[1]

C. A. Robarchek and I have addressed the question of Semai nonviolence more recently, working independently. My first, paleo-Freudian attempt at analysis is available on microfilm (Dentan, 1965). It strikes me nowadays as unsatisfactory because it postulates psychic aggressiveness before it "discovers" it. I touch on the topic elsewhere, in a short book and a long article (Dentan, 1968a, 1968b). C. A. Robarchek (1976, 1977a, 1977b) approaches the problem from the viewpoint of systems analysis.

TRANSLATION PROBLEMS

Since this chapter attempts to give a Semai point of view, it is often necessary to use Semai words, which look harder to pronounce than they are. The glossary and pronunciation guide at the end of the chapter may therefore be useful. Translators are traitors, of course. Trying to translate the questions addressed by this book into meaningful Semai terms illustrates the difficulties involved.

The mandate for this chapter was, roughly, to describe the ways in which the Semai enculturate their children to be nonviolent. From a Western viewpoint, this is a sensible question. Phrasing it this way, however, invites certain misconceptions. The terms "enculturation," "nonviolent," and "Semai" require a closer look.

"ENCULTURATION"

The word "enculturation" might raise two false expectations. The first is that Semai might have stumbled on a technique, applicable anywhere, for producing nonviolent people. The other is that Semai think of themselves as moulding their children the way Euroamericans do.

The context of learning. The traditional context within which a child learns to act Semai is much less differentiated than the Euroamerican one. In a sense, the settlement in which the child lives is its school. Education occurs there all the time, implicit in whatever is going on. Analyzing educational techniques out of this context distorts what actually happens. Furthermore, because the nature of this total context determines what Semai children grow up to be, it is implausible that Semai enculturative practices could be transplanted successfully into a milieu which is not, like the Semai milieu, homogeneous, egalitarian, intimate, and peaceful.

Indeed, in a differentiated, hierarchical, impersonal, and violent setting, even adult Semai may act very differently from the way they act in their own settlements. For example, Semai say that when they were recruited into the Malaysian government's counterinsurgency forces during the Communist uprising of the 1950's, they were fiercer than people from other ethnic groups, partly in reprisal for terrorist acts committed against Semai. Some former troops say, "We were drunk on blood," *buul bhiip,* a condition which apparently only occurs when aggrieved Semai are taken out of their own social context and are dealing with non-Semai. Most of the violence Semai fantasized to me in 1962, 1963, and 1975 was directed against outsiders. In 1962, some Semai in the remote interior thought the counterinsurgency war might be a prelude to a genocidal war against them. "Outsiders," said a Semai who had been a "corporal" in the *Polis,* "are bad. They call our food unclean and rape our women. I tell you, if they try to kill us, we have poisons known to our ancestors, and we will poison the rivers, and they will die in their cities."

Moving out of their traditional context does not, of course, automatically turn Semai people violent. Although Semai try to keep to themselves ("We hinterland people gain nothing by mixing other peoples' affairs; we only lose"), when pressure is put on them to get involved in what they say is an outsiders' quarrel, they may simply refuse. As one spokesman put it in 1962, "During the war they asked for bearers from our people. There were those who obliged them, for money. I myself like money, but I said to them, 'For rubber, I'll take money. For chickens, I'll take money. For bananas, I'll take money. But I won't take money for blood.' "

In short, nonviolence makes sense in the traditional Semai context. Violence in that context would seem insane, not only to Semai but to anyone else. But enculturation has not incapacitated Semai for violence in response to the violence of others.

Instructing children. Semai emphatically deny that they teach their children. Playing to what he sees as an unsympathetic stereotype of hill people held by an outsider, a man might say, "We don't worry about our children. We don't mess with them. They grow up here in the jungle like animals. We look after ourselves, they look after themselves." This sort of comment is part of the deliberately misleading, Goffmanesque "line" whose ironic theme is that Semai are bestial savages. This line gets Semai off from doing what outsiders want them to do and affords them some amusement. Like most good lies, it is plausible in its context.

In a more serious vein, the mostly pagan Semai contrast their behavior with that they attribute, often mistakenly, to the Moslem Malays who are the dominant people in the area and whose culture, as Semai see it, is a counterculture to their own. For example, "Malays hit hit hit their children. We love our children. That is why our children are strong and healthy, and Malay children like baby rats." Semai thus speak of training children as a form of coercion. For Semai, all coercion is ultimately physical coercion. As physical coercion, it can do physical damage. In a couple of sentences a Semai can move from a question about training children to a counter-question: "Suppose you hit your child and it died?"

"NONVIOLENCE"

Semai nonviolence is an interesting topic for Westerners. It is not a central Semai concern. People express no worry that their children might become violent adults. Such a worry would be bizarre in the traditional Semai context. There, the traditional reluctance to hit people, for example, may be expressed in a commonsensical way: "Suppose he hits you back?" On this level, nonviolence is just being reasonable.

There are three major justifications for calling the Semai "nonviolent" in the face of their expressed indifference to the matter. The first is contrastive. They do not brawl like Americans nor feud like many other Southeast Asian hill peoples. The second is that they openly and often express fear that outsiders will attack them. They therefore do teach their children to fear and shun strangers, especially non-Semai. Flight seems always preferred to fight.

The third justification is that the Semai concept of violence seems very broad and seems almost always to involve a notion of ultimately increasing the risk of physical injury. Any loss of self-control is disastrous. This statement requires a brief exposition. The Semai notion of what constitutes a physically violent act seems far broader than the Euroamerican one. Any type of coercion, for instance, is said to increase the victim's chances of falling sick or being injured or dying. As noted above, teaching = coercion = violence. To take another example, Semai talking in Malay about hitting children almost invariably slip from using the word *pukul* (hit) to *bunuh* (kill), without expressing any sense that they have changed the subject. Furthermore, frustrating someone, ordering someone around, not sharing freely with someone, and so forth: all, say the Semai, may make that person likely to brood, sicken, have a bad accident, or even die. Such results, Semai say, are not inevitable, but their likelihood is increased. In other words, the Semai notion of aggression is more inclusive than the Euroamerican one, although the content of the two notions is different. Moreover, the Semai notion differs in that the results of aggression are always ultimately physical. In short, the third justification for calling the Semai "nonviolent" is that the acts they define as physical violence which decent people do not commit include a broad spectrum of behavior which other people might think of as merely being unfriendly or as necessary discipline.

Students who have read *The Semai* (Dentan 1968a) often seem to form a stereotype of Semai as a people who, due to genetic deficiency or benign personality disorder, are preternaturally gentle and compulsively Apollonian. No Semai, and no one who has spent much time with Semai, thinks of them that way. For example, Semai backbiting, which is frequent, is almost a dramatic art. Six months in a Semai settlement will see at least three or four serious quarrels in which voices are raised and threats of physical violence are at least alleged, if not actually made. Robarchek (1977b) records quarrels so bitter that only a full meeting of the whole settlement could calm people down. At least two murders have been committed between 1955 and 1977, and there is gossip about a couple of others. In short, Semai are nonviolent only in the three senses discussed in this section.

"SEMAI"

The word "Semai" is a Western linguistic and ethnographic convenience not much used by Semai. It may be a Temiar word. Semai call themselves "people," "we people," or "hinterland people." In the 1960's Semai were not quite sure who was and was not "Semai." I use the word because the Semai seem to be a "people" in the sense that term is defined by Karl Deutsch (1966). Geoffrey Benjamin (1966) makes a similar defense of the word "Temiar."

There are about 16,000 Semai. They live mostly in mountain rain forest along the border of Perak and Pahang States. They speak about forty different dialects of a language related to Cambodian and to the languages of some South Vietnamese *"montagnards."* Until recently, they cleared fields in the forest, cultivated them for a few years, and then cleared new fields elsewhere, a pattern anthropologists call "shifting horticulture." Since the population density in Semai areas was less than seven people per mile, considerably lower than this sort of horticulture could support, they could move on easily. Where other peoples are crowding into Semai lands, Semai are turning to cash cropping and wage work. Settlements are usually dispersed and distant from each other. Except during the abortive insurrection of the 1950's, however, people rarely traveled more than a dozen miles from home.

Except where noted, the present tense in this chapter refers to 1962 and 1963. In 1962 I spent about seven months with deep forest "east" Semai, and in 1963 I stayed about the same amount of time with "west" Semai near a thriving Chinese town. I visited the latter settlement for a couple of weeks in 1975. The Ford Foundation supported this research.

CONCLUSION

This translation changes the original question from "How do Semai enculturate their children to be nonviolent?" to "How do children grow up in the Pahang-Perak borderlands?" I hope an answer to the second question helps answer the first. I would be pleased if it also resembles the way a Semai might answer.

"PREGNANCY" (MNAKƆƆ')

Semai begin to pay attention to a child's development from the moment that they realize the child has been conceived. At that time, both parents become *makɔɔ'*. This adjective (the noun is formed by infixing an "n," i.e., *mnakɔɔ'*) is broader than English "pregnant" but implies a more significant biological connection than "expectant parent." Its use expresses the close, symbolically biological connection between both parents and the child. This ritual connection persists even after the child is physically separate from the parent, although the Semai (unlike the Temiar) do not practice the couvade. Thus, for example, the parents' acts may influence the child's health.

When a woman misses her period, she and her husband consult a midwife. The midwife should be a healthy older woman who has borne many healthy children, since her health will, like the parents', affect the health of the child. If the diagnosis is positive and if this is a first pregnancy, the mother and father get their first teknonyms, *KiMakɔɔ'* and *BiMakɔɔ'* respectively. They start to restrict their conduct, particularly their eating. The mother is under many more restrictions than the father. The underlying principle of these restrictions is to avoid taking chances with the health of the mother or child. For instance, one should stick with familiar and routine foods, which one "understands." Careless or happy-go-lucky people, or people who have already had uncomplicated pregnancies resulting in healthy children, are less likely to follow the protective ritual rules than worried neophytes. A number of other factors influence the extent of the rules and compliance with them. Space does not permit a discussion here (see Dentan, 1965). Table I lists foods which neophytes of people with a history of difficult pregnancies should aviod.

Since there is not much news in a traditional Semai settlement, everyone soon becomes interested in the pregnancy. Sooner or later, in a dream, a familiar spirit will bring news of the pregnancy to a local "adept" (*halaa'*). He thereafter is responsible for the public ceremonies called "sings," held to treat the pregnant woman and her midwife.

HOUSE AMULETS

Amulets over which an adept or spell expert has whispered a Malay spell hang by a dried banana stalk string over the door(s) of any west Semai house in which a pregnant woman lives. The usual amulet is a sharp-toothed fishhead dyed bright blue or a sack holding henna, ginger, areca nut husk, garlic, black peppercorns, rice

TABLE I   FOODS WOMEN SHOULD BE CAREFUL ABOUT EATING

Place	Dangerous Situation	Land Animals		Fish Spp.		Plant Spp.	
		N	%	N	%	N	%
East	Pregnancy	175	49.2	44	27.3	206	16.9
	Menstruation	147	70.1	44	27.3	182	20.8
West	Pregnancy	142	36.6	20	30.0	191	8.9
	Menstruation	165	3.6	20	0.0	211	1.9

N is the number of species in the sample for which data were available.
% is the percent of N *makɔɔ'* women should be careful about eating.

husks over two years old, a scrap of umbrella (Southeast Asian symbol of royalty), and some yellow coconut hairs (yellow being the royal color in Southeast Asia). The amulet is to protect the woman and her child from the beautiful, long-haired Bird Spirit(s), which are said to combine the characteristics of the Malay Specter Huntsman and Princess Spirit. An abbreviated Semai version of the origin of house amulets runs as follows. Ngah Hari bin Yeop and Itam Bluug bin Alang Judin, good friends and good informants, told it to me.

A man and a woman (a *klamin,* roughly "couple," the basic social unit) of the Ancient People cleared a field in the rain forest far from any settlement. After the felled wood was burned, they built a house in the center, following Perak Semai custom. They planted rice, and the woman became pregnant. As the crop ripened, so the pregnancy progressed. Right after the harvest, labor pains began, but the woman was unable to give birth. Next morning at daybreak, the man began the long trek to the nearest settlement to find a midwife. The woman lay writhing in pain and crying out.

In the heavy morning mist that lay over the jungle, Bird Spirit, lurking near the house as it always does when people are pregnant, heard her cries. "Aha," it thought, "I'll help her out and make a little profit on the deal." It assumed its usual form, a beautiful nubile woman, and strode toward the house, thinking of how it would steal the umbilical cord, loss of which would kill the baby. It stuck its long-haired head over the doorsill.

"What's the matter?" it asked.

"There's nothing the matter with me. Only, my stomach is giving birth, and I can't bear it."

"Okay, I'll help." Bird Spirit collected some fresh tapioca leaves, warmed them over the fire and rubbed the sick woman's stomach with them until the child was born. Bird Spirit laid the child and the afterbirth beside the mother and cooked up some rice paste, which it put in a special cup and gave her to drink in order to keep wind out of her womb. Then it cut the navel cord.

"Where do you keep the wild ginger?" it asked.

"In the bag."

Unknown to Bird Spirit, in the bag was the head of a snakehead fish. When Bird Spirit reached into the bag, its fingers got caught in the head's sharp teeth. Round and round it danced in panic, trying to shake the thing loose from its fingers. Finally, in a desperate attempt to escape, it turned into its true shape, an argus pheasant, and flew away shrieking.[2]

When the man returned with the midwife and the couple's parents, they found the baby safely delivered. Ever since, couples about to have a child have used fishhead amulets.

RITUAL BATHING

Semai "sings," held only at night, involve contrapuntal singing by an adept calling on his familiars and a chorus repeating his phrases. Women set the rhythm by pounding bamboo stampers against a log, producing a mellow, almost crystalline two-note sound. Young men may dance into trance after the fires are out, and young people flirt in the dark.

A pregnancy requires a ritual bathing "sing." Additional "sings" should be held in the following circumstances: 1) after a miscarriage or the death of a young child, to bathe the mother, midwife, and responsible adept; if the dead child was old enough to get around outdoors without supervision, the parents need only bathe the adept; 2) after an adoption, to bathe the child's midwife; 3) when the child is sick and someone has a monitory dream; 4) when the midwife or adept is sick or has a suggestive dream; 5) when anyone has a dream indicating that anyone needs ritual bathing.

When the woman's stomach "looks big enough" that she seems nearly ready to give birth, the familiar spirit should appear in the adept's dreams to order a ritual bathing "sing" for the woman, her midwife plus any other pregnant women in town and their midwives. The adept asks competent people, preferably the parents-to-be and their kin, to prepare the appropriate equipment. In the east, this equipment includes two bathing cups, an asperger, two or more bamboo bathing tubes, and a spirit perch.[3]

Like most important work, making these items is under certain taboos. Ominous phases of the moon (notably, in the west, its 15th, 16th, 20th, 21st, and 22nd night) increase the risk that people involved in the ceremony will become "hot," as discussed below. Spirits will not accept an object near which someone has sneezed, since, like people, they are afraid of sudden loud noises.

No ritual object should be made for three days after a funeral, and east Semai would prefer to wait a month. West Semai would wait a week if the funeral were for one's kinsman, i.e., until after the entombment feast. Finally, stepping over a ritual object makes it less attractive to spirits.

Bathing cup. Ordinarily the father makes the bathing cup from an internode of a certain species of bamboo (*rngrɔd*). Other bamboos are too full of water, too spiny, or too small-bored, characteristics which might have dire effects on the birth. He leaves a tapering "foot," 2 to 3 cm wide, on one side of the cup. The foot is thrust through the slats of the floor to hold the cup upright. The midwife's cup is 20 cm tall, the cup for the mother and child about 30 cm. Men and women bathing the child should use its cup until the child can "get around on the ground by itself." One should not throw even a cracked cup away, for, if the child's "soul" sees it discarded, the soul will flee (see below). West Semai women were using tin cans instead of bamboo bathing cups by 1963, but remained careful about bathing when ritually appropriate.

Asperger. The asperger is much like a Malay shaman's whisk. It is a brush about 30 cm long made of magical leaves (especially those of *slbɔk* and a laurinaceous plant called "coolness") whose coolness and fragrance attract spirits.[2] The women who have gathered the leaves should tie them together with the fragrant barkcloth made from a particular sort of fig tree, although other barkcloth and even rattan will do.

Asperging plays an important part in most Semai rituals. An adept, medicine man or in some rituals an elder holds the asperger over a censer filled with coals and benzoin, then dips it into a bathing cup which holds a thin paste made by mixing rice flour and water and called by its Malay name *tepung tawar*

> which properly means "the Neutralizing Rice-flour (Water)," "neutralizing" being used almost in a chemical sense, i.e. in the sense of "sterilizing" the active element of poisons, or of destroying the active potentialities of evil spirits (Skeat, 1900:77).

He shakes the asperger almost dry and asperges the patient, calling on his familiars' spirits to come and invoking healing coolness by crying *"la'ap!"* (cool!). This coolness attracts familiar spirits and healing powers which normally live in cool places like hills, rivers, and oceans. By the same token it drives away the heat associated with illness. A euphemism for adepts is "cool bodied people." Asperging may be by sprinkling or by pressing the asperger against an object or body part and pulling downward in short jerks. There is no prescribed way to discard a used asperger, but any ceremony requires that a new one be made. Ritual objects like bathing tubes and spirit perches are normally asperged before and after use.

Bathing tube. The ritual bathing tube is bamboo, one end of which is closed by the natural septum, with an ornamentally carved protruding lip on the open end. The father should collect the bamboo and do the carving under the supervision of an adept. Men or women paint on ornamental designs with ashes, lime, and the reddish juice of a specially cultivated fruit.[2]

A rectilinear 7-runged "ladder" ornaments the midwife's tube, representing the 7-tiered cosmos and the 7 primordial Midwives. A child's tube gets 6-rayed "stars" or "suns" whose rays conjoin to make a lattice. People seem more careless about getting the right number of rungs on the ladders than they are about the rays of the stars, perhaps because two and six are traditionally Semai magic numbers, while seven is a Malay magic number. The dream that led to the ceremony may suggest such other patterns as "tiger paw," "toad eggs," or *"bʉn buus* flower." *Bʉn buus,* which is closely related to basil and is, with *slbɔk,* the most widely used Semai sacred plant, is also sacred to Hindus and used medicinally in the Philippines.

Women make a decoction of water and fragrant plants they have collected. Besides *bʉn buus* and the plants used in aspergers they may use citronella grass; jasmine, "vine jasmine," frangipanni, and amaranth flowers; and other fragrant plants.[2] After steeping for an hour, the leaves are taken out and pounded. The women then pour the decoction through a cloth into a bowl from which it is poured into the bathing tube. They stopper the top with the fragrant leaves and amaranth flowers, leaving an ornamental fringe of *slbɔk* leaves hanging from the lip. They put the pounded leaves on a small mat next to the wall, on which they have set the censer for the asperger. The midwife should weave this little mat, but an ordinary mat will do as long as the ritual objects do not touch the floor.

Bathing tubes are one to four meters long, depending on how many people are to be bathed. That number depends on the space available, how difficult the course of the pregnancy, whether a more modest ceremony has failed, and the number of people with other ailments who seek simultaneous treatment. If small, the tubes are set upright against the wall on the little mat just mentioned. Men tie two ornamentally frayed sticks onto each larger tube in preparation for hanging them on a rack slung from the rafters. There should be one tube for each person to be bathed.

Spirit perch. The spirit perch is a flat-topped leaf cylinder with a long fringe hanging from the bottom. Through it women thrust two needles of bamboo or the central spine of an attap leaf, at right angles to each other and to the long axis of the perch. They hang a pair or two of leaf necklaces from them, made of the plants used for ritual bathwater.

A RITUAL BATHING

The following step-by-step account of an actual West Semai ritual bath is given in preference to a more general description for three reasons. First, it captures some of the flavor of the occasion. Second, rituals are hard to condense without omitting points which may be crucial to Semai or to anthropologists with interests different from mine. Finally, although the occasion for this particular instance included a case of "soul loss," ritual bathing is pretty much the same on all occasions.

> A spirit perch hangs from the rafters near the right inside wall of the house, which belongs to the family of an infant who has just lost his soul. On the little mat opposite to and just right of the door stand the bathing tubes, an old sardine tin brazier, and a small bowl of rice paste. Next to the mat and nearer the door is an earthenware pot holding the decoction for the bathing tubes. In an east Semai longhouse the area defined by these objects and the near right wall (by which the bathing tube will hang), would be a five-meter-square curtained off by palm leaves and called by the Malay word *kandang*. An

ornamented circular frame (*jrmun*), concentric and level with the spirit perch, would hang from the rafters for the spirits to sit on when they flit in to admire their perch. The time is evening; the place, the house of Itam, the pregnant woman's brother.

7:45   Itam, 31 years old, fills the bathing tubes with the fragrant decoction.

8:23   Into each tube he puts 70¢M to provide the "aura of silver." The amount should be 75¢M (about 20 cents U.S. in 1963), but Itam cannot afford that much. Two male kinsmen support the tubes at a 25 to 30 degree angle while he clambers on the rafters and ties them on very securely, even though the nubile young men will not shake the floor with their dancing as they dance into a trance, as they would in the east. Fallen bathing tubes would bring disaster to everyone involved. The knots are those used in rituals, "macaque grasps."

8:50   As a sign to the spirits that the ceremony is getting under way, the father censes the bathing tubes.

8:55   He wraps the sick boy in a blanket and carries him to a spot between the tubes and the spirit perch. His wife tells her eldest child, a girl, ten, to clean off the mats covering the floor. Her other children, boys aged seven and three, look on, as do her husband's elder sister's daughters, aged seven and eight.

9:01   The pregnant woman, KinLii, thirty-three, Itam's sister, enters with her three oldest children, a boy, Lii, eight and two girls aged six and seven. She sits by the door. Her husband, BiLii, enters shortly thereafter.

9:20   KinLii takes home her two girls, who have fallen asleep.

9:35   The adept, a thin and tubercular septuagenarian, and his wife, a husky midwife in her mid-forties, enter and sit down. She sits with one bare knee up, exuding competence, in a posture most women would find a bit daring.

•   The adept sits to her left. She is Itam's next door neighbor as well as his maternal grandmother's sister. Marriage between midwives and adepts is not typical.

9:43   Itam finishes making two aspergers, one of *slbɔk* leaves, the other of the almost equally magical leaves of *pmoleh*.[2] Then he makes an adept's whisk, which Semai call "nurturing leaf," from areca palm leaves. Any palm with stiff, rattling leaves can be used for the whisk, which is about a forearm long.

9:45   The adept puts *kijai* sap[2] in the censer, sending up a cloud of fragrance, and censes the bathing tubes again. He warms his hands over the censer to take in the healing smoke.

9:46   He and his wife begin to pray aloud, each taking over when the other falters: "Ah, I call on you, Primordial Midwives, Seven Midwives, Mecca (?) Gate, Cumulus Gate, Thundercloud Gate. I urge you to come and stand by the bathing tubes. I urge you, take the aura of your flowers, the aura of gleaming bathing tubes. I would care for your descendent. I want coolness, cold, chill, frigidity, as my bodily state, for the sake of your descendent. I want revitalization to whisper spells with Primordial *Pmoleh-Plant*."

9:50   Adept asperges the bathing tubes once and the sick boy three times, then calls KinLii to him and asperges her breasts and head, once each. She returns to her seat.

9:56   Itam spreads a white cloth on the floor between the adept and the baby and puts the earthenware pot on it, as earnest to the adept's familiars.[4]

9:57   Squatting, the adept slaps his whisk against the palm of his left hand to attract the attention of his familiar spirits. Then, arm resting on knee, whisk against forehead in the usual posture of a lowland Semai adept, he resumes praying. The whisk in this posture cuts out the light, letting him see what evil force afflicts the patient.

9:59   As prayer continues, Itam mashes coagulated rice flour and drops it in the pot to "neutralize" the disease poison.

10:00   Group singing begins. Itam's wife accompanies by lackadaisically pounding two bamboo internodes of different lengths on the floor beam between the kitchen and the main room. As usual, the adept sings a couplet, and the audience sings it back.

10:01   Midwife interrupts to ask for an asperger. As adept sings, she prays. Still singing, adept takes off his shirt and fans himself with his whisk so that his body will not get too hot to attract his familiar spirits. Prompted by his wife, he invokes his familiars by name, urging them to come "in great numbers and multitudes."

10:10   Left fist loosely clenched in front of his mouth, adept sucks air noisily through the passage thus formed, to relieve the feeling, common to adepts at this stage, that his mouth is clogged up. At the same time he ritually shakes his whisk (-*gar*). The audience is getting impatient with the familiars, as usual, and more people join the singing.

10:12   Itam's mother, who lives next door with another son and his family, and who is also a midwife, calls testily on the spirits. People stop singing to discuss why the spirits are taking so long. Perhaps the room is too big; familiars are agoraphobic. Perhaps it is the strangers; familiars are xenophobic too.

10:20   Adept goes to sick boy and "blows" his breath at him through the narrow passage made by his clenched fist, in order to pass on the healing virtues of the familiar spirits and of the smoke from the censer. This complex ritual action is called -*tlhool,* glossed here as "exspirates."

10:22   Adept shakes his whisk over the boy in order to cool his body, another complex ritual action here glossed as "whisks." Adept prays.

10:24   Adept exspirates, whisks, exspirates, whisks, and slaps his rattling whisk against the palm of his left hand to shake loose any evil influence it may have caught.

10:25   Adept sings briefly, shaking his whisk, exspirates the boy. He repeats these actions twice more, then takes a break.

10:34   He exspirates the boy again, while Itam's mother prays.

10:37   He turns to a man with a sprained wrist, who is Itam's near neighbor and maternal uncle's son-in-law. Adept prays for exorcism of "sharp things, hot things" that pain the wrist.

10:40   Adept "inspirates" (-*trheer*). Inspirating, Semai say, differs from exspirating in that, besides infusing healing powers, it sucks sharp and hot "things" out of the patient's body, and in that one need not clench one's fist to do it. The words are probably cognates. Adept whisks over the wrist and prays. He draws the whisk slowly down over the sprain, inspirating. Again he slaps his whisk against his palm to knock off the "things" it has drawn out.

10:43   Patient returns to his seat by the door. KinLii takes his place in front of the squatting adept, who extends his left hand over her swollen belly, shaking his whisk back and forth parallel to the floor as he prays.

10:45   Adept whisks hard, twice, inspirates, slaps whisk against palm, inspirates twice more, invoking his familiar spirits to help him.

10:47   Whisks, prays.

10:48   Inspirates again and kneads her womb with both hands to draw out any sickness, then extends his arms and claps his hands to shake off whatever sickness he may have drawn out. Again he kneads, this being the way to treat any stomach problem, from dyspepsia to pregnancy. Again he claps his hands, then picks up his whisk and whisks vigorously as he prays.

10:50   Kneads, claps, whisks over her stomach.

10:51   Inspirates, whisks, inspirates, whisks.

10:52   Shakes his whisk over the pot to infuse the bathing decoction with the virtue of his familiar spirits. Sings briefly and sends spirits home with a wave of the whisk.

10:54   The people go home.

Early next morning, adept and midwife return to Itam's house. Holding his hand over the mouth of the pot to keep sodden leaves from falling out, Itam pours the fragrant decoction over the squatting midwife. Ideally, he should repeat last night's prayer while he bathes her, but he stumbles over the words and adept has to pray for him. Adept, KinLii, and sick boy squat under their bathing tube. Under the fourth tube sits KinLii's younger son, four, who was delivered by the same midwife and is receiving routine postnatal care. Reciting last night's prayer, midwife breaks open the bottom of the bathing tubes, one after the other. After the bath, Itam puts some fragrant *kijai* sap in the brazier. The bathers gather around to absorb the healing smoke. Adept asks a blessing, invokes coolness, then sprinkles the bathers with a *pmoleh* leaf asperger. People sit around for a while, chatting in the desultory Semai way and then go home.

The ceremony that night follows the same pattern but a spirit "meeting hall" (*balei*, see below) is brought into play for the sick boy.

On the Telom, adepts order the fires relit after the first part of the ceremony and invite people to examine the bottoms of the tubes which, although they look solid, have been supernaturally weakened by the familiar spirits. ("Probably the adept hits it with a machete in the dark.") After everyone has looked, the midwives and pregnant women squat under the bathing tubes and an adept easily snaps open the weakened septums of the tubes with his fingers. The release of the water guarantees easy childbirth. Sometimes the spirits do not help much, and the adept must publicly open the bottom of the bathing tubes with his machete. The bath over, people sing and dance late into the night, a few diehard nubile men persisting until dawn.

Childbirth

Place of childbirth. A woman goes home as soon as labor pains begin. Birth should occur in a place with slatted floors, so that the blood and afterbirth will pass through and not contaminate the house. All east Semai floors are made of springy bamboo slats about 3 to 5 mm apart, so that garbage can pass down and cooling breezes up. Some west Semai are well enough off to floor all the house but the kitchen with planks. In such houses childbirth must take place in the kitchen. Housemates screen off the area with blankets or palm leaves.

Danger of childbirth. Puerperal blood and afterbirth are so dangerous that people use euphemisms to talk about them, leading early observers to conclude that there was a wide geographical variation in words for afterbirth. The odor of the discharge attracts evil forces, notably Bird Spirit(s). A trace in the river brings evil water spirits. The husband, therefore, should take precautions that it does not touch the ground. If labor begins where the couple cannot reach a settlement, he should hack out an earthen couch with his machete and cover it with dry leaves to catch the afterbirth. East Semai husbands formerly plaited a platform about a meter square, covered it with earth and hung it below the birth area. The platform stayed in place until the navel cord fell off, after which it was hung on a tree in the cool rain forest away from the settlement. The west Semai usage described below may be like that of south Perak Malays but differs from normal Malay practice.

ATTENDANCE AT BIRTH

Although P. D. R. Williams-Hunt (1952:64) reports that men in the area he lived in normally do not attend births, and although Semai men generally profess to fear "all that blood," anyone can attend birth. Friends, kinsmen, and neighbors drop in and out continuously, bringing food and helping with the chores. One feels slighted otherwise, as one Telom man did when his wife's labor attracted fewer visitors than another's, which the whole settlement had attended.

Visitors try to keep out of the way, so that only the midwife, adept, husband, and female kinsmen bringing hot water or warm leaves and stones enter the birth area proper. No one would want to endanger the mother, midwife, and baby by inadvertently carrying the scent of the puerperal discharge outdoors where evil forces could sniff it.

DANGERS OF CHILDBIRTH

Census data graciously made available by the Department of Aborigines show a preponderance of men over women in all age categories. This ratio, anomalous in comparison with most human populations, suggests a high mortality rate for women in or after childbirth. Alan Fix (1971) shares this conclusion. His data from Satak, Pahang, in southeastern Semailand, show that childbirth is by far the greatest peril faced by women in their reproductive years, accounting for 13 of 29 deaths, (45%), and half of all deaths from known causes. Richter (1975) suggests that a probable cause of this inferentially high death rate is hookworm infestation (see below), citing Chandler and Read (1961).[5]

> The effects of hookworm infection are particularly severe during pregnancy, when the demand for protein and iron by the developing fetus puts an extra drain on the mother. Hookworm is the cause of a tremendous number of stillbirths and is believed by some to be a more serious complication of pregnancy than even syphilis or eclampsia. The reduction of labor efficiency from hook-

worm infection may amount to 25 or even 50%, and there may be additional loss from sickness and death (432–33).

The danger to the child is less clear. Cases of children dying from loss of mother during their first year (9 of 77 deaths from known causes), and of dying in the first week of life (17 of 77), suggest that as much as a third of Satak infant mortality may result from puerperal complications, according to Fix (1971).

ACCOUNT OF A BIRTH

Trying the reader's patience with another detailed account seems proper here, not only for the reasons given in the first paragraph of the introduction to this paper and in introducing the account of ritual bathing, but also because, since births tend to occur when the mother's blood sugar is low and therefore at ungodly hours, it is the only birth we actually watched. Semai do not deliberately awaken people, lest a sleeper's soul, which may be far away dreaming, be too startled to return to the body (see "soul loss" below).

The place is the slat-floored main room of a small nuclear family house. KinLii, the pregnant woman, lies propped against the wall at about a 30 degree angle to the floor. When indoors, BiLii, her husband, sits to her right against the wall facing the door. On his right sits same adept who performed the ritual bathing described above. Next to him sits his wife, the midwife. On her right is the door to the tiny kitchen. Other adults, including the Dentans and a teenage neighbor girl, sit along the wall between the kitchen door and the entrance door. KinLii's little girls sit in a corner on their mother's left. KinLii's mother and mother's sister are working in the kitchen.

At 8:45 P.M., BiLii closes the entrance door to announce that labor has begun. Lii and other little boys gather outside.

8:45   Midwife and adept enter. Midwife arranges her materials and falls into a preparatory reverie until Uda, KinLii's mother, brings in coffee for everyone. Midwife kneads KinLii's stomach, asking her how she feels, whether she is in pain, and so on. Then she kneads with both hands for about 3 minutes.

9:07 The adept asks for the usual fragrant gum for the censer so that he can pray over it. There is some question whether the women have remembered to collect it. The adept worries that sand may blow in from an abandoned tin mine nearby. Uda takes some wild ginger leaves into the kitchen. The adept sends BiLii out to get some leaves of the other appropriate kind of wild ginger.[2] The sorts of leaves used when someone is sick are inappropriate here, since they connote disease.

 The adept whispers a Malay spell over a tin can holding the water and the two types of wild ginger leaves. BiLii returns and makes an asperger. The adept passes the can to the husband, saying, "Rub it on." BiLii rubs it on his wife's stomach and back. He tucks in the blankets wrapped around her. Uda brings the adept rice paste for the asperger.

9:25 Uda brings in a coconut shell brazier holding embers and fragrant gum. The adept warms his right hand over it, absorbing the healing smoke. He exspirates and inspirates KinLii and draws his hand over her stomach. He repeats this process, then holds his hand over the brazier. He squats on his heels, arms stretched out straight in front of him, hands dangling over KinLii's stomach, head between his arms. His wife coaching him, he prays to the Primordial Midwives of the 7 gates. "Completed the agreement, completed the days. Already this woman has been in labor a long time, since morning. Already she is tired. Perhaps alien forces are interfering. If so, help me."

 "Perhaps her womb is tied up," interpolates the midwife. Whenever during the prayer the adept asks a blessing (-smain slamad), BiLii asperges, echoing "Slamad!"

9:33 Having summoned his familiar spirits, adept asperges KinLii's stomach, prays briefly, asks a blessing, asperges twice more. Uda gives him a scrap of newspaper with wild ginger on it, over which he says a Malay spell.

 Under the house BiLii sets up a lime-smeared machete whose "iron" should scare away evil entities attracted by the blood. Around it he builds a rough wall of discarded attap shingles to fence off the evil forces and to keep the "dirt" of the birth from being blown into neighboring houses. Inside the fence he lights a fire, also to ward off evil entities.

9:57   Midwife moistens KinLii's stomach and forehead to keep her cool. KinLii's younger sister brings in some coconut oil her father has said a Malay spell over.

10:05   BiLii, on his wife's left, whispers a Malay spell over her, while adept mutters another Malay spell over some wild ginger.

10:10   KinKupa', another midwife, peeks in, explaining, "Mostly, I stay outside because they're relying on another midwife. I'm looking after the outdoors business." She sits in the doorway. BiLii continues rubbing his wife's stomach with the decoction of wild ginger. Adept sits by her head, occasionally praying aloud. KinLii: "I'm hot and tired."

10:50   KinLii groans loudly. Midwife moves into position between her legs, calling the other women to gather around. KinKupa' joins them, praying aloud. Midwife calls for a cigarette. Adept prays, "Hurry and help her. I'm old, I have a cough, I want to go home." He chuckles a little.

Midwife hauls out the baby, calling for someone to take the cigarette out of her mouth and for a cloth to put the wrinkled red baby on. She sends the oldest of KinLii's little girls out for tapioca leaves and calls to the women in the kitchen for hot water. When the clean cloth arrives, she puts the baby on it and devotes her whole attention to the mother.

11:05   Uda hands in a newly made, razor-sharp bamboo knife from the kitchen. KinKupa' calls for black cloth, midwife for warm stones.

11:07   A bundle of warmed fresh tapioca leaves are handed in from the iktchen. "Go get more leaves," a midwife tells the eldest daughter. "Bring some coffee," she tells Uda.

11:10   Midwife, kneading KinLii's belly to bring out the afterbirth, glances for the first time at the baby and comments, "A boy." Uda passes in a tin of hot water.

11:12   Uda brings adept some coffee to whisper a Malay spell over.

11:14   Midwife washes her hands in the hot water, calls for a cigarette and continues massaging KinLii's stomach.

11:15   Midwife gets a new bundle of warm leaves. Adept gives her the coffee to warm her up.

11:16   KinKupa' tears a strip of ordinary cloth. Uda hands adept a strip of black cloth. He unwraps a razor blade, ties the black cloth into a knot and puts it on a scrap of an old Portland *Oregonian* with the razor blade. Traditionally, he would have used a banana leaf and the bamboo knife which he now lays on a joist under the floor. Uda hands him some pounded wild ginger root on a scrap of newspaper. He puts the razor blade and cloth knot on the new scrap and smears the root over them, muttering a Malay spell.

11:26   KinKupa' rolls the strip of cloth she tore at 11:16 in wild ginger root on another scrap of newspaper from the kitchen.

11:27   Adept finishes his spell, gives the materials to midwife, takes the cloth from KinKupa' and begins a spell over it.

11:28   He returns the cloth to KinKupa' who hands it to midwife.

11:30   Midwife, who has rejected some water because it has cooled off, now rejects a new tinful. "It's too hot. Cool it off with cold water." Uda hands in another warm stone. KinKupa' puts it on KinLii's stomach, since midwife is still kneading out the afterbirth with both hands.

11:35   Uda hands in a large bowl of cooled water. Mother sits up, drinks coffee.

11:37   Uda hands adept a cup of warm rice water. He starts a Malay spell over it.

11:39   Cold water from kitchen. Midwife bathes baby in warm water, gently squeezing the fontanelle closed with one hand. Older women exclaim at the size of the navel cord.

11:40   Adept finishes spell, hands cup to KinKupa', who gives it to KinLii to drink. Midwife ties and cuts the cord.

The father should put the afterbirth in a bamboo internode, take into the shade of the forest so that it will not get "hot" and discard it in the fork of a tree so that the scent will not enter the ground. East Semai say they should lay the baby face down and swaddle it in soft barkcloth, commercial cloth being too harsh, arms by its sides and buttocks bare so that it can defecate. Midwife, mother, and baby should remain isolated until the navel cord falls off, ideally to be disposed of like the afterbirth. East Semai estimate that process takes six days, west Semai say seven.

Twins "embarrass" their parents because they are unusual. Identical twins may both live, but, of fraternal twins, one would die. This notion corresponds with the rationale given for planting at least two of every cultivar, so that no cultivated variety of crop will be lost. Triplets are rare: "The mother'd die"; "Women only have two breasts"; "Sounds like mice." Polydactyly and adactylia are known. No one seemed interested in the two cases we noticed in the east. Semai tend not to get as upset about "deformities" as Euroamericans do.

Concepts of Early Childhood

The following generalized account rests on statements made by Semai. My own remarks are in parentheses, although some interpretation slips into any translation. What people say about childhood, of course, need not be what they believe.

(Semai seem more aware of the fragility of children's lives than are people with lower infant mortality rates (see Table II). In the east, where children have less than an even chance of surviving their first year, people seem more sensitive to this fragility than in the west, where the infant mortality rate is about half as high. For instance, ritual restrictions to protect the infant affect more kinds of food, last longer, involve more people, and seem to be more scrupulously observed in the east (see Table III). These subcultural differences may represent different ways of dealing with different disease ecologies.)

SOCIAL IDENTITIES

In the Semai "age grade" system the first grade is that of "child," to which people belong until they are nubile. A newborn baby is a "new child." It automatically gets a name (*muh*) which specifies its position in the birth order. It may also get a general name (*mɔl,* "handle") which simply specifies its gender, like Cɔng for boys or Doi for girls. A title, *Bah* or *Wa',* goes in front of the name, e.g.,

TABLE II   FREQUENCIES WITH WHICH SEMAI CHILDREN
PREDECEASE THEIR MOTHERS

State	Altitude (meters)	Source	Total Births	Total Alive	Mortality
Pahang	Over 700	Polunin (1953:81)	168	68	59.5
Pahang	Intermediate	"East," 1962	34	16	52.9
Pahang	Under 200	Polunin (1953:81)	174	111	36.2
Pahang	Lower than Telom, over 200	Satak (Fix, 1971:61)*	76	43	43.8
Perak	Lowlands and foothills	Hogan-Shaidali (1950:3)	263	177	28.9
Perak	Under 200	"West," 1963	328	248	24.4

* Fix uses only births of (1) living mothers over 40 and (2) dead mothers aged
25–60, so that his figures are roughly but not strictly comparable with the others.

TABLE III   POSTPARTUM FOOD RESTRICTIONS
Numbers refer to number of species avoided.

Restriction ends after	East	West
1–3 weeks	47	124
1–2 months	54	55
2 mos.–1 year	102	53
Over 1 year	22	12
Not recorded	33	0
Total restrictions	258	244
Total "safe" foods	95	101
All foods	353	345

Bah Cɔng, *Wa'* Doi, although people use the titles only in a joking way for "new children." *Bah* is the address form for parent's
younger brother, *Wa'* for parent's younger sister. The connotation
is that a person so titled need not be "listened to" as deferentially
as a more mature person. Referring to someone as *Bah* So-and-so
during an argument is thus a dirty trick.

(Earlier I commented that one of the ways in which the symbolically physical link between parents and child appeared was in the parents' taking the names KiMakɔɔ' and BiMakɔɔ' when they realized the mother was pregnant for the first time. Semai teknonymy, in which the parents' name incorporates the name of their first viable child, seems similar.) By teknonymy parents of a girl named Doi become KinDoi and BiDoi or simply Doi for short. Other people may still address or refer to the parents as *Bah* or *Wa'* So-and-so, using their personal names. But having a teknonym indicates that one is passing out of the "nubile youth" age grade and is becoming a person of some importance in the community. Therefore people in their twenties who have not yet had children also get teknonyms, KinManang or BiManang, *manang* meaning "sterile." (West Semai addressed both the Dentans and the Robarcheks as Manang; the term is not abusive.)

On the other hand, since a "new child" is likely to die, these naming procedures tend to be tentative and unserious. People typically wait until they are fairly sure the "new child" will live before a close kinsman gives it an autonym, i.e., a personal name referring only to itself. The autonym (also called *mɔl*) is a nickname based on the "new child's" first word, idiosyncrasies, and so on. The parental teknonym incorporates the child's autonym. Like Americans confronted with a childhood nickname, Semai often become "embarrassed" by their autonym as they mature, particularly since it can be used as a put-down, as noted in the last paragraph. Therefore people often change their autonyms when they move. (I changed mine, "Incest," when I moved west.)

Finally, there is a teknonym (in anthropological jargon, a necronym) for parents whose first child has died. If they have another child, the whole naming procedure begins again, although the more recent "new baby's" birth order name (*muh*) will indicate that it is the second born. (In short, the birth of a child has ramifications throughout the community, as the complex naming process makes clear.)

New children are ignorant and uneducable. No blame attaches to what they do, since, "they don't understand." (A person makes no fuss, for example, if an infant wets him or her. He or she holds it at arms length over the slatted floor until it is through, then passes it to another adult. Often there is no effort to wipe off the urine.) New children are always cute, and people play with them a lot.

MOTOR DEVELOPMENT

Adults pay attention to an infant's acquisition of motor abilities, an important index of the child's general health (see Table IV, which bears comparison with that reported by Williams [1968] for "Dusun," Austronesian hill people in the east Malaysian state of Sabah). This sequence is a natural unfolding, not a learning process. Adults do not try to hurry it, although they may put an infant in a sitting-up position or hold it erect. As it passes each stage, the parent worries less about it and therefore observes fewer precautionary restrictions than before. Although there is wide local and idiosyncratic variation in these restrictions, the mother observes more and for a longer time than the midwife, and the midwife more than the father.

A SAMPLE OF CHILDHOOD DISEASES

Sniffles (*sĩĩh*) are a children's ailment, amusing in adults. *Sĩĩh* also refers to more serious respiratory diseases, which are the second greatest cause of death among Satak Semai less than a year old (18 of 152 or 11.9% of all cases and about a quarter of all deaths from known causes) and over a fifth of deaths from known causes between one and fourteen years old, according to Fix (1971). To ward off such ailments, west Semai people make a string necklace for their children from fragrant eaglewood bark. The parent rolls strips of bark on his or her thigh to make string in the usual way, then ties six granny knots in it. An "expert" (*malib*) in Malay spells, who may be an adept, says a spell over it. It does not always work, but will minimize the severity of an attack. A child with a cold bathes in or drinks a cold infusion of the fresh bark over which a spell has been said in Malay, the only language for spells. A wan child who coughs a lot is bathed in a warm, pinkish decoction of psychotria.[2]

Diarrhea is also an important cause of "new children's" death. (Fix [1971] reports it accounted at Satak for seven out of twenty-three deaths from known cause of children between the ages of one

TABLE IV   STAGES OF CHILD DEVELOPMENT ("EAST" VERSION)

Sequence	Semai Term	English Gloss	Remarks
1.	-brhood pai	is-born new	Umbilicus should fall off on 6th day for long life.
2.	kbuu' lua'	skin of fig (*ficus* Sp.)	Skin blotchy, "red" and "white" like fig fruit. A couple of weeks old.
3.	cngoog mad	focussing eyes	Recognizes mother; makes noise to signal hunger.
4.	crneer	lying on one side	
5.	knpkɔɔ p (or) knpɔɔ p	lying prone	Kpnɔɔ p also means "upside down (Diffloth, 1975).
6.	wnnuud	crawling	Raises up on elbows and tries to pull self towards mother.
7.	prngoi kiil	making sit ? upright	Tries to sit but falls; held upright by parents. A *keel* is a banana "heart" (*sc.* flower). Thus this phrase may be a mistranslation for something like "made to sit while dangling from its upheld arms like a banana heart."
8.	-gigoi btul	sits up really	
9.	-brsadar ninig	is-propped up by wall	Tries to stand, leaning on wall.
10.	prncud	making-planted	Stands alone, with help from adults (see text).
11.*	-gryur	toddles	Father cries "A-ah!"
12.*	prnhe' cug	helped (?) to climb-down	Keeps heading for door; have to watch it lest it fall.
13.*	-cgrug ma rangkal	climbs-down on ladder	Gets around by itself.

* 11–13 may be summed up as -*ciib*, walks. Cf. Williams (1968:68) and Fortes (1949:187n).

and fourteen.) East Semai parents bathe a continuously fretful child in a warm decoction of canarium leaves, and in the west parents rub the ashes of the leaves around the baby's eyes, reciting a spell. Alternatively, Semai, like Malays, may tuck the leaves of a sensitive plant under the fretful child's pillow, hoping that it will "relax" the way the leaves do.[2]

Another common childhood disease is *klab,* a form of malaria caused by parents' or midwives' eating sweet, acidic foods like fruits and marked by a hot, swollen spleen. (From a quarter to two-thirds of most Semai populations were carrying malaria parasites in the late 1960's.) If an east Semai child with *klab* is wan, feverish, and torpid the mother cuddles it on her lap and laves it with a warm decoction of uncaria bark scrapings, then pours the leftover liquid over the child's head and binds the scrapings over the child's spleen. The idea is to get rid of the "disease thing," in this case a *sampuu'* "disease thing" in the spleen. Kneaded out by an adept, the "disease thing" looks like a small, pale stone. (In this case, *sampuu'* seems to refer to the debilitation caused by malaria. In other cases, as *nyani' sampuu',* it seems to be "anemia disease-causing entity." As such, it is the major cause of death of children under a year old: in Fix's sample, 75 of 152 or 17.8% of all deaths; over 35% of deaths from known causes; and 10 of 23 deaths from known causes among children between the ages of one and fourteen. This discussion of what at first seems to be a simple disease category should indicate how complicated Semai theories of disease and healing are.)

SOUL LOSS[6]

Semai notions of soul loss. Soul loss is the most feared childhood affliction. Since souls in general and childrens' souls in particular are as timid as familiar spirits, almost all children lose their souls at one point. The precipitating event is a startling stimulus, like a loud noise, e.g., toads croaking, a bird call. The classic symptoms are pallor, listlessness, and lethargy. The eyes may be closed as if in sleep. Speech may be irrational. Other symptoms include anemia, diarrhea, fever, or convulsions. When the soul has fled, someone in the settlement, probably an adept or a midwife, has a diagnostic dream. Diagnostic elements in the dream may be children or such symbols of the soul as birds or butterflies, which are as prone to flight as souls.

Possible causes. Many of the allegedly precipitating events in case histories of soul loss do not seem very startling. For example, the toads just mentioned set up a pleasant chorus every evening at the west Semai settlement; their croaking seems unlikely to startle anyone. The salience of startle in the Semai etiology of soul loss may stem from the salience of the Moro reflex in an infant's limited behavioral repertoire. Acting out how children respond to the presumptive startling stimulus, informants jump slightly, open their eyes wide, and fling wide their arms and legs, as in the Moro reflex. This explanation also suggests why the Moro reflex does not figure in the otherwise meticulous Semai account of infantile motor behavior.

The symptoms of soul loss seem to be those predictable when a child burdened with parasites is exposed to a variety of serious diseases. In this connection, it is noteworthy that soul loss seems more common in the east than in the west, although the number of case histories obtained is too small to permit a definite assertion. Acculturated Semai settlements at low altitudes generally have a greater morbidity of parasites and heavier parasite burdens than remote settlements at relatively high altitudes (Table V).

Since Westerners often assume that systematic beliefs like the west Semai notion of "soul loss" are the product of "primitive superstition" and not intellectual responses to real problems in the real world, it is worth examining the following information on

TABLE V   PER CENT MORBIDITY OF HELMINTH ("WORM")
INFESTATION AMONG SEMAI

| Helminth Genus | Lowland Semai | | Highland Semai | |
	Perak (1930s)	West (1963)	Low Level	High Level
Ascaris	56	67	18	0
Trichuris	83	13	6	0
Enterobius	1	—	0	4
Hookworm	58	25	82	94
N (Sample)	85	104	33	55

parasite burdens provided by Fred Dunn (1964) and Malcolm Bolton (1963, 1968). Roundworm burdens in the west Semai settlement are heavy, often very heavy. Amebiasis is common, but the large pathogenic *Entamoeba histolytica* affects only about 5% of the people. Almost half the people, however, carry the flagellate *Giardia lamblia*, the highest rate in the world. By contrast, east Semai children sometimes have "wet" sores that may be symptomatic of oriental forest leishmaniasis but show no other ill effects. The hookworm rate is high, but individual burdens rarely pass the anemia threshold. Amebiasis is rare, as is *Giardia* infestation.

These data suggest the possibility that "soul loss" is a composite of anemia and secondary shock, often resulting from a heavy roundworm or *Giardia* burden, complicated by other diseases and some malnutrition. Clinical reports on west Semai children hospitalized by their families for "soul loss" confirm this possibility. The symptoms certainly match the *sampuu'* syndrome of lethargy, pallor, anorexia, malaise, precipitating "shock," and so on. Moreover, the symptoms of *Giardia* infestation are almost precisely those of "soul loss," so that it is possible that the different rates of *Giardia* infection account for the different salience of "soul loss" among the east and west Semai.

Balei. There is no medicine for "soul loss." Treatment involves the construction of a spirits' "meeting house" (*balei*) and a ritual bathing "sing" of the sort already described. An east Semai spirits' meeting house looks rather like a four-vaned propellor with a long shaft. The vanes are about 15 cm long, the shaft half a meter long for one type of *balei,* a meter for the other. In the latter, a second set of four vanes hangs from the top of the shaft, just below the first set, at a 45° angle to the shaft. They are propped away from the shaft by wooden "needles." In the first type of spirits' meeting house, two circular frames hang from the vanes, encircling the staff. Black charcoal dots and orange tumeric juice zigzag ornament the vanes and shaft of both types.

Long shredded leaves of magical plants[2] lift up jauntily from the ends of the vanes, trailing an ornamental fringe. More such leaves hang from the circular frames. There is a "collar" just above the "foot" of the shaft so that the *balei* can be stuck upright through the floor slats.

One kind of spirits' "meeting house" is the "thought" or "conscious" *balei*. Its shaft is enclosed in a tight-fitting length of bamboo. The singing adept twists the shaft, making the eerie squeaking associated with familiar spirits.

The father of the sick child makes the *balei* of soft white wood on the morning of the ceremony. Making it earlier would risk disaster for the maker and his family. Women are "reluctant" or "too shy" to make a "meeting house" for spirits, but they could if they wanted to. Close female relatives of the patient make the leafy "necklaces" for it. Once made, the spirits' "meeting house" is stored on the rafters or in a sleeping chamber, so that no one will step over it, ruining it and himself.

That night the men set up the spirits' "meeting house" in a *jrmun*, an enclosure of magic leaves and flowers, where the adept sits in the dark with his patient(s). As he sings his invocation, spirits land by the dozens on the vanes of their "meeting house" and scurry to hide in the magical leaves. Later the souls of the young men who dance into trance will join them. The familiar spirits may also flit into the dark rain forest to snatch the child's lost soul from the clutches of evil forces ready to consume it.

When the dancing is done and the fires relit, the *balei* is left in place for a few days, ideally six. The adept then discards it in the trunk of a shade tree in the rain forest, so that it will not get hot.

In the west, a spirits' "meeting house" consists of a square frame of slats 3 to 4 cm tall and a little over a foot long, with ornamentally carved finials. These "walls" enclose a slatted "floor" on which is laid a foot square mat of woven pandanus leaf, banana leaf, or old newspaper. The father of the sick child makes the frame of soft magical wood.[2] Women closely related to the child string parched rice on a thread, putting a *slbɔk*[2] leaf cylinder every 7 to 10 cm to make a "twining ornament" that is to hang in dangling loops around the sides of the *balei*. The spirits' "meeting house" should hang just north of the "spirit perch" described in the section on ritual bathing above.

Into the spirits' "meeting house" go 7 betel nut sections; areca leaf, lime, and gambier to make 7 tasty cuds; 7 nipa palm leaf cigarettes; half a tael, *i.e.* about 2/3 oz. of parched rice; and half a tael of saffron rice. There should also be a statuette of the sick child, perhaps in the form of a bird or butterfly. If the diagnostic dream indicates Bird Spirit(s), "the long-haired ones," a bird statuette is needed. A dream of dragon(s), "Mr. Backbasket" (because of the scale pattern) or "they beneath the earth," requires a dragon statuette, and so forth. If a ghost is indicated, the statuette's head should be turned backwards, the leafy ornaments inverted, and the whole ceremony oriented to the west ("day's eye dies," i.e., sunset), rather than as usual to the east ("day's eye lives").

The spirits' "meeting house" comes into play on the second night of the bathing ritual. The idea is that the evil entity which caught the soul will release it to take the "spiritual essence" of the statuette, as a person holding something will put it down to pick up something else. The ceremony usually goes on for a third night. The *balei* and other paraphernalia hang in the house for about a week, after which someone should take them out and hang them on a tree in primary forest so that they escape the heat of the sun. Sometimes, however, people just leave it hanging. If possible, after the child has recovered, the father should pay the adept about M$7.25 (about U.S. $2.42 in 1963), in coin because the glitter of coins is an "aura" which paper money lacks.

SUMMARY

The new child is the focus of much emotional, cognitive, and ritual attention, which stems from affection and concern. Its fragility is linked to its alleged timidity, epitomized by the supposed timidity of the soul. Its whims are indulged, and it is not rebuked, because, being unable to talk, "it cannot understand."

Childhood

THE TRANSITION FROM INFANCY TO CHILDHOOD

The transition from "new child" to "child" has definitely begun when the child "goes down the house ladder to the ground" by itself. It is over when the child can talk. By then the child has a personal name which marks it as a social being, deserving, for example, a full-scale funeral.

Developing verbal skills gives the child some power over its surroundings, particularly in the Semai context, where interpersonal power lies wholly in persuading others to do what one wants and therefore depends mostly on verbal facility. Talking also means the child can "understand." It therefore becomes subject to correction and deliberate enculturation.

The chances of dying drop rather sharply at this time, as does the incidence of soul loss. The intense adult concern for the child also drops off rather abruptly. The end of ritual concern in the east comes about two years post-partum, when the mother can resume sexual relations without fear of having more children than she can give proper care to or of damaging her womb—although a score of foods remain dangerous until the child is six or seven, by which time it is almost completely weaned. In the west, where sexual relations resume after 2 months or 44 days ("but who can wait that long?"; cf. Satak where "coitus begins 'as soon as the woman feels like it' " [Fix, 1971]), a dozen foods remain dangerous until the child is six or seven, but most are safe when the child is no longer "new" (see Table III). Other children take up an increasingly large part of the child's social life, becoming, at a guess, as important as agents of enculturation as adults are.

In short, the transition is rather abrupt and occurs mainly during the child's second year. Adult attention dwindles rapidly and other children become more important. My impression is that children in this situation tend to become edgy, quiet, and withdrawn.

CONCEPTIONS OF CHILDHOOD

This section is impressionistic, based on conversations with Semai and unsystematic observations.

Hearts. Diffloth (1975) reports that Semai at Tngrig in southwestern Semailand say that a child under five or six has the inquisitive and imitative "heart of a macaque." An older child has the snappish and quarrelsome "heart of a dog." By contrast, responsible adults have "elephant hearts," always remembering.

Acquiring skills. Besides being coercion that might make the child sick, training is unnecessary because "our children learn by themselves" (see "Enculturation" above). Children tag along after adults, especially parents or grandparents, imitating their activties in ways that shade imperceptibly into helping out. Seeing the child's interest or in response to its initiative, the adult may show it how to do something better or may make a small version of the appropriate tool. When no adults are around, children often play at adult activities by themselves.

"Dumbness of children." Children are "dumb" because they have not completely mastered verbal skills. It may be stretching a point to say that, whereas Euroamericans regard the mentally retarded as "like children," Semai regard children as "like retardates," but it is close to the truth. A child is a completed presence, a dumb miniature adult. Its cultural skills will unfold naturally, as its motor skills did. If not, it will be because of the sort of person the child is, not because some adult failed to teach it. The idea that a parent is responsible for what his or her children can do, let alone how they "turn out," seems alien to Semai. In this sense, no Semai child has "potential" which adults need encourage. So Semai treat children like retardates: doing for them what they cannot do for themselves, letting them get away with some things adults should not do, expecting of them only what they are capable of.

Conclusion. Within this social and ideological context occurs what might loosely be called the "socialization" of avoidance and aggression, fear and anger. Obviously more goes on in Semai childhood than these rubrics cover.

"Fear" and "Embarrassment"

Discussing someone else's emotions, even when you share a common language, is tricky. When the topic is emotions differently categorized the problem is worse. The first draft of this section used English glosses for the Semai words *snngɔh* ("fear" or "caution") and *slniil* ("embarrassment" or "shyness"). Using the English words as the Semai use their words, however, quickly produces sentences that are preposterous or wildly untrue. After all, the English word "panic" has lost its religious significance, and "fear" in the King James Bible is used in ways that would be inappropriate in modern English. If Angloamericans lose touch with the root meanings of their own language so quickly, it is not surprising that trying to force Semai words into English distorts them.

The following glosses, therefore, are only to help introduce the Semai notions of "fear" and "embarrassment." If you -*sngɔh* some-

thing, you avoid contact with it. If you -*siil,* you refrain from doing something because of how people might respond. To -*srngɔh* is
to "induce *sngɔh,*" to threaten or yell at someone.

"FEAR" AND ITS CONTEXTS

Teaching caution. "Being afraid" (-*sngɔh*) is not reprehensible
but "smart." Making children afraid (-*srngɔh*) is basically protective, although adults enjoy teasing the children at the same time.
Whenever we first visited a Semai settlement, adults who knew our
harmlessness by reputation would take the opportunity to -*srngɔh*
children about strangers. For example, a man who took us to his
home village thrust his head forward, opening his eyes wide and
smiling, and said to the gaggle of quiet children who had gathered
two or three meters away to have a look at us, "*Sngɔh! Sngɔh!* The
Pale People have come to inject you! Haaa . . ." (looking around)
"Who -*sngɔh* the most? That's the one we'll inject first!" Or a
mother might point us out to a baby on her hip: "*Sngɔh, sngɔh,*"
she would croon until the child started to cry, then, after covering
the child's head and starting away, would look over her shoulder
at us and say, smiling, "Myself, I don't -*sngɔh,* I just -*srngɔh* her."

Adults say that children should and do -*sngɔh.* Although some
children do not, the Semai stereotype of the timid child with the
yet more timid "soul" is almost universal. One should -*srngɔh* a
forward child, even if its behavior is otherwise good. For instance,
one man said that his 5-year-old boy, who burst into wails and fled
whenever he saw us, was better behaved than his 9-year-old girl
who was always helping us out around the house. "You should
-*srngɔh* her the way I do," he said, although in fact he rarely
threatened his children. In this sense, *snngɔh* means something like
"proper reserve," and to -*srngɔh* a child is to "teach it respect."

In short, besides trying to make their children -*sngɔh* tangible
dangers like fire and heights, Semai apparently try to inculcate
timidity almost as an abstract virtue. They also expect their children
to -*sngɔh.* Often the children seem to respond to such expectations
by acting shy and timid. In this sense, *snngɔh* means something
like "caution."

It should be remembered that adults do not spend much time instructing children in anything, including *snngɔh*. Although Semai children are timid and xenophobic, they are not sunk in terror. They are initially shy in unfamiliar places or with unfamiliar people. When experience shows them there is no danger, they become more forward until finally they are behaving quite freely. At most, the training seems to produce a tendency to opt for flight or at least initial caution in the face of danger or the unknown, rather than being "daring." It is a matter of priorities rather than deep seated compulsions.

CONTEXT OF TEACHING CAUTION

Neal Miller and John Dollard (1941), dealing with another Malayan hill people, seem to be the first to have suggested in a rigorous way that overwhelming defeat at the hands of the technologically advanced Malays forced the hill peoples to retreat to the rain forest, where the avoidance patterns learned in cultural contact generalized into a pattern of intracultural caution transmitted by enculturation. P. M. Gardner (1966) gives a similar but more sophisticated explanation, stressing the importance of an unpopulated refuge area and referring to some of the peoples described in this volume.

One of the earliest Malay "fabulous histories" describes a great battle in which the hill peoples were routed forever, and there are a few tantalizing hints, currently under investigation, that hill peoples in remote times enjoyed a "higher level of civilization" than they do now. Times were bad for Semai until about fifty years ago, when slaving finally stopped, and not good until Malaysia won its independence, after which there was a rapid and marked improvement. In 1962 and 1963 there were many Semai who remembered the bad old days and governed their relations with Malays accordingly. Under these circumstances, teaching one's children to be leery of strangers is simply sensible.

The real fear that Semai children and adult Semai in remote areas have of strangers is much more marked than the general caution Semai show of the unfamiliar and dangerous. Thus, confronted with a blindsnake or phallic fungus,[2] both reputedly of supernatural significance, east Semai stayed about three meters away, patting their chests in amazement and saying, "O, I -*sngɔh*,

I *sngɔh.*" They were clearly going through the socially proper motions. The three meter distance, to use Miller and Dollard's terms, marked the point where the gradient of avoidance (fear) crossed the gradient of approach (curiosity); but the response was as much customary as motivated by fear.

Psychoanalytic speculation. Whiting and Child (1962) suggest that, when the universally occurring aggression they postulate is frustrated, as it would be in the Semai case, people will project their aggressive impulses onto others, in the Semai case onto strangers and the evil disease entities with which parents explicitly identify strangers to their children. This speculation seems supererogatory here, since strangers historically and diseases currently are in fact dangerous, and only a foolish person would not fear them. The instability of east Semai marriages might produce something similar to the "absent father syndrome," which psychoanalysts believe increases mistrust of strangers. The discontinuity between "new childhood" and "childhood" might have similar results. Again, these speculations seem supererogatory but possible.

Slniil

An angry Semai or a Semai at whom someone else is angry feels an emotion called *slniil* (loosely, "shame" or "nervousness" or "reluctance"). *Slniil* observedly makes people avert their eyes from people at whom they are angry and refuse to talk or listen to them. A politically sophisticated west Semai man explained that, given the absence of an accepted hierarchy, "the only authority here is *slniil.*"

Slniil in response to anger seems to be learned in many of the same contexts as *snngɔh.* For example, a stranger one knows to be friendly makes one -*siil* rather than -*sngɔh.* The only teaching of *slniil* observed, however, came (1) when parents of a "new child" going through the transition to childhood would pat the child's hands away from its genitals, saying gently, *"siil, siil";* and (2) when larger east Semai boys would lift up smaller ones, exposing their genitals and yelling, "Take a picture! Take a picture!" at us.

The conceptual equation of exposing one's anger with exposing one's genitals presumably has an inhibiting effect on the former.

Aggression

The following two examples of aggression in childhood were picked randomly from our files. They seem to be typical, however. The first illustrates how children deal with their own anger, the second how adults usually respond to it.

> Kioh and Kuup, girls about 8, compete for our attention. One day Kioh holds the door of our house shut when Kuup tries to come in. Kuup lets out a great wail, cries for about two minutes and walks away, despite our entreaties to come in. A few minutes later she is beating a stick against the ground, presumably in anger. After about five minutes we cajole her into coming in. She shows no anger at Kioh and is soon playing with her.
>
> Siti, a 7-year-old girl, grabs a stick toy belonging to Hamid, a boy about 5. She tries to loose his hands, he to bite hers. His uncle and aunt (*bah* and *wa'*) say "Stop it," but do not interfere. Awa, Hamid's 11-year-old boy cousin, who is under the house, bangs a stick against the floor to get them to stop. Siti finally gets the toy and leaves the house, after which the aunt says, once, "Give it back." Hamid wails for about ten minutes, getting no response. In the midst of his wails, the aunt's baby starts to cry, and its parents concentrate on comforting her. "He -*srngɔh* her," says the uncle. Awa comes in and plays with the baby for a couple of minutes, then goes and sits by the wailing Hamid, not touching or speaking to him. Finally, Hamid's grandmother enters to ask what is wrong. Awa takes him to her by the hand. She carries him off on her back as she did when he was a "new child," the usual way to comfort older children who cry for a long time.

As the second example illustrates, adults and older children rarely interfere actively with the quarrels of younger children, who, having "hearts like dogs," are expected to squabble, until a child seems to have lost its temper completely. Then they swoop on the child at once and carry it off wailing to its parents. This abrupt intervention must be all the more frightening because, as in the second example, adults usually ignore children and almost never interfere with someone else's child.

The most aggressive game we saw east Semai children play involves everyone between the ages of 3 and 12 and generates a lot of excitement. Children square off with each other, assume dramatically threatening poses and flail away at each other with large sticks. The terrible blows they smite, however, always freeze about an inch from their target, just like the gestures of a parent threatening (-srngɔh) to strike a child. Probably such parental gestures serve as the children's model. The game must be a fine rehearsal of self-control. In a similar game, two children, often of disparate sizes, put their hands on each other's shoulders and wrestle, giggling, but never quite knocking each other over.

Whenever these children become too boisterous, as they do many times a day, adults cry out, "Trlaid! Trlaid!" in reference to behavior that will bring on one of the terrifyingly violent Malaysian thundersqualls. The adults are usualy laughing, however, and the children rarely stop what they are doing. It seems to be mostly a *pro forma* reminder that cautious reserve is proper behavior. Just possibly, however, the actual occurrence of a thundersquall, during which parents cry "Sngɔh! Sngɔh!" to their children, serves to remind the children that failure to maintain such cautious reserve can be disastrous.

Probably one of the most influential inhibitors of childhood aggression is the fact that children see so few examples of it. Even in the west, where boys sometimes play at shooting each other and falling dead in imitation of American movies, which Semai regard as newsreels ("If you're not killing your aborigines, why would you want to watch it?"), violence is clearly defined as non-Semai behavior. In the absence of hierarchy, adults cannot even boss each other around. Parents make threatening (-srngɔh) gestures at their children, but only rarely actually hit them. Therefore, even if a child wanted to become violent, it would have no very clear idea of how to proceed. Euroamerican social psychologists contend that this situation, in which ignorance of violence combines with parents' not expecting children to become violent, not punishing it with violence, and not permitting it to occur is one maximally geared to producing nonviolence.

Summary and Conclusions

The foregoing account emphasizes what seem to be central Semai concerns in raising children. It therefore allots a good deal of space to physical and spiritual nurturance. This emphasis stems from a sense that, for an anthropologist, the concerns of the people with whom he or she has worked must take precedence over other concerns.

The secondary focus is on nonviolence. Making children -sngɔh and -siil seems to lead them to opt for avoidance rather than violence. Semai apparently conceptualize the shyness observable in their children as due to a phobic soul, whose tendency to flee requires ritual attention almost from the time of conception. A psychoanalyst might see in Semai ideas of children, of souls, and of familiar spirits a projection of adult fears. The observed timidity of children may be reinforced by the discontinuity in adult behavior which parallels the transition from "new child" to plain "child." Moreover, the adult response to children's aggression is exactly that which, in a Euroamerican context, leads to nonviolence.

Enculturation, however, is only one of about five factors conducive to nonviolence among the Semai. As Semai experience during the Emergency shows, Semai are not nonviolent if these conditions are not met. The other four factors may be labeled ecological, economic, historical, and social.

The important ecological fact, salient in Gardner's (1966) study of nonviolent peoples, is that the almost unpopulated interior of the Malayan peninsula has always provided refuge areas to which people could flee from community or interethnic quarrels. Flight has always been a viable alternative to fighting. The strong tendency to opt for flight, due not merely to enculturation but to the realistic assessment of the historical situation discussed in the next paragraph, results in the demographic "fission-fusion" profile elegantly demonstrated by Fix (1971). Semai are explicit that, in the absence of a refuge area, they would stand and fight to the death.

Historically, Semai have been vastly outnumbered and outgunned by their neighbors. Unlike their American counterparts, Semai can count on a reasonably sympathetic hearing from the Department of Aborigines. Although they tend to trust high government officials, they know that they cannot expect to swing much weight in national policy-making, because they are so few. They say that violent resistance to national policies with which they might disagree would be suicidal and that they would not resist that way unless they felt they were being driven to extinction and could not flee.

The traditional Semai economic system has been discussed elsewhere in terms of indefinite reciprocity. Price (1975) more recently distinguishes between reciprocity and "sharing." Without his italics, he writes that "sharing is usually an unequal exchange . . . characterized by the attitude that each person will do what is appropriate, not by an expectation of equivalent return as in reciprocity" (1975:6). It is clear that, like the other nonviolent peoples in this volume that Price (1975:13) mentions, Semai traditionally place an "extreme emphasis on sharing" to the point that it is almost the only form of distribution of goods. Violence, like the failure to share, which Semai say is its equivalent, would effectively isolate the perpetrator from participating in this distribution. Such potential isolation may serve as an effective sanction against violence within the community.

Finally, Semai, again like most of the nonviolent peoples described in this volume, do not have segmentary social groupings like clans and hierarchies, which combat violence by freezing the threat of counter-violence in perpetuity. As Euroamericans have known at least since Roman time, the ultimate rationale of hierarchy is violence, the *ultima ratio regum.* For Semai, resisting both violence and hierarchy, the external order rests on *snngɔh,* the internal one on *slniil.* Segmentary social groups, implicitly violent, might destroy the traditional cautious Semai strategy of avoiding situations in which violence might occur.

In short, although Semai enculturation seems to foster nonviolence, it can probably only succeed in the sort of total context which Semai share with other peoples described in this volume. Within this context there is a simple answer to the question, "Why are the Semai nonviolent?" It is the only sensible way to be.

ROUGH GUIDE TO PRONUNCIATION

Semai stress the last syllable of a word. A difference in the length of a vowel, here shown by doubling long vowels, may be the only difference between two words of very distinct meanings. Vowel sounds are as follows:

a, as in f*a*ther
e, as in b*e*t
i, as in s*ee*k
o, as in r*o*pe
u, as in b*oo*t
ɔ, as in *ou*ght
ʉ, as in th*e*.

This last sound, a schwa, is not usually written for unstressed syllables. Thus *bʉʉl bhiip* "intoxicated (by) blood," would, in standard English spelling, be pronounced like "BULL buh-HEEEP."

Most final consonants are pronounced roughly as in English:

j, as dg in e*dg*e
r, trilled
s, midway between "s" and "sh"
c, as tch in e*tch*
', a glottal stop, as in Brooklynese "li'l" for "little"

NOTES

1. I am currently writing a paper on Stewart's work. His major publications are Stewart (MS, 1953–54, 1954, 1962, 1972). American references to his work include Coxhead and Miller (1976), Regush and Regush (1977), and Tart (1972). *Psychology Today* has carried articles on Senoi dream therapy.

2. This note lists tentative identifications of plants and animals used by Semai. Such a listing seems useful for three reasons. It is intrinsically interesting, like any archival material. Second, as Lévi-Strauss (1966) demonstrates, one needs a minute knowledge of the natural environment to understand how people use it. Finally, Westerners have usually described Malays and Semai as enemies. As noted below, there is evidence that a complete ethnobiology of both peoples would show a great overlap. Such an overlap sug-

gests that traditional indigenous intellectuals respected knowledge too much to let their traditional enmity stand in the way of disseminating useful knowledge.

In the story of Bird Spirit (pp. 101–02), the wild ginger is *brda'*, possibly *Zingiber* sp. The name, however, may derive from Malay *bedak*, used for the white spots left by touching rice paste to certain spots on one's body. The fish are *ka' bakap* ("ruby fish"), *ka' kadag*, and *ka' ruan*. The "specific" names are of Malay derivation and refer to *Ophiocephalus* spp.; *ruan* may be *O. striatus*. The argus pheasant is known to Semai as *ceep mard'*, "elder bird."

In the description of the asperger (pp. 103–04), the preferred source of barkcloth is *ipad* (*Ficus* sp.). One can, however, use regular barkcloth, made from trees of the breadfruit genus, e.g., *smkab* and *slamei* (*Artocarpus* spp.), the more often used *s'ug* (*A. elastica*) or *dkɔh* (*A. polyphema*); or of the eaglewood genus, *gaalug* (*Aquilaria agallocha, A. malaccensis*). The famous ipoh or upas tree, *dɔɔg* (*Antiaris toxicaria*), is another good source of barkcloth. If no barkcloth is available, a very useful rattan, *coog stɔ'*, may be used instead.

The plants used in an asperger may include *pmoleh* (*Filetia ridleyi, Justicia gendarussa*), *ppulud* (*Urena lobata*), *slbɔk* (*Ouratea crocea, Susum malayanum*), *spad* (*Mallotus* sp.), and *tabar* (*Costus speciosus, Kalanchoe pinnata*). Compare Malay usage (e.g., Burkill and Haniff, 1929–30: 178–79, 202, 223–24, 257, 315, 324; Dentan, 1971: 152, 154; Gimlette, 1971: 191, 221; Skeat, 1900: 79–80).

Besides these plants ritual bathing water (p. 104) may include *bʉn buus* (*Ocimum sanctum*), *bʉn srey* (*Cymbopogon nardus*), *bʉn kalib, ckor*, and *pngkras*. *Bʉn* is the short form of *bood* or *bʉʉd*, plants whose fragrance is especially likely to attract helpful "spirits." Amaranth (*Celosia argentea*) leaves and the sap of *kijai* (*Trigonochlamys griffithii*) may also be used.

The manufacture of lime is discussed by Dentan (1968c). The reddish fruit which produces the dye used on bathing tubes is *sumba'* (*Bixa orellana*), a plant of Caribbean origin.

Kijai sap (*T. griffithii*) is used for childbirth. The appropriate wild gingers are *brda'* (see Bird Spirit story above) and *rmpuyig*, which might be *Zingiber* spp. Both are medically used by Malays.

The following tentative identifications are of plants used to medicate "new children." Malays also make medicinal use of eaglewood, Semai *gaalug* (*Aquilaria agallocha, A. malaccensis*). I have *salung* as the Semai word for the unidentified *Psychotria*. *Salung* seems to be a portmanteau word for Malay *salang, sesalang,* and *sulong,* terms Malays sometimes use interchangeably (Burkill and Haniff, 1929–30: 218, 223, 317, 322, 323). Contextual evidence suggests the species in question might be *P. stipulacea,* though east Semai use *gilik* (*P. sarmentosa*) to facilitate childbirth and Temiar use *P. rostrata* for headache. Semai call the *Canarium* (*C. littorale*) "soother" (*prsnlir*) from the verb -*slir,* which seems to mean "cease fretting." The sensitive plants used seem to include *Biophytum sensitivum, Mimosa pudica,* and perhaps also *B. adiantoides.* Although the name may be a variant of Malay *senduduk,* Semai *kado'dak* seems to be *Uncaria pteropoda,* whose bark may contain tannin.

The *tabeg* accused of frightening souls are *tabeg kangkiig* (*Bufo melanosticus*).

Magic plants on east Semai spirits' "meeting houses" include *slbɔk* (*Ouratea crocea, Susum malayanum*) and *bʉn pnreh* (*Goniothalamus scortechnii*), as well as white costus (*C. speciosus*), the leaves of which west Semai boil to make a lave for someone whose fever has broken. The word *tabar* apparently refers to *Kalanchoe pinnata* as well as white costus. The ideal wood in the east is *stoog* (*Hibiscus macrophyllus*). West Semai prefer the wood of *pulei* (*Alstonia* spp., most likely *A. augustiloba, A. scholaris, A. spathulata*) and *bdɔ'* (*Dyera* spp.). Both trees are the reputed haunts of supernaturals (*nyani'*). *Bdɔ',* in particular, is infested by Bough Spirit(s), perhaps because its sap is red, "like blood."

The blind snake is *Typhlops diardi muelleri,* a "headband of Thunder." The toadstool is *btees kemɔɔc,* "ghost fungus" (*Amorphophallus* sp.), said to be a corpse's penis. The story of Thunder's problems in Dentan (1968a) involves this fungus.

3. The American Museum of Natural History has an extensively documented collection of Semai artifacts, including those mentioned in this chapter. Dentan (1968a) lists other collections, to which list should be added the Temiar collection at the Muzium Negara (Kuala Lumpur) and the collection at the Muzium Negara (Singapore).

The bathing cup is called *takɔɔ',* a word which may be related to *makɔɔ',* "pregnant" (see pp. 99–100). The asperger is a *cnau,* a noun formation from the verb -*cau,* "to asperge." The bathing tube is called by the Malay word *pancur,* "conduit," or *pancur takɔɔ'.* East Semai call the spirit perch a *sngrig,* perhaps a noun formation from the word *srig,* "a basket fish trap." West Semai call it a *tamu',* from a Malay word meaning roughly "to entertain, as a host a guest." In both cases, the idea is that the "spirits" are so shy that they must be inveigled into attending the "sing."

4. To become adept, a man (very rarely a woman, but they are said to be exceptionally good) has a dream in which a familiar gives him a melody. Thenceforward the "soul" (*ruai*) or "spirit" (*kloog*) of the familiar will come to help him when he sings the melody under the appropriate circumstances described in the text (Dentan, 1968a:82–85) of a familiar (*gunig*). The adept in the text had the unusually high number of nine familiars, viz., in decreasing order of potency:

Nyani' lata'. Waterfall spirit, in dreams of a friendly old Semai.

Bah Ta' Kuali'. Mr. Old Man Wok. In dreams a Chinese man infamous for breaking the taboo against mixing ritually immiscible categories of food as Chinese do. It bears a carrying pole with two large baskets holding cups, bowls, chopsticks, a rice pot, pork, fish, fungi, tumeric, and so on. Also appears as a beast, basically a pig, composed of immiscible foods, e.g., the ears are bracket fungi. Diagnostic of hepatitis.

Bah Karau. In dreams, a tiger outdoors, a youngish Semai indoors. Tigers are the commonest familiars of the Semai and Temiar.

Bah Lingsar. Like *Bah Ta' Kuali'*, a beast composed of immiscible foods.

Nyani' Ceeb. Bird Spirit. See text.

Karim. A wind spirit, a young Sinhalese man in the class "sea spirit" (*vs.* inland spirits), i.e., spirits knowledge of which comes from the coast where Malays live.

Tambi. Young Tamil man. Like most "tree spirits," lives in *bdɔ'* (*Dyera* spp.; see *balei* under "soul loss" in text) trees. Cures skin diseases called *tma'*.

Mara' Tunggul. Elder Treestump. The tall *tunggul* (branch reentering the ground, as on banyan trees) in question is in a secondary forest near specific "west Semai" swiddens. People take a break in its shade during horticultural work. Connected with immiscible foods and hepatitis.

Putri Mayang Murei. Princess palmflower straits-robin (*Copsychus saularis.*) Probably a mispronunciation of *mayang mengurai*, the opening palm flower which recalls curly hair or gradually unfolding beauty in Malay literature. Lives in a pool called Princess's Bath by local Malays, just under the high falls near the sacred Mt. Rlau.

5. Since 1963 the Department of Aborigines has drastically reduced this rate. Its medical program has been superlatively good since Malaysia became independent. I hazard the guess that Malaysia has the most enlightened policy towards its indigenous minorities of any country in the world, definitely including the West. For documentation, see, e.g., Ahmad Shaffie, 1971; Bolton, 1965 and 1968; Ministry of the Interior, 1961; Moss, 1962; Ng, 1961.

6. This is a cursory discussion of a complex topic. More detailed discussion is available elsewhere (e.g., Dentan, 1968a, 1968b).

BIBLIOGRAPHY

'Abdul-Hadi bin Haji Hasan 1925 Sejarah 'Alam Melayu. *The Malay School Series* #7.

Ahmad bin Embun n.d. Hantu dengan Kerja-nya. 2 vols. 2nd. ed. Singapore: Sinaran Brothers.

Ahmad Ezanee Manssor, Mohd. Razha Rashid, Syed Jamal Jaafar, Tan C. B., and S. Nagata 1973 Peringkat-peringkat umur di kalangan Orang-crang Kensiu di Kedah dan Orang-orang Kintak dan Temiar di Ulu Perak—satu lapuran pendahulan. *Manusia dan Masyarakat,* 2:117–25.

Ahmad Shaffie 1971 Temiar di Pos Brooke. *Dewan Masharakat* (Oct): 32–35.

Ainsworth, L. 1933 *The Confessions of a Planter in Malaya.* London: Witherby.

Alwi bin Sheikh Alhady 1962 *Malay Customs and Traditions.* Singapore: Eastern Universities Press.

Baharon Azhar bin Raffiei 1966 "Engku—Spirit of Thunders." *Federated Malay Museums Journal, 11*:34–37.

Barber, N. 1971 *The War of the Running Dogs.* London: Collins.

Benjamin, G. 1966 "Temiar Social Groupings. *Federation Museums Journal, 11*:1–24.

Bolton, M. 1963 Personal Communication on Semai Disease.

Bolton, J. M. 1965 "Jungle Rescue." *Straits Times Annual for 1964:* 26–28.

Bolton, J. M. 1968 "Medical Services to the Aborigines in West Malaysia." *British Medical Journal, 2*:818–23.

Brau de St.-Pol Lias, M. F. X. J. J. H. 1883 *Perak et les Orangs-Sakeys.* Paris.

Burkill, I. H. 1935 A Dictionary of the Economic Products of the Malay Peninsula. 2 vols., London.

Burkill, I. H., and M. Haniff 1929–30 "Malay Village Medicine." *The Gardens' Bulletin, Straits Settlements,* 6:167–332.

Cerruti, G. B. 1908 *My Friends the Savages.* Milan. [Mes Amis les Sauvages.]

Clifford, H. C. 1925 *In a Corner of Asia.* New York: McBride.

Cole, F.-C. 1945 *The People of Malaysia.* Princeton: Van Nostrand.

Collings, H. D. 1949 "Aboriginal Notes." *Bulletin of the Raffles Museum, Series B,* 4:86–103.

Coxhead, D., and S. Hiller. 1976 *Dreams.* New York: Avon.

Dentan, R. K. 1965 "Some Senoi Semai Dietary Restrictions." Ph.D. dissertation, Yale University.

———— 1967 "The Response to Intellectual Impairment among the Semai," *American Journal of Mental Deficiency.* 71:764–766 (To be reprinted in a reader on Southeast Asia edited by Forrest McGill).

———— 1968a *The Semai.* New York: Holt, Rinehart & Winston.

———— 1968b "The Semai Response to Mental Aberration." *Bijdragen tot de Taal-, Land en Volkenkunde,* 124:135–58.

———— 1968c "Notes on Semai Ethnomalacology." *Malacologia,* 7: 135–41.

———— 1970a "Labels and Rituals in Semai Classification." *Ethnology,* 9:16–25.

———— 1970b "Hocus Pocus and Extensionism in Central Malaya: Notes on Semai Kinship Terminology." *American Anthropologist,* 72:358–62.

———— 1971 "Some Senoi Semai Planting Techniques." *Economic Botany,* 25:136–159.

———— 1975 "If There Were No Malays, Who Would the Semai Be?" *Ethnic Pluralism in Malaysia,* J. Nagata, ed. Toronto: Canadian South Asian Society.

———— 1976a "Identity and Ethnic Contact: Perak, Malaysia." Intergroup Relations: Asian Scenes, T. Kang, ed. *Journal of Asian Affairs,* 1 (#1).

———— 1976b "Ethnics and Ethics in Southeast Asia." *Changing Identities in Southeast Asia,* D. J. Banks, ed. The Hague: Mouton.

Deutsch, K. W. 1966 *Nationalism and Social Communication.* 2nd. ed. Cambridge, Mass.: M.I.T. Press.

Diffloth, G. F. 1968 "Proto-Semai Phonology." *Federation Museums Journal,* 13 (ns):65–74.

———— 1975 Personal communication.

———— 197x Ms. "Body Moves in Semai and French."

Dunn, F. 1964 Personal communication.

Fix, A. G. 1971 "Semai Senoi Population Structure and Genetic Micro-differentiation." Ph.D. dissertation, University of Michigan.

Fortes, M. 1949 *The Web of Kinship among the Tallensi.* London: Oxford University Press.

Gardner, P. M. 1966 "Symmetric Respect and Memorate Knowledge: The Structure and Ecology of Individualist Culture." *Southwestern Journal of Anthropology,* 22:389–415.

Gimlette, J. D. 1971 *Malay Poisons and Charm Cures.* London: Oxford University Press.

Gimlette, J. D., and H. W. Thompson 1971 *A Dictionary of Malayan Medicine.* Singapore: Oxford University Press.

Green, R. 1949 "Anthropological Blood Grouping among the 'Sakai.' " *Bulletin of the Raffles Museum, Series B,* #4:130–132.

Hogan-Shaidali, S. A. E. 1950 Report on Sakai statistics. Unpublished letter in file of Department of Aborigines.

Ismail, Munshi; J. D. Gimlette; and I. H. Burkill 1930 "The Medical Book of Malayan Medicine." *The Gardens' Bulletin, Straits Settlements,* 6:333–499.

Leech, H. W. C. 1880 "About Kinta." *Journal of the Straits Branch of the Royal Asiatic Society,* 4:21–33.

Machado, A. D. 1900 "The Hot Springs of Ulu Jelai." *Journal of the Straits Branch of the Royal Asiatic Society,* 33:263–64.

McHugh, J. N. 1959 *Hantu Hantu: Ghost Belief in Modern Malaya.* Singapore: Eastern Universities Press.

Miklucho-Maclay, N. V. 1878 "Dialects of the Melanesian Tribes in the Malay Peninsula." *Journal of the Straits Branch of the Royal Asiatic Society,* 1:38–43.

———— 1879 "Ethnological Excursions in the Malay Peninsula, November 1874 to October 1875" (preliminary communication). *Journal of the Straits Branch of the Royal Asiatic Society,* 2:205–21.

Miller, H. 1960 "The Fighting Senoi." *Straits Times Annual 1960:* 17–19.

———— 1972 *Jungle War in Malaya.* London: Arthur Barker.

Miller, N. E., and J. Dollard 1941 *Social Learning and Imitation.* New Haven: Yale University Press.

Ministry of the Interior 1961 *Statement of Policy Regarding the Administration of the Aborigine Peoples of the Federation of Malaya.* Kuala Lumpur: Ministry of the Interior.

Moss, P. 1962 "She Patrols 400 Miles of High Jungle." *Sunday Mail* (11 November 1962).

Needham, Rodney 1964 "Temer names." *Journal of the Straits Branch of the Royal Asiatic Society,* 37:121–25.

—— 1972 *Belief, Language, and Experience.* Chicago: University of Chicago Press.

Ng Yook Yoon 1961 "Science Reaches the Jungle Folk." *Sunday Mail* (5 November 1961).

Polunin, I. 1953 "The Medical Natural History of the Malayan Aborigines." *Medical Journal of Malaya,* 8:55–174.

Porteus, S. D. 1937 *Primitive Intelligence and Environment.* New York: Macmillan.

Price, J. A. 1975 "Sharing: The Integration of Intimate Economies." *Anthropologica,* 17:3–26.

Regush, J. V. and N. M. 1977 *Dream worlds.* New York: Signet Books.

Richter, L. B. 1975 Personal communication.

Robarchek, C. J. 1976 "Tradeoffs in trading with traders." Paper presented at the Western Conference of the Association for Asian Studies, Annual Meeting, Flagstaff, Arizona.

Robarchek, C. A. 1976 "Learning to Fear: A Case Study in Emotional Conditioning." Paper presented at the Western Conference of the Association for Asian Studies, Annual Meeting, Flagstaff, Arizona.

—— 1977a "Semai Nonviolence: A Systems Approach to Understanding." Ph.D. dissertation, University of California, Riverside.

—— 1977b "Conflict, Emotion, and Abreaction: Conflict Resolution among the Semai Senoi." Paper presented at the Southwestern Anthropological Association, Annual Meeting, San Diego, California.

Schebesta, P. 1926 "Sakai in Malakka." *Archiv für Rassenbilder,* 9: 81–90.

—— 1927 "Religiöse Anschauungen der Semang über die Orang hidop" (die Unsterblichen), part 2. *Archiv für Religionswissenschaft,* 25:5–35.

Skeat, W. W., and C. O. Blagden 1906 *Pagan Races of the Malay Peninsula.* 2 vols. London: Macmillan.

Skeat, W. W. 1900 *Malay Magic.* London: Macmillan.

Stewart, K. MS "A report on Porteus Maze Test results from some of the racial groups of southeastern Asia and the peripheral island." (Excerpts in S. D. Porteus 1937 *Primitive Intelligence and Environment.* New York: Macmillan.)

—— 1953–1954 "Culture and Personality in Two Primitive Groups." *Complex,* 9:3–23.

―――― 1954 "Mental Hygiene and World Peace." *Mental Hygiene,* 38:387–403.

―――― 1962 "The Dream Comes of Age." *Mental Hygiene,* 46: 230–37.

―――― 1972 "Dream Theory in Malaya. In Tart, ed. 1972 (*q.v.*)

Tart, C. T., ed. 1972 *Altered States of Consciousness.* Garden City, New York: Anchor.

Tweedie, M. W. F. 1961 *The Snakes of Malaya.* 2nd. ed. Singapore: Government Printing Office.

Wheeler, L. R. 1928 *The Modern Malay.* London: Allen and Unwin.

Whiting, J. W. M., and I. L. Child 1962 *Child Training and Personality.* New Haven: Yale University Press.

Wilkinson, R. J. 1915 "A Vocabulary of Central Sakai (dialect of the aboriginal communities in the Gopeng valley)." *Papers on Malay Subjects, 2nd. series #3.*

Williams, T. R. 1969 *A Borneo Childhood.* New York: Holt, Rinehart & Winston.

Williams-Hunt, P. D. R. 1950 Unpublished filed notes of January 21. In files of Department of Aborigines.

Williams-Hunt, P. D. R. 1952 *An Introduction to the Malayan Aborigines.* Kuala Lumpur: Government Press.

CATHERINE H. BERNDT

In Aboriginal Australia

The Problem

Some urban Aborigines today take a nostalgic, golden-age view of the traditional past—a past of which they themselves have had no firsthand experience. Their impressionistic image underplays the notion of aggression or conflict. It concentrates on the traditional Aborigines as a gentle people living in harmony with one another and with the world around them, sharing all their possessions as well as their labor and their natural resources.

Some traditionally oriented Aborigines look back at their past—their own, local past—rather differently. Take Lamilami, for instance, a Maung-speaking man from the northwest coast of Arnhem Land. Brought up in a mission dormitory, he was later ordained as a Methodist minister, but deliberately kept up his interest in his traditional culture, including the religious belief and practice that are still important to many Aborigines in that region. This combined foothold was made easier for him because of the Methodist Mission's stated ideal of "keeping what's best in the Aboriginal culture," even though there were formidable difficulties in translating the ideal into practice. In his autobiographical account (1974), which he sets in the context of the changing scene in and around the Goulburn Islands, he certainly conveys a picture of basically cooperative living. But he does not hesitate to include the friction and even physical violence that to him were also an intrinsic part

144

of that scene. Farther along the coast, in the mid-1940's, north-eastern Arnhem Landers used to boast about their reputation for forceful behavior, their quick emotional reactions to supposed slights or insults, and their ability to get their own way, if necessary through violence or threat of violence. They would refer in matter-of-fact terms to episodes in their own experience where, for instance, a man was killed for the specific purpose of taking over his wife or wives. With greater gusto, some of them would recount rare happenings in their parents' or grandparents' generations and before, where wanderers whose craft had drifted off course were roughly handled and any goods they had were eagerly seized.

Another example of an Aboriginal perspective on the past, in this respect, comes from a person who is physically part-Aboriginal and until a few years ago was socioculturally Aboriginal only in a negative sense—defined as Aboriginal in the sense of being legally and politically disadvantaged, living on the fringes of the wider Australian society. Now, in the changed sociopolitical climate, he not only identifies himself as an Aboriginal (not a "part-Aboriginal") person but also is regarded by many people, Aboriginal and otherwise, as a leader and a spokesman, an authority on Aboriginal affairs. His earlier contention, which he expressed strongly and unequivocally, stressed the "harmonious past" approach. But this gradually changed. When trouble between some people of Aboriginal descent living in Perth made headline news in the Western Australian press, culminating in the death of one of them in the main city area, he explained this as a feud between two "families" going "right back to tribal times," back to the traditional past.

Of course, these perspectives are not mutually exclusive. For people like Lamilami, the inference one might draw is that Aborigines have behaved more mildly in the conquest situation than they might have done if they had had a chance to do otherwise. For urban Aborigines, the contrast is sometimes drawn explicitly and deliberately to point up the shortcomings of the Australian-European society which formerly rejected them and which they in turn are now rejecting (at least up to a point). Traditional Aboriginal harmony and cooperativeness are depicted as an ideal mode of life, as against the overbearingly aggressive and rapacious life style that has supplanted and destroyed it.

Because the traditional situation was actually mixed, as in Lamilami's version, the balancing of aggressive and non-aggressive elements within it can be presented in varying ways, including an extreme emphasis on one at the expense of the other. Aside from the general circumstances just mentioned (Aborigines looking at the past from the vantage point of an unsatisfying present), a number of factors come into this: notably, who is asking what questions about the past, and maybe anticipating the answers? How much relevant material is available? And how far do the questioners actually draw on such material? What about regional variations? Not least, there is the problem of how aggression and aggressiveness are defined in framing the questions: the extent to which they are implied, not merely gauged on the basis of overt behavior, and how verbal and dramatic evidence, such as myths and rituals, is analyzed in relation to them.

So far, there has been no comprehensive study of this overall topic in regard to Aboriginal Australia, though a fair amount of data has been published on particular regions. Much of this has to do with sociocultural features; some touches on personality issues, and following Róheim's earlier work on women's dreams in Central Australia there has been a growing interest, in the past few years, in psychoanalytic and psychiatric themes—but these inquiries, and their reported findings, require more discussion than can be accorded them here.

Needless to say, not everything that could be labeled "aggression" is spelled out under that heading in the literature. Kaberry's *Aboriginal Woman* . . . (1939), one of the few to provide an index-entry for the term, seems to lack clear criteria for it and excludes a number of relevant page-references. Warner (1937/58), despite the numerous examples he gives, has no such entry. Nor have we, either in our Gunwinggu study (R.M. and C.H.B., 1970) or in our more comprehensive general account (1964/77). Instead, like most others, we have noted specific topics—conflicts, disputes, fighting, retaliation, revenge, and the like. Nevertheless, almost every volume and article that deals with Australian Aboriginal life contains some material that bears either directly or obliquely on the subject of aggression. Interpersonal fights and quarrels, injuries and deaths, sorcery accusations and charges, sharp dealing in the economic sphere, bear witness to the range of actualities as well as possibilities in this direction.

Learning What To Do about It

Aboriginal children grew up in surroundings where *people* were regarded as important, and the people they came into contact with could all be easily identified. Although they moved about from one place to another, the relationships that they developed were long-term, continuing ones.

The process of growing up went on in a physical environment that was difficult at times, especially in bad seasons, but in a social environment that was fairly secure. A child learned his or her place in the scheme of things—that he or she *had* a place, an assured place. The emphasis was on spiritual continuity. This rested partly on links with the land—and, through the land, with spirit beings and with other people: for example, people connected with the same sites or with various spirit manifestations. In addition to these spiritual links, there were physical links with other people, through parents who supplied flesh and blood and bone structure.

A baby was always close to its mother, from the time they emerged from birth-seclusion together. Small children slept with their mothers, cuddled against them, in warm bodily contact with them. Even if they were left with "baby-sitters" during the day— grandparents, for example—it was their own mothers who were (it seems) the most important persons in their lives until they were able to run about by themselves. Until then, a child's mother was the main source—not just *a* source—of food as well as shelter, comfort, and love. A crying baby was the signal for its mother's instant attention—and demand-feeding was the rule. If a small child tripped or fell or took fright at something and ran to its mother, as often as not she would take it in her arms and push her nipple into its mouth to quieten it. Weaning could strain the relationship for a while, but that might be delayed for a youngest child or an only child.

Children would sit among the women watching the dancing at a camp ceremony, or would curl up asleep in their arms or on the ground beside them. By day, if they were not out with a group of women gathering food, and learning how to do this themselves, they would play together—but always within sight and earshot of somebody they knew was there to look after them. Because of the wide spread of the kinship network, people used the terms "mother" and "father," "brother" and "sister" for more than one person. But they always knew the gradations, the range between (for instance) "own father," father's brothers, and more distant fathers.

From childhood through to old age, everyone was enmeshed in a network of close relationships with some people, shading into more distant relationships with others. The social and emotional security that this involved outweighed the minor insecurities that went with it.

Because the Aborigines were human beings, they quarreled and argued and fought, they worried about what other people did or didn't do in relation to them or what they would do to or for other people. Children took notice of such things, watching and listening and sometimes participating. They learned about breaches of the rules, what *not* to do, just as they were taught about the rules themselves. Competition and competitiveness, aggressive behavior and stances, were not absent, but they were played down. The stress was on cooperation. And this was a matter of urgent, day-to-day necessity. Cooperation between people was essential for physical survival, and so was cooperation with the land and the other living things that shared it with them. The people in a community belonged together, and their natural environment was part of that belonging.

The general message that was handed on to children, to be handed on in turn by and through those children as they grew older, was that life had meaning. All they had to do was to follow the guidelines that had been set down. This did not mean following them slavishly—there was some room for variation, but the guidelines were there.

The Aborigines did not suppose that the information they considered necessary for adult living could be transmitted mystically or through genetic inheritance. In many areas they believed that a spirit-child, a preexistent spirit, brought life and animation to the physical part of a baby before it was born. The spirit would appear in a dream or in other ways to the baby's father or his sister or some other appropriate person. But they did not believe that this spirit came ready-made as far as knowledge of everyday living was concerned. What it signified was a person's bond with his or her country and the people who shared it, and with the spiritual past (and present and future).

Aboriginal philosophies of education were not wrapped up in involved discussion of words and concepts. They focused on the actualities of the situation and on "why" statements that were framed in religious terms. All Aboriginal societies paid tremendous attention to both teaching and learning, as a two-sided process. It is true that the main stress was on *teaching,* and learning was expected to follow almost automatically if the conditions were right and the children were properly receptive. But they did allow for contingencies, and for differences in individual response. They believed that children had to be taught and that it was adults' responsibility to do this.

For children, then, and for adults, the social context was one of primary relationships—known, identifiable persons. It was also one of warmth and closeness between such persons, even though there were inevitable disagreements and problems. The Aborigines were a gregarious people. Hermits and social isolates, individuals who withdrew from others to meditate in solitude, had no place in their culture.

This closeness and recognition of personal ties extended outward beyond the immediate family, beginning with mother and father, brothers and sisters, and spreading to include everyone in the particular area where a child was living. Children learned about the identification of "we" as against "they"—a shifting identification, as it always is. And this was a basis for learning both rules and actual practice in a variety of situations. For young children, it always began in the setting of family relationships, in an atmosphere of affection and personal attention. In the ordinary way, small children were loved and wanted—and were made to feel loved and wanted. In spite of what some writers have suggested, infanticide was rare.

The domestic family was the source of teaching and discipline, in these early years. This meant primarily a child's mother. Fathers were important too, but mothers had much more to do with babies and children up to about three or four years old.

That circumstance altered as a child grew older, especially for a boy. His father became more consistently involved, and later this extended to other men too. His mother's brothers were particularly important to him in some areas, but in any case the religious leaders of his community came to have more of a say in his upbringing —a controlling say. In northeastern Arnhem Land, for example, a boy would be taken for circumcision between six and eight years old—taken, literally, from his mother as he clung to her or rode astride her shoulders (a customary way of traveling, for a young child), to signify the break with his family-controlled life up to that time. After that, he no longer lived in his parents' camp.

For a girl there was more obvious continuity, and growing identification with women and with women's roles. A girl's break with her parents' camp came when she married—in some areas at puberty if not before, in others later. Then, as a rule, she would not only leave their small cluster of home fires and shelters. She would move farther away, out of their camp-complex into another. Traditionally, this would not mean going into "foreign" territory. It would not be a sudden, abrupt happening, because usually she would have been betrothed since she was quite small—or there would have been a lot of talk about this, getting her used to the idea. And she would not be going among strangers. The ideal kind of marriage, in all Aboriginal societies, was one where a husband and wife were already linked through a kin relationship, although the particular type of relationship that was preferred in one area might not be the same in another. So, the wife's own family, her close relatives, were already related to her husband's family even before the betrothal and marriage were arranged.

But to begin with, the keynote in teaching-and-learning situations was indulgence. Discipline was gentle. The atmosphere was fairly permissive. Parents didn't expect adult behavior from children. They were lenient in regard to such things as toilet training, and what would be defined as naughty behavior in older children was likely to be tolerated in younger ones—children who "hadn't learnt to understand properly yet." Difficulties were graded. Children were not expected to cope with tasks that were "too hard for them." Also, their squabbles and fights were allowed to proceed only so far before adults (notably, their mothers) intervened. A boy could get away with being cheekier to his mother than a girl could. But in northeastern Arnhem Land, for instance, temper tantrums that could go on even up to adolescence among girls were assaults on people's ears (and eyes) rather than attacks on their persons. Typically, a girl would lie on her back, kicking and screaming, a process that could go on sporadically for several hours. Adults sitting nearby might shout or moan in exasperation at intervals, but mostly would not intervene directly, except perhaps to provide a diversion—food, for instance.

In any traditional camp setting, a fairly wide range of people would participate in teaching. They did this informally and tolerantly, but consciously and continuously. They would talk to small children, tease them, and joke with them, fondling them, addressing them by the right kinship terms. Without seeming to teach, they taught them the polite forms of speech and polite expressions they should use in dealing with other people. For example, never to address others by personal names, except nicknames or joking names, only by kinship terms or various social-category labels, or even place-names. Sometimes there would be a lot of people around, sometimes only a few. In this open, almost public kind of environment, among sociable people, a child was hardly ever alone with only parents and brothers and sisters for company. Everybody in a community helped in some way with rearing the children of that community.

Nevertheless, when it came to discipline, the field was much narrower. The main control over a child was vested in its parents, and particularly in its mother. In the round of daily life, a mother was responsible for her small children. She could smack them or punish them, as even their grandparents or uncles or aunts (for instance) would hesitate to do. If she treated them roughly or unfairly, however, or neglected them, her husband (and her brothers, in some areas) would proceed to punish *her*. This prospect could have deterred a few mothers from ill-treating their children, but if so, it was mostly a background threat.

In general, a mother was expected to be loving and protective, not punitive. It was up to her to ensure that her children were safe and properly fed, that they didn't go near dangerous or forbidden places, or eat dangerous or forbidden foods. Whoever else might help her, she was accountable for them. And this was more than simple protection and prevention, sheltering them from harm. She was expected to teach them how to deal with such matters on their own behalf.

Another point in which mothers had a pivotal role, in conjunction with other women, is one that is often overlooked by outsiders (non-Aborigines). It is even forgotten in some cases by Aborigines looking back on their own past.

In many parts of Aboriginal Australia, traditionally, small children were introduced to religion most directly and most consistently through women, especially their mothers. This was not an introduction to detail, or even to the general content of religion. It might include some elementary teaching about subject matter, in areas where there were children's versions of religious myths and songs, but mainly it had to do with something less specific—with the inculcation of atmosphere, and attitudes.

This was tackled through the same two-barreled approach that the Aborigines used in almost all of their teaching programmes.

One side of it was negative, concerned with "what *not* to do." There might be preliminary warnings, or general statements, like "when such-and-such happens, this is what you must remember," but these would come into sharp focus at the appropriate time and place. In a ceremonial-ritual context, for instance, children might be told forcefully "Don't look!" as their mothers and other women covered their heads and shoulders or averted their faces during certain parts of the performance. Or they might be warned, as they sat with a group of women waiting for a group of decorated men to come chanting from their sacred ritual ground, "Don't call out!" "Don't laugh, don't smile!" To small children, the unfamiliar figures that looked so unlike the men they knew in ordinary life could seem either frightening or funny, like a new game—so women used to say. And some women might add, hushing the children, "Don't do that, or the men might kill us!"

The second approach complemented this, impressing on children in a more positive way the importance of such occasions. In this way they laid the foundations for acceptance, positive acceptance, of religious manifestations. Even more telling, they worked at building-in attitudes of respect, reverence and awe, a feeling for the sacred. These were a vital preliminary to the specific information that children were expected to acquire as they became older.

Children, then, learned (were taught) how to establish and maintain relations with people, with their human environment, and also how to deal with nonhuman environment. At first, they saw all of these in the frame of everyday activities but with a growing awareness that they existed within a religious context. Later still, came more direct understanding and participation.

Aboriginal societies come into the category of what have been called "repetitive" societies. This means first, that the past was used as a guide to behavior in the present and in the future, and secondly, that children were expected to use adults (and older children) as models on whom to base their own behavior.

Almost no scenes were barred to children, apart from the sphere of the secret-sacred, and its offshoots such as women's seclusion shelters. Children had plenty of opportunities for observing "wrong" behavior and the punishments that should or might go with that. They learned that in many situations of everyday living there was not a single, fixed way of behaving: that there was nearly always a range of acceptable alternatives. The further away those situations were from the domain of the most sacred beliefs and rites, the greater was the possibility of choice. But it is probably safe to say that in most cases, if not all, people were not concerned with the general issue of freedom of choice, *as* an issue. Their basic values and assumptions were not open to serious questioning, let alone serious dispute. How the rules were translated into practice—this was seen as a problem-area where things could go wrong. But the rules themselves were virtually "givens." Children learned about things and people, about food tabus and about social tabus, just as they learned about preparation for marriage and adulthood—through a combination of soft and hard teaching. The softness was more obvious on the surface, particularly in early childhood. The hardness was associated with the core-rules, most notably with the religious rules, but spilling over into the whole field of social activities.

Conclusion

This generalized outline does not go into the question of local variations, but it sets out some basic points that would have to be taken into account in a more comprehensive study.

One intriguing area of enquiry here concerns initiation procedures in relation to their sociocultural context. Physical initiation rites varied throughout the continent, from no physical initiation at all, to (for instance) depilation, tooth evulsion, circumcision, and subincision. Some non-Aborigines seem to regard such operations, especially subincision, as harsh and cruel if not actually sadistic, if not in themselves, then in the scope they afforded for dominating, bullying, and punitive behavior. (So, in this view, they were a means of inducing and perpetuating such behavior.)

To examine this subject satisfactorily it is not enough to take, say, the mother-son relationship as one variable and the nature of the initiation procedure (the physical-operation aspect of it) as another. What is called for is a study of the whole system of social control in a particular society, together with the verbal and dramatic material that children are exposed to, the manner in which they respond to it, and an analysis of that material itself. Initiation-type is only one small facet of all this, albeit an important facet. It provides visible physical signs that the people themselves can interpret as clues to other things (ritual status, knowledge of religious symbols, and the like). But can it provide clues of a different sort to an anthropologist who is interested in broader contextual issues on a comparative level? Interestingly, the Aranda, who became widely known through the work of Spencer and Gillen, taken up by Durkheim, were for a time almost the archetype of the mild, gentle Aborigines. Yet their initiation rites included head-biting and the tearing-out of finger nails (a painful process), as well as fairly autocratic domination of younger by older men on such occasions. In contrast, the Gunwinggu-speaking people of western Arnhem Land traditionally did not circumcise or subincise or in fact include any physical operation at all in their quite lengthy initiation sequences. Nevertheless, their life style made provision for a pattern of small-scale fighting, or small-scale warfare, which partly resembled that of the circumcising northeastern Arnhem Landers to their east. (See R. M. and C. H. Berndt, 1970, for the Gunwinggu; W. L. Warner, 1937/58, for the northeastern groups, in his case from the standpoint of Milingimbi on the north central coast.) Correlations along these lines, on a broad comparative scale, could yield some fascinating combinations and contrasts; but again, they would have to be seen against a *total* framework which brought in other aspects as well—views about treatment of the human body, specifically one's own and other people's but also bodies in general, as manifested in mortuary rites, for example. (The analogy between physical initiation procedures and bodily death and rebirth is or was made explicit in many Aboriginal societies, but it has other implications too.)

Whether or not flesh-eating populations ("flesh" including fish, game, and so on as well as meat) are more aggressive than vegetarians, or whether that particular variable is not directly relevant in measuring aggression has not yet been rigorously tested. After all, as Ashley Montagu has pointed out (in Ashley Montagu, ed., 1968:7), the actual killers are not necessarily the sole consumers. Also, tending cattle, pigs, fowls, or other creatures specifically for killing as food is not fundamentally different from hunting for the same purpose. It does have the connotation of hunting-in-order-to-destroy, but choosing victims from one's own household if not from one's own family and kingroup, as against "outsiders" or strangers. In the Aboriginal case they need not be "outsiders" as far as species is concerned, but individually they are almost certain to be strangers—unlike, say, household pets or members of small domestic flocks or herds.

In the Aboriginal case, the relationship between people and the creatures they killed for food was not confined to these two facets of their association (killing, and eating). It was both closer and more extensive than that. The identification between certain persons or groups or categories of persons and certain species was not merely nominal. It was an emotional, personally significant bond. Even in one society it could take a number of forms, and not all of these precluded or discouraged the killing or (for vegetable and fruit foods) digging or collecting of the non-human manifestation. Inequality was built into the relationship in the sense that it was not evenly reciprocal. Human beings used other living things for food—but not, normally, vice versa. Australian Aborigines had few predators, few carnivores to fear—notably, sharks, crocodiles, and pythons. When these attacked people, the reasons were usually sought in the human sphere, in terms of sorcery, not through attributing responsibility to the visibly obvious killer. Human enmity, human grudges, and human aggression were believed to provide necessary and sufficient reasons without invoking ill will on the part of the creature-as-agent.

By the time people were adults they were expected to know about such things, not only in relation to themselves but also in relation to other members of their community—about their human and nonhuman connections. But there is not much information on how this knowledge was acquired. More is available on the teaching side than on the actual processes of learning and internalizing and responding. What evidence there is suggests that two overlapping dimensions were involved. One was the sphere of personal and social identification, with its implications for answers to transcendental questions. The other, linked with it but focusing on practical considerations of physical survival, was the pattern of killing-for-food in nature. This, and the attitudes associated with it, seem to have been grasped more easily by children than the general idea and the particular commitments which together mapped out the various facets of their identity.

Aside from observation of actual human behavior, songs and stories acquainted children with the ways in which natural species drew on one another and on the world around them for nourishment and life. Children's songs from western Arnhem Land, for example, were short but concentrated sketches of the habits and characteristics of creatures who shared the natural environment with human beings. In some of these, the allusion to hunters' ruthlessly stalking and catching their prey reflected the same basic theme that was relevant to human hunters. The wild dog or dingo song was one, like others that dealt with fish-eating birds in and around the billabongs and rivers. In the light of such "natural" behavior, children's apparently callous treatment of little, helpless creatures that fell into their hands could perhaps be seen as "functional," a necessary hardening-preparation for people who needed to kill animals and the like in order to survive. (Even though the Aborigines' diet was fundamentally vegetarian in most areas, it was supplemented by protein-rich foods, large and small.) The way some children handled baby kangaroos, for example, that were given to them to play with could not be called deliberate torture. It was more casual than that, and might be mixed with sporadic displays of affection and caressing (hinting at or foreshadowing the adult scene in this respect, in regard to the instrumental and affective sides of their place in nature). It was a kind of sport, with no pretence of utilizing the victim as food, even on a make-believe level—whereas the spearing-practice games of killing small inedible lizards and grasshoppers and so on were more clearly part of a total sequence, cooking and pretend-eating and all.

One further example comes from western Arnhem Land, in this case a story that some thirty years ago was told to children. It is almost a just-so story, about how the inedible Loglog lizard came to be like he is now. In summary, it tells how old Loglog, when he was a man, tricked two young brothers who were helping him to catch rock-possums in deep, narrow caves in the escarpment country. They called him "grandfather" (mother's father), but not "own, actual grandfather." He killed them by blocking up a cave-mouth with dry grass and then setting it alight so that they suffocated in the smoke. Then he cooked them, mixing their flesh with possum meat, ate some, and took the rest to eat on his journey. He made a special basket to carry their bones in, as he carried the death-message to their parents and other relatives in a conventionally correct way. But when he poured out the bones onto the ground in front of the assembled people, the men attacked him with spears while others gashed themselves in mourning. He turned into a little shiny-skinned lizard: but finally they caught him and burnt him to death in a tree, gathering extra wood to incinerate the few tiny bones that remained. The story is replete with dramatic details to hold the attention of listeners, from the early scenes where the brothers go far into the caves while the old man listens to their voices from outside and runs to collect dry grass, to the cave-closing, burning and suffocation episodes (which appear in a number of western Arnhem Land stories), the cooking and basket-making, the journey (Loglog skipping and dancing along, so that the bones jumped up and down in the long basket), and the final chase and destruction of Loglog. The main points for us here are the assertion by Loglog's killers that "people are not to be used for food," and, especially, that the killing of one person by another must be adequately justified. Loglog didn't have a good enough reason for killing the two brothers; and they were at least nominal kin to him, which made his action all the more reprehensible.

A further point, outside that regional situation, is also pertinent. When I was asked a few years ago to suggest a few stories which could be used, in translation, in general Australian schools, I included this one partly because of its vivid imagery and its lively story-line. The educational authorities at the time claimed to find it too aggressive and frightening for children: it would give the children nightmares, they said, not because of its unfamiliar cultural setting, but because it conveyed a threatening atmosphere that children would be unable to cope with.

Perhaps this simply points up the importance of sociocultural context in regard to any kind of verbal or dramatic material that brings in aggression or violence.

Statements about Australian Aborigines as mild, unaggressive people are often misunderstood, because they are *relative* statements. They say something about Aborigines in general, as contrasted with other peoples. It was not that, traditionally, Aborigines never fought, never wounded or killed one another in the heat of the moment or in planned revenge, and so on. But such statements do mean that, as far as we know, they did not delight in violence for its own sake, or in inflicting harm and injury on others. They were on the whole humane people. The few exceptions *were* exceptions. And these values and attitudes were taught, and learnt, in childhood.

The problem, then, is not whether there *is* some modicum of aggression in any given society, or whether there are expressions of what could be called aggression. It is whether there are checks and balances which restrain or contain these, how successful or otherwise they seem to be, and how they are transmitted. Aboriginal societies varied on this score. But all of them had some features in common, features that in combination served to "damp down" the range and intensity of aggression. The absence of reported, openly acknowledged suicide in the traditional past may or may not be a pointer to this: but it is something that needs further exploration.

In particular, however, it is important to remember that territorial defence and territorial conquest were not salient issues in Aboriginal Australia. The land was regarded as god-given, not subject to negotiation. The boundaries were not open to change by human beings. Religious gatherings when members of different groups met together were, at least by implication, occasions for reaffirming ownership of sites and the country around them. This limited (not obviated) the possibility of conflict between neighboring groups.

Internally, within communities, conflict and open expressions of aggression took place within a framework of interdependence. It was what I once called "community through necessity." Networks of cooperation, of cross-cutting obligations and duties, were an inescapable setting in and for individual decision-making. Territorial mobility was limited by these, by the close interpersonal links which bound people together in a regional framework, and by the religious imperatives which governed their relationships. Ultimately, it was religious rules and religious authority which underlay the virtual absence of protest. Children growing up in Aboriginal societies accepted the discipline imposed by their elders because they had no effective alternatives. And in this context, while they learned about "bad examples" and self-assertion at the expense of others, they learned also about the penalties that could be expected to follow. Expectations and ideals along with actualities made up the sociocultural fabric where strands of violent, aggressive behaviour and attitudes were only a small part of the overall pattern.

SELECTED BIBLIOGRAPHY

This list is brief, because a) references to socialization in the traditional setting are so scarce and b) references to aggression and non-aggression, not necessarily under those headings, are so numerous as to cover virtually the entire range of published literature on most traditional-Aboriginal topics. The C. H. and R. M. Berndt (1972) reference is an overview of socialization, traditional and otherwise. The R. M. Berndt (1965) and T. G. H. Strehlow (1970) references draw attention to some important issues in the sphere of social control and authority. Further reading-sources are included in some of the items noted here (especially in R. M. and C. H. Berndt, 1964/77).

Berndt, C. H. and R. M. 1972 "Aborigines." *Socialization in Australia,* F. J. Hunt, ed. Sydney: Angus and Robertson. (New, revised edition forthcoming 1977; in press.)

Berndt, C. H. and R. M. 1978 *Pioneers and Settlers: The Australian Aborigines.* Melbourne: Pitman.

Berndt, R. M. 1965 "Law and Order in Aboriginal Australia." *Aboriginal Man in Australia.* R. M. and C. H. Berndt, eds. Sydney: Angus and Robertson.

Berndt, R. M., and C. H. 1970 *Man, Land and Myth in North Australia: The Gunwinggu People.* Sydney: Ure Smith.

Berndt, R. M. and C. H. 1964/77 *The World of the First Australians.* Sydney: Ure Smith.

Kaberry, P. 1939 *Aboriginal Woman, Sacred and Profane.* London: Routledge.

Lamilami, L. 1974 *Lamilami Speaks . . .* (An Autobiography.) Sydney: Ure Smith.

Montagu, M. F. Ashley, ed. 1968 *Man and Aggression.* New York: Oxford University Press.

Strehlow, T. G. H. 1970 "Geography and the Totemic Landscape in Central Australia." *Australian Aboriginal Anthropology,* R. M. Berndt, ed. Perth: University of Western Australia Press, for the Australian Institute of Aboriginal Studies.

Warner, W. L. 1937/58 *A Black Civilisation.* New York: Harper.

COLIN M. TURNBULL

The Politics of Non-Aggression

What follows may appear to be a needlessly lengthy and overly detailed descriptive account of pregnancy, childbirth, and child training. Far from being irrelevant to any study of aggressivity, however, the pity is that I cannot provide *more* detail. The crux of the learned aspect of aggressivity, at least, is the relationship the individual develops with the world around him. It is a *total* relationship. We divide it into artificial segments and talk of man's relationship with the human or animal worlds, with the natural and the mechanical or technological worlds, and in many other ways. But for true non-aggressivity and nonviolence to be learned the individual has to gain confidence in his relationship with all the various segments of his experience, and perceive it as a single totality rather than as the mere sum total of separate relationships.

While the extent to which the human being is biologically programmed to be an aggressive, predatory animal may be questionable, there can surely be no question as to man's *potential* for aggressivity. His physiological capability in this direction is not unimpressive, but his mental capacity is staggering, for it not only

Much of the data that follow was acquired during a field trip funded by the National Science Foundation (1970–72) for whose support I am much indebted. I am also grateful for the advice and help of my colleague, Dr. Barbara Ingersoll, of West Virginia University.

enables him to devise and fabricate weapons, it also enables him consciously to plan and chart his course of aggression and execute it with malice aforethought, which is perhaps the most dangerous and destructive form of violence.

In this discussion I am not ignoring the possibility of biological programming, and am well aware that there are indeed many significant biological and physiological factors that have to be taken into consideration; but the discussion will focus primarily on cultural factors that can undeniably be shown to have the power of overriding whatever impulses (biological or cultural) the individual may have towards violence, except in the most extreme cases. We should be equally concerned with those specific social institutions that serve, usually among other things, to avert, control, or rectify any outbreak of individual or group violence.

However, if man has a seemingly limitless capacity for violence, for aggression, he has an equally great potential for nonviolence and non-aggressivity, and a notable feature of many small-scale societies is the great amount of concern shown, in a wide diversity of institutionalized forms, for the reduction of man's potential for aggressivity and violence to a remarkable minimum. It is not that "primitive" man was or is any more moral than ourselves, nor necessarily more pragmatic; if he sees the wisdom of minimizing violence and aggressivity, reducing hostility to a level far below his mental and technological potential, it is perhaps simply because that best answers his overall needs for survival just as our own maximal development of the aggressive potential may answer our needs, if not our tastes.

It is not the objective to argue here that one is better than the other, nor even that one is better suited to its context than the other to another context; nor is the argument meant in any way to demonstrate that the cultural factor overshadows the biological factor. Here we shall merely look at one single society at the most "primitive" and of the scale (by which I refer to the level of technological complexity) and pay attention to the numerous ways, formal and informal, in which man's tendency to violence and aggressivity is reduced to the point where its destructive potential, both for the individual and the group, is almost totally eradicated.

The Mbuti hunter/gatherers of the tropical rain forest in northeastern Zaïre accept that man's nature is not angelic, and they expect, with typical pragmatism, that however divine our essence may be (and they have such a concept) our social self may stray. Therefore, by stating at the outset our potential for harm, they defuse that potential to a major extent, which allows them time to put considerable energy into averting that harm while, and by, developing their potential for nonharm.

I have discussed their social organization and their relationship with neighboring peoples elsewhere,[1] but must here at least briefly outline the factors contributing to the explosive potential of the Mbuti context, which makes their non-aggressive and nonviolent life style all the more noteworthy. One of the major areas of potential conflict facing the Mbuti is, in a sense, external to their "real" world, an inner world by which they regulate their daily life. It is the profane nonforest world of the immigrant cultivators who now encircle the sacred inner domain of the Mbuti, the forest world. It is a classic binary opposition that finds its nonhostile resolution in a third realm common to both, the forest; and that is the context in which both sides conceptualize the opposition. The manner of resolution followed by the nonforest cultivators is different from that of the forest hunter/gatherers, and falls outside the scope of this study. But the dramatic potential of the situation is clearly enough recognized in the opposed and potentially exclusive subsistence economies of the two populations; the cultivators depend for their survival upon cutting the forest down for their ever shifting plantations, whereas the Mbuti depend for *their* survival upon retaining the forest uncut. The success of their joint resolution of this major area of possible conflict is seen in the peripheral distribution of the cultivators, who until well after Zaïre achieved independence seldom penetrated into the inner forest preserve, and never moved their plantations inwards when the soil became exhausted but confined such movement to a linear drift back and forth around the perimeter.

While for the cultivators the conceptualization of this essentially territorial conflict and its resolution lay embedded in their definition of the forest as profane, rather than in any positive definition of their own nonforest world as sacred (a secondary factor), for the Mbuti the resolution had its source in their definition of the forest as sacred, the profanity of the nonforest world being a secondary factor and secondary focus of interest. While the rest of the discussion will confine itself to the inner, forest world of the Mbuti, it is important to remember the existence of the outer world, for however clearly the Mbuti differentiate the two, maintaining the opposition in structure, values and behaviour, there *is* interaction. It is also important to recognize that in defining the forest as sacred a conflict is created within the inner world of the Mbuti, who, as hunter/gatherers, can survive only by the taking of forest, therefore sacred, life.

The beginning as well as the end is the forest, and the Mbuti concept of the forest and of the quality of forestness. While any outsider's attempt to penetrate the conceptual life of another people is fraught with danger and must remain largely conjectural, the anthropologist, through prolonged participation in the way of life of that people, through being subject to the same pressures, the same hopes and fears, through sharing in joy and sorrow, may begin to order all these experiences increasingly in terms other than those proper to his own culture, and more approximate to the terms of people with whom he is living. But while much of what he has to say (and much of what I shall say) is to this extent conjectural, he also has a pretty solid array of facts to help him get still closer to this foreign conceptual world.

One such fact, here, is that the Mbuti, young or old, male or female, whenever going through the forest (except at critical moments of the hunt, obviously) talk, shout, whisper, and sing to the forest (*ndura*) addressing it as mother or father or both, referring to its goodness and its ability to "cure" or make good (from the same root, *bonga*). The choice as to whether to address the forest as mother, father, or both is an individual matter depending, the Mbuti say, on how they feel at the moment. It is significant that in the Mbuti system of kinship terminology the only term of address or reference where a distinction between male and female can be made is at the parental level. The terms for grandparent, sibling, and child do not vary according to sex. Further, there is one significant point in the life of a young child when he or she accepts the father as "a kind of mother," a point to which I shall return later.

I refer to it now because for the moment I want to consider the forest as mother rather than father, in an attempt to translate an Mbuti attitude into our own cultural terms, though I suspect the Mbuti would prefer me to use our term "parent."

A second fact that underlies the conjecture that follows is that in explanation of this usage of terminology the Mbuti say: "Like our father and mother the forest gives us food, shelter, clothing, warmth, and affection." I use "affection" so as to err on the right side for as long as I can, though the word *kondi,* which the Mbuti use in this context, is also the word they use for love and need, between which they seldom differentiate when discussing human relationships. This imagery is reiterated by every Mbuti practically every day of his life, and many times in every day. It is no formality, it is no courtesy, it is something done with joy and meaning. Sometimes there is conscious intent, to make sure that "the forest" is alert and watchful, thus to assure protection. Perhaps more frequently it is without conscious intent, being rather a spontaneous expression of emotion. What is that emotion? Again one may detect by the gestures or facial expression, or by the tone of voice, or by supplementary words or phrases, or by all of these observable and relatable facts, that it is an emotion of sexual love; for the sexual relationship between a man or a woman, a boy or a girl, and the forest, is sometimes demonstrated overtly enough by an erotic gesture of the body, in imitation of the act of copulation. More playful youths may even specify verbally that they want to copulate with the forest. This is sure to arouse mirth amongst their companions, particularly if the accompanying body gestures are well executed; but as a motive that hardly holds ground when a youth behaves like this, as I have observed, in privacy. Then, at least, it is a private, if sexual, communion between self and forest. The emotion is sometimes more one for which I can only use the word adoration; and I do so without shame, rather with the joy felt by Teleabo Kengé when he slipped out into the *bopi* (children's playground) one moonlit night, adorned with a forest flower in his hair and forest leaves in his belt of forest vines and loin cloth of forest bark. Alone with *his* inner world he danced and sang, in evident ecstasy. And his answer to my stupid question (for to question the obvious is surely stupid) was: *"me bi na'ndura, me bi na songé"*—"I am dancing with the forest, dancing with the moon."

Such recorded examples of this intimate relationship between the Mbuti and the natural world around them are amongst the most frequent items in my field notes. But as evidence in the present argument the above will suffice, for there is a compelling inherent logic and a consistency that is evidence in itself. Let me move a little closer to the heart of the matter, ignoring such questions as to how an Mbuti girl, in this way, can wish to copulate with her "father" or a boy with his "mother," questions the Mbuti find infinitely tedious because they miss the whole point, and to which they have replied to me "Why then not a boy with his father or a girl with her mother?" neatly avoiding my profanity with well-aimed ridicule. Sex *per se* and sexuality are not the heart of the matter, as the Mbuti see their world. And since it is their world, I prefer to rely on their categories.

Their world, as they expressed it to me at a time when I was living in the nonforest world, though still clearly belonging to their forest, is like a "sphere." Within this sphere we as individuals (or as a people, they stressed, though each talked in primarily individual terms) are normally always in the center. When we move in time or space the sphere moves with us, so we remain in the center. This is consistent with their almost exclusive usage of the present tense, although they have a past and a future tense; and it is also consistent with a vocabulary that makes it difficult to indicate that which lies ahead (in time or space) as distinct from that which lies behind. The concern is with the here and now, and if it not here and now it does not very much matter where it is, in front or behind. Why not to the side, in time or space?

However, the Mbuti say, if one's movement in time or space is too violent, too sudden, one can reach the edge of the sphere before it has time to catch up, and that is when a person becomes *wazi-wazi,* or disoriented, and unpredictable. And if the violence of the movement, the disregard for the security that comes from remaining in the center of one's sphere, is too blatant, one may pierce through into the other world. If you do that, you may let something else in to replace you. At this point the Mbuti generally start discussing the nature of water and its reflective qualities. They ask, what is the image that you can see, that looks like you, and does everything you do, and which you can even touch and *feel* if you place your foot ever so carefully onto the surface of the water, so that the other foot comes up to touch yours? And what happens if you place your foot *in* the water. The other comes up and disappears into your leg. The deeper you submerge yourself the more of that image-self enters your body, passing through you into the world you are leaving behind. And if you completely submerge yourself, say to cross underwater through to the other side of the river, on emerging the reverse process takes place. Then which is the real self and which the real world? This is something like what happens, they say, when you pierce through the safe and known boundaries of your sphere. The word they use for sphere is one of their words for womb.

They are not thinking of a womb in a literal sense, of course, and they made this plain by trying alternative words on me; stomach, for instance. But dissatisfied with that, and fearing that I might think they meant a real stomach, or more likely press the analogy in the wrong direction, or too far, they qualified it as "the stomach of birth," another way they sometimes refer to the womb. Another alternative word they tried, more to their satisfaction than stomach, was *endu,* which is the spherical-like dwelling of sticks and leaves in which they live, which they build out of forest materials for shelter and protection, for warmth and comfort.

From this womb, then, within our own conceptual sphere, let us move to another womb, that of a pregnant mother. The child in the womb was conceived out of joy, for the sexual act to the Mbuti is a supremely joyous act, as any act of creation should be. It is also a sacred act, when conception is the goal. This attitude is manifest in various ways that will be discussed shortly in relationship to youth. For the moment that youth is not born. I shall refer to him as male simply to make it easier in writing to differentiate him from his mother, though to the Mbuti such differentiation itself would be questionable. I want to follow this child from the womb into adulthood, and discover what are some of the various factors that help young life grow up into such an essentially non-aggressive, nonviolent adulthood.

Intercourse between husband and wife continues after the first indisputable signs of pregnancy, but it is a matter of individual choice. Some say that continued intercourse right up to delivery helps matters along, even speeding them up. Others argue differently. In my experience of Mbuti couples I have known well, it has been the woman who makes the decision, according to whatever makes her and the child within her "feel good." The same woman may not follow the same pattern of behavior for every child. But by and large the young mother-to-be pursues her normal everyday life without much change right up to the moment of delivery. She increasingly avoids activities that might tax her strength unduly, and she equally avoids situations that might tax her emotionally. More significantly, one can see small ways in which she responds positively, rather than negatively, to her condition. Again it is an individual matter, but the most common ways in which she recognizes her pregnancy include adornment of the body with leaves and flowers, perhaps in readiness, like Kengé, for *her* dance of adoration. It is clearly a form of consecration, as it is when in the last few months she takes to going off on her own, to her favorite spot in the forest, and singing to the child in her womb.

This lullaby has certain distinctive features. It is the only traditional form of song that can be sung as a solo (was Kengé, therefore, a mother singing to his child, the forest? It is entirely possible). It is composed by the mother for that particular child within her womb. It is sung for no other, it is sung by no other. I should here state again that I must ignore possibly significant biological factors, if for no other reason than my own incompetence to consider them properly. But we are all aware of certain physiological effects upon the unborn child that may result from physiological changes in the body of the mother.[2] It seems accepted that intelligence becomes alive in the womb, and this to me is highly significant, for from my standpoint as a mere ethnographer, trying to describe what I have observed, Mbuti mothers (and others I have seen in Africa) treat their children as intelligent beings three or four months before them giving birth. Further, they accord them the intelligence, though not the knowledge, of adults. No baby-talk is used, unintelligible to mother and child alike. The subject matter is clear; it is informative and it is reassuring and comforting, just as are the mother's actions.

The young mother composes and sings a quietly reassuring lullaby, rocking herself, sometimes with her hands on her belly, or gently splashing her hands or feet in the water of her favorite stream or river, or rustling them through leaves, or warming herself at a fire. In a similar way she talks to the child, telling him of the forest world into which he will soon emerge, repeating simple phrases such as those perhaps already "heard" by the unborn baby as his mother is joyfully singing to the forest while off on the hunt: "the forest is good, the forest is kind: mother forest, father forest." I have heard them enter into more detailed conversations, describing the place where the child will be born, the other children he will meet and play with, grow up with, and relating that somewhere there is another unborn girl-baby that one day he will marry. Both the physical and the social world may be described to the child in this way.

In one sense it is not of the slightest importance to my argument that the child, not yet having learned to speak, can hardly be expected to understand the words. Nor am I troubled by the doubts that many may raise as to whether even the emotional content of what the mother is thinking and doing and saying and singing is in any way transferred to the unborn baby's consciousness, though personally I share no such doubts. It is enough for me that the mother, at least, is reinforcing *her* own concept of the world, and is readying *her*self for the creative act about to unfold, giving *her*self confidence that the forest will be as good and as kind to her child as it has been to her; providing food, shelter, clothing, warmth—and affection. That confidence alone would be an auspicious beginning to any life, and until it is proven otherwise I am not about to believe that nothing of this is transferred to the child in the mother's womb, because I have seen that child born, grow through infancy, childhood and youth to adulthood, secure in an otherwise almost incredible trust and confidence in each of the new worlds into which he successively enters as though each were another form of that first and primal sphere, or womb.

A few days before her time is due, the mother may restrict her activities and perhaps refrain from going off on the hunt each morning, though it is common enough for a girl to give birth while actually on the hunt, merely staying back either by herself or with a friend and rejoining the hunt an hour or two later. But always, a few days before, while on one of her solitary trysts with the forest, perhaps singing to her child more as a lover, she selects a vine that will yield her favorite bark. She cuts it, brings it to the camp, and with a hammer made from the tusk of an elephant she beats out a soft piece of bark-cloth, sweet-smelling and clean and light in color, like *le-engbe* or *esele*. The smell should be pleasing to the infant, the color light perhaps to reflect more light inside the dim interior of the hut in which the infant will spend most of his first three days or perhaps, as most mothers say, because a light-colored bark-cloth shows the baby off to better advantage. But above all the smell must be sweet, not acrid like some barks; and the texture should be smooth enough to be comfortable, but rough enough to assure the infant that he is enveloped in the all protective womb of the forest. Some Mbuti assert that the first Mbuti were indeed born out of trees, so what could be more reassuring to the child than the smell and texture of a tree? Once made, the mother may decorate the cloth with free-flowing designs painted with a twig dipped in the dark juice of Kangay, the gardenia fruit.

The infant was conceived in love and joy, and that is how he is born. If the mother is by herself she may sit on her haunches, or on a log. If she feels there may be any difficulty at all she may place herself with her feet against a tree. Some say they put a vine around a tree and hold on to that. But then I have only seen the preparations, and believe that what may have been lost by not intruding on the delivery in the name of science was more than made up for in other ways. When telling me about childbirth, for instance, if there was something they did not wish to discuss Mbuti women simply told me so. In return for not having their inner world violated I believe they respected *my* inner world by telling me the truth, if they told me anything. In any case it is unlikely that so many mothers who talked with me, denying me access to only the moment of delivery, would come up with the same fabrications so consistently. Many asserted, for instance, that if they felt there would be any difficulty they would have a friend sit opposite them, feet to feet, "like trees in the forest."

But even minor difficulty in delivery seems to be rare. The infant emerges easily, helped only by the mother's hands or those of a friend, and is immediately placed to the mother's breast as she lies down. The cutting of the umbilical cord never takes place immediately, but may take place in anything from a few minutes to as much, they say, as an hour or so. When the umbilical cord is cut, or soon after, the father and close friends may be invited to see the child, who by then is happily suckling. Women say this is a decision made by the mother, *and* the child. I cannot remember ever having been alerted to the moment of birth by loud and prolonged crying. When I have been present in the camp at the time of birth the newborn infant has sometimes given two or three tiny bleats, as though aggravated at having been made to do something he really did not want to do. But then he has better things to do than cry, such as explore his mother's body, feel her warmth, try the new and satisfying experience of drinking his mother's milk, while being reassured by the familiar sounds of her voice, singing his own special lullaby, rocking in a familiar rhythm.

At this point the reader may well ask what all this descriptive detail and conjecture has to do with non-aggressivity and non-violence. It may well have everything to do with it. For if the child were not born into the world with such confidence, if birth were not both a glorious adventure safely achieved and a movement from one kind of womb to another, similar in so many ways, and if this educational pattern were not consistently followed throughout childhood and youth, how else could that child as a child or as an adult, face the world with such invincible faith in its ultimate goodness, as Mbuti manifestly do? If his initial experience of the outside world bore no resemblance to his secure mother-womb world, he would be born in insecurity and understandable fear. If *that* same model or initial shock and surprise at the unfamiliar, that same unpredictability, that same infamous demand on his ability to cope with the unknown, was followed throughout the life cycle instead, a perfectly reasonable response to any new situation might well be one of fright, fear, suspicion, hostility, if not violence. And Mbuti simply never react in that way. Nor do they react in other ways that have been suggested as even more likely responses to early violent changes and unpredictability, namely, passivity, helplessness, depression; nor do I have any evidence in my own notes or in the literature of stress-related illnesses.* Why should the Mbuti infant learn aggressivity when he is at his mother's breast any more than when he was in his mother's womb, so long as his mother satisfies his needs just as did the womb? Challenge is productive and necessary to be sure, but the Mbuti ration it out in doses that never for a moment threaten to destroy confidence in ultimate success, confidence in the ultimate goodness of the forest/sphere/womb.

Usually about three days after birth, during which time the mother and one or two close friends stay in her spherical hut, with the child in almost constant contact with only the mother, the mother emerges and presents the child to the camp. Everyone has been waiting for this moment; it may even be the first time the father has seen his tiny son. But now the mother comes out of the hut, the infant boy wrapped in that sweet-smelling *le'engbe,* and she hands the boy to a few of her closest friends and family, not just for them to look at him but for them to hold him close to *their* bodies. Another educational event has taken place in that young life: at the age of three days the infant boy is learning that there is a plurality of warm bodies, similar in warmth (which is comforting) but dissimilar in smells and rhythmic movements, which he may find disconcerting enough to make him cry, in protest. If that happens his mother immediately takes him back and puts him to her breast. Enough schooling for the first day in yet another world. In this way an initial model of predictability and security becomes multiplied, and so it is throughout the educational process: vital lessons, such as in non-aggressivity, are learned through a plurality of models.

The infant's visual image of that world is blurred, no doubt, like most if not all of his other visual images; but vision is only one form of perception, the Mbuti give equal importance to all the senses. Inside the hut the light is always subdued, though you can see mothers sitting close to the doorway in those first three days, as if accustoming their newborn to the light of day. Even the light in

---

* I am much indebted to Dr. Barbara Ingersoll, of the Department of Behavioral Medicine at West Virginia University for comments of this kind made while reading through the typescript of this article.

the camp is quiet and cool, the trees meeting high overhead, making yet another kind of sphere that in time proves to be just as protective and satisfying as all other spheres. But after that initial introduction to what will be the major social sphere of the child's life, the hunting camp, the mother takes him back into their home. Now the father can follow and friends can visit, as long as the infant does not protest. It seemed to me that this was invariably the guiding factor; that when a child was faced with something too unfamiliar, something he could not deal with and to which he responded by crying, the mother instantly put him to her breast, restoring the familiar sense of security and protection.

But infancy was by no means a time of total protection, it was rather one of controlled experimentation and perpetual learning. Oddly enough, after birth mothers seldom talked to their infants in the same way they did during pregnancy, and children seemed to learn to speak more by listening to their mothers talk with other adults than by much direct instruction. As before, no baby-talk was employed. Usually the child was named shortly after the presentation to the camp, and from that moment onwards he would be treated as a full person with certain individual rights. The first name was usually decided on by family and friends together, often after some favored form of forest life, animal or vegetable. At this early stage the mother gave her child a great deal of freedom to explore, leaving him to explore for himself rather than by putting opportunity in his way. While cooking, for instance, she simply put the child on the ground and let him explore the leaf bed they shared, secure in its increasingly familiar smell and texture. Soon the infant boy would crawl to the edge of the hut and explore: the sticks with which the hut frame was made, the leaves with which it was roofed down to the ground. There the sticks were a new experience to deal with, but at least the leaves would be familiar, for the same phrynium that is used for roofing is chosen for making a sleeping mat.

Still the young child's life has been devoid of willed violence, physical or mental. The pain of emerging from the womb, or of filling the lungs with unaccustomed and unfamiliar air, of opening the eyes to light and visual sensations totally foreign to the world of the child's first womb/sphere, all such pain has been adequately dealt with, if the lack of much audible protest is any indication. More familiar sounds than screams, from a newborn infant, are gurgles, not of suffocation (for the passageways are quickly cleared), but rather of apparent delight at finding that this new world is not all that strange after all. While left alone on the leaf bed there is little that can cause discomfort, let alone pain, and his total experience until now, and for some time to come, is that his mother, his prime refuge and first contact with humanity, his first model of human behavior, is totally without any violence that his developing senses can detect. But if his education is gradual, and so far without violence, it is not without order; and if it did not soon incorporate violence in such a way that he could learn to handle it, that education would be sadly lacking. How then is it organized?

For the Mbuti there are four major principles of social organization, which correspond to the four major areas in which conflict is most likely to occur in their lives. These areas are clearly recognized by the Mbuti; the inherent potential for conflict in each is made manifest in ritual form and is further guarded against by appropriate social institutions. These areas are territory, family (or kinship), age, and sex. These areas are progressively explored in approximately that order, both as principles of organization and as dangerous areas within which conflict can arise and violence erupt, as the newborn passes from infancy through childhood into youth. In this way he is equipped to be a part of a highly integrated, organized community, in action and belief, and the nature of his educational experience is that he is also equipped to deal with conflict as it arises without the fear that comes from individual isolation and competitiveness. On the contrary, his total experience has led him, by youth, to enter any situation of stress with the very confidence that is one of his chief weapons against stress. This confidence is well supported by a whole repertoire of specific conflict-resolving skills and techniques well learned and practiced throughout childhood. While he may feel a degree of uncertainty, he feels none of the fear and perceives nothing of the threat which could lead ultimately and exclusively to a violent solution to conflict.

The child's education is not rigidly programmed by adults; to some extent his education in all four areas is simultaneous, but whereas the first tools available to him, his senses, are adequate for a preliminary exploration of territory and kinship, age and sex are more readily explored at a later stage, when the intellect and power of reason are more developed.

Infancy is certainly the time for exploring territory. The womb, after all, was a very clearly defined territory; and the newborn utilizes every sense available to him to explore the new territory, his mother, even before he is severed from her by cutting of the cord. There is not an inch of that new world that the infant has not explored within his first few weeks of life. And while the child is exploring the relatively familiar confines of his mother's body, in total security, he is constantly being introduced to other sensations which he will, in future life, also associate with total security. When born, for instance, the child is bathed in water. That water does not come from a forest stream, though any such water would be healthy enough. But rather it comes from one of several enormous vines which, when cut, give forth a sweet tasting water that, sacred as everything is that is of the forest, must surely be closer to the very essence of the forest. The mother herself prefers, usually, to bathe in this water and drink it during the first week following childbirth. The child is enveloped in bark-cloth. Little circlets of vine are placed around his neck, wrists, and ankles: onto some of these are threaded little pieces of wood. All these things the child can and does explore even before he can crawl. He smells, feels, tastes, listens to, and squints at them, just as he smells, feels, tastes, listens to, and squints at his mother. He finds she has similar vines around her wrists and waist and neck and ankles; similar pieces of forest wood, and is perfumed by that same scent of the water of forest vines.

But then it is time to be born again, into yet another sphere, that of the *endu*, the dwelling made of forest sticks and leaves. Once he can crawl the young child will explore the floor of the *endu* just as thoroughly as he explored his mother's body. He may run into trouble; a thorn that was brought in when his father returned from the hunt, a biting ant, or the sharp edge of a leaf; but rather than prevent him from discovering these things the mother will either leave him to discover them for himself or may help him discover them, discover their harmful potential, and discover the fact that harm can be avoided or readily alleviated. The child may already even try to explore vertically, pulling himself upward on the stick frame of *endu*. If he is so inclined, the mother is again more likely to help him than not, and certainly would not prevent him. If he falls, however, or in any other way comes to minor harm in his explorations of space, she quickly comforts him before turning him loose to try again. In a matter of weeks the *endu* has been fully explored, all but its upper reaches, and the young child is ready for yet another rebirth, this time into the sphere of the *apa,* or camp.

Having countless times lain on my back in my own tiny *endu* in the Ituri forest, I am only too aware of the similarity of the experience to that of lying on one's back in the middle of the *apa,* or camp. The walls and roof of both are of wood (sticks/trees) and leaves; it is just a question of magnification. The patterns formed by the trees and leafy canopy of the *apa* are less regular, and unlike those of the *endu* they are constantly shifting and changing. That same all-pervasive smell of a wood log fire is in both spheres, but in the *apa* it is the smell of many fires (plurality of models again) in many directions, all to be explored with confidence that smelling so much like the fire in the thoroughly safe and proven *endu* the other *endu* hearths could not be anything but safe also.

So the crawlers crawl all over the camp, and the child learns another vital lesson that has to do with both territoriality and kinship. He learns that the farther he strays from his own family hearth the more dangerous it is likely to be: more exciting too, and it is as if he is driven to explore every last nook and cranny until you expect him to crawl out of the camp and into the forest itself. But that is an adventure, primarily of the mind and soul, that is yet to come; for now he is kept to the confines of the camp. However, he may crawl to a part of the camp where everyone is away, perhaps off on the hunt. Young parents are more free than others to stay behind when the hunt goes off; they help guard the deserted camp with any others who stay because of sickness, old age, or sheer laziness. But during the hunt the camp is largely deserted. The child learns two things in such a situation. One is that if he keeps to the territory defined by sounds, smells, taste, feel, and appearance associated with his *endu* and mother spheres, then if he runs into trouble he will quickly be comforted. He learns that if he wanders into another similar but plainly different territory, and similarly runs into trouble, he can still expect to be comforted, but by a different kind of mother, with a different smell and taste and touch and sound and appearance. In point of fact it could be an old man or a young girl. This somewhat enlarges the child's concept and experience of motherhood, and his sense of security, for now he obviously has a plurality of mothers and safe territories. However, they are not quite as predictable as his original womb/mother, and if he wanders into a territory where there are no mothers at all, and gets into trouble there, something quite new is likely to happen. Even his own womb/mother is likely to come over, and after pulling him out of the hot ashes into which he has crawled, instead of putting him to her breast, feeding him, and comforting him with his familiar lullaby, she is likely to slap him, carry him back by an arm or a leg to his own safe primary territory and dump him with unaccustomed roughness onto the ground. He has had his first lesson in true sociality, or reciprocity.

Up to this point he has learned a subtle combination of dependence and independence. He has had independence of action while exploring his successive worlds, but for his basic needs and comfort, for his survival, he has been totally dependent on his mother. Now, however, he has learned that there are certain restrictions on the way the game is played, especially on his independence of movement. There are certain territories that are safer than others, certain territories that should not be violated (he will be slapped or shouted at, for instance, if he crawls into another *endu*), and that while all these mother-like people are likely to provide him with what he needs, just as his own mother does, they and his own mother alike are beginning to make certain demands on him. For the moment these demands are associated with his own good, for at this stage the Mbuti only discipline a child for endangering himself, such as by crawling into a fire. Only when he learns to walk, in another few months, and can walk well enough to join others of his own age and create his own territory with them (the *bopi,* or playground), is he likely to be disciplined for merely "being a nuisance" to others.

Meanwhile his first lesson in classificatory kinship is formalized. He has already learned that he can be dependent on a number of people, mostly so much older than himself that he classifies them as "*ema*" (mother), but at some time in his second year, probably near the end, the person who has been sharing that familiar leaf bed with his mother, and whose body smell and sound and taste and appearance and rhythm he knows almost as well, and which he has found to be every bit as safe and secure, begins to fondle him as his mother does. At the age of two, if not before, a child is taken to the breast of his father and held there, even encouraged to try and suckle. The child finds everything else familiar, so the fondling, just like that he knows from his mother, leads him to explore for milk. Instead of milk however, he receives his first solid food. Here is another kind of mother indeed, one that offers everything the mother has always given, the warmth and shelter and affection, and who offers food also, but instead of from the breast it is from his own mouth or from his fingers. In this way the child learns to distinguish between *ema* and *eba,* between mother and father, but also to equate them. Essentially the relationship is the same one of trust and dependency, and of increasing obligation, for here is yet another person who will slap him instead of comfort him if he hurts himself.

While such slapping is increasingly frequent, it is never hard, nor is it in any sense violent. There is always a point at which the child is comforted, if he cannot cope with the situation by simply crawling off to do something for which he knows he will *not* be slapped, within the safer confines of his own territory. But his lesson in kinship, or family, has been unmistakable. It has nothing to do with shared smells or sounds, with human biology; it has to do with the larger territory, the *apa,* as distinct from that smaller, rather safer but more confining sphere, the *endu.* Anyone appearing to his now clear vision as being like his mother or father in general size and shape (or by whatever sensory images he uses) he is expected to address in exactly the same way, as *ema* or *eba,* and he can expect much the same treatment from any of them. He can expect this new kind of solid food he is learning to eat, whenever he wants it; he can expect comfort and affection; he can also expect discipline if he infringes on the few simple rules of the game.

He learns that other kinds of people, clearly distinct to his senses, he must call *tata* ("grandparent"), regardless of sex or biological kinship, and on them he can make certain demands but

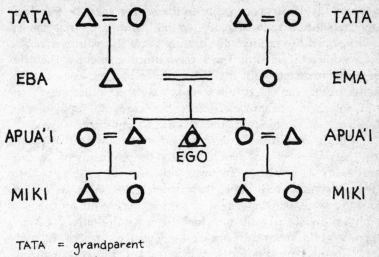

TATA = grandparent
EMA   = mother
EBA   = father
APUA'I = sibling   △ = male
MIKI = child   O = female

Figure 1. GENERATIONAL/KINSHIP TERMS OF ADDRESS AND REFERENCE: From point of view of EGO, sexual differentiation only made at parental level.

seldom need he expect discipline of the same kind. On the contrary they are people to whom he can go for comfort when it is denied by his plurality of *ema/eba*. Another distinct group he comes to recognize is less easy to define; in some ways they behave like *ema/eba*, in some ways like *tata*, and they call him and each other *apua'i* (sibling). But by the age of two, when he has learned these terms and many others, and can already talk with ease and walk and run, he is beginning to associate more with the children of other *endu*, some of which *apua'i* will take him to yet another territory, the *bopi*. Those older ones who call him *miki* (child) seldom come to the *bopi*. Now he is being introduced to that all-important principle (for the Mbuti, at least) of social organization, age. In the same way that he has been made aware of differences between different territories, and different "families" and "kin," but has not yet developed the faculty* for dealing rationally with conflict, so he does not yet have to deal with the conflict, inherent in the principle of age, merely with the fact of difference between children, youths, adults, and elders. All seem to have their appropriate territories and their appropriate activities; they are recognizably distinct categories, and plainly relate to each other in an ordered way.

It is in the *bopi* that the child, from between the ages of two or three and eight or nine begins to face the problems of conflict, aggressivity, and violence. To begin with, his world is still primarily physical and emotional rather than rational. *Bopi* activities are primarily physical, but they begin to provide a sense of direction for emotional outlet that will come into use in a more rational manner when the child leaves the *bopi* and becomes a youth. But the problems of conflict are still not faced directly, rather are they faced indirectly by an ever increasing clarification and expansion of the principle of opposition that lies within each of the four major areas of potential conflict. For instance, the child will already have noted not only the distinction between the various *endu* territories that make up the overall, inclusive territory of the *apa,* but also that *endu* tend to group themselves within the camp in opposition to each other. He will have sensed the opposition, perhaps, through his increasingly sensitive awareness of emotional relationships within the camp, but being the incredibly sharp observer that an Mbuti child seems to be, he may well also have noted that in the same way that these groups are physically opposed to each other, so sometimes are individual *endu*. Plotted on paper these oppositions invariably indicate the lines of fission and fusion within a camp (see Fig. 2). They provide clear examples of opposition (in the physical sense) without hostility, for to face your *endu* directly across the camp, or across the subgroup, at another *endu,* is to offer special friendship and trust, or to demand it. Like looking another directly in the eyes, as the child has learned to do, however, it is also to create just the intimate kind of relationship from which conflict can spring.

---

* Nor the interest, judging from the disinterested reactions of children of this age to conflict situations.

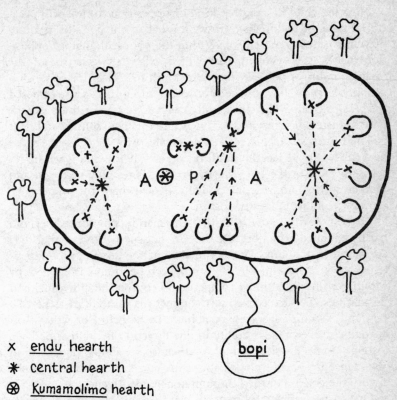

x   <u>endu</u> hearth
✳   central hearth
⊛   <u>Kumamolimo</u> hearth
     (<u>molimo</u> hearth)

Figure 2. *endu* hearths are seen as being affectively opposed to each other, across the camp.

Approximately where the lines of opposition intersect there may be a central hearth, built from embers from the individual hearths, symbolizing the alliance of one group of *endu* in opposition to a similar alliance in another part of the *apa,* or camp.

The *bopi* stands outside these internal alliances and is not affected by them.

Now the child has another kind of opposition to deal with, that of the *bopi,* or children's territory, to that of the *apa,* the territory of youths, adults, and elders. Within the *bopi* still another opposition makes itself evident, that which exists between two of the major bonding principles, age and kinship. The primary kinship group, the *endu,* has now been cross-cut and in that sense opposed to the age group. The child easily, with the familiarity of experience, transfers his trust and confidence to this new sphere, and does not find his trust misplaced. His age-mates provide the same sense of security that he has felt in all his other spheres, and when he returns to the *apa* the old security is still there, and his *endu* and mother spheres are still intact. He can take them for granted, he senses no conflict in loyalty or trust.

To begin with, *bopi* activities are mainly physical. They can hardly be called games because they are not competitive; rather they are pastimes or sports. The significance of the absence of competitive games is inestimable. The only competition encouraged by Mbuti pastimes is an inner competition between the individual and his abilities. To succeed he must conquer his disabilities as best he can, and restrain any excess of ability. To be better or worse than anyone else is to fail. If ability in one direction is limited, perhaps through some physical handicap, then some ability possessed in abundance may be developed above the norm, in compensation. In a word the goal is equality, through noncompetitiveness.

One pastime illustrates more clearly than any the kind of education that takes place in the *bopi.* The youngest children, with accustomed freedom to explore their relationship with the natural world, begin to explore hanging vines, pulling themselves upwards, developing their young muscles while getting to know the vines. They climb and they swing, and soon they learn skipping and hoop jumping which, like climbing and swinging, can be done in a wide variety of ways, and can be done alone or with others. This leads ultimately to the most difficult of all these vine pastimes, in which an enormous vine is strung from high up between two trees. Only youths are strong and agile enough for this, but the groundwork is done in the *bopi.* Swinging from an axis perhaps thirty feet above ground, but with the loop a bare two feet from the earth, one youth sits in the swing and swings higher and higher. Then the others join in. As their companion starts his backward arc one runs after him, grabs one side of the vine swing, and when it soars upwards he leaps with it, does a somersault over the head of his companion who jumps to the ground allowing the other to take his place. It requires perfect coordination as well as considerable strength and agility. There are variations, which at first may look like competitiveness, but if they are it is only in the Mbuti sense. The jumper may swing himself right over the head of the youth sitting in the swing, and land on the ground in front of him as the swing descends. If the "sitter" does not sense what is happening, and also jumps, expecting the "swinger" to take his place, there is a moan from the spectators; the perfection of the ballet has been spoiled. Alternatively, the sitter may decide to remain sitting, and the swinger has to make the extra effort demanded to complete the swing over his head and land safely. There is no question of the one trying to outdo the other, for the fun is in developing daring maneuvers spontaneously and executing them together.

Similarly climbing leads gently and steadily from individual development to social development. The children are all adept at tree climbing by the age of four or five, limited only by their physical size and the size of the trunk and limbs of the tree. They climb singly, alone, exploring every branch, testing every way of getting from one branch to another, one tree to another. The idea is never just to get to the top, it is to know more about the tree. The younger are constantly stopping, riveted with fascination at a tiny detail of the bark they had not seen or felt or smelled before, or to examine the movement of ants up and down the tree, or to taste some sap oozing from its side. Put your own ear to a tree, one day, and see if like an Mbuti child *you* can hear it sing with happiness or cry with sorrow. But then the Mbuti develop tree climbing into a pastime that, like the vine swing, has serious educational import at a social rather than personal level. A group of anything up to about ten children in the *bopi* climb a young sapling. When they reach the top of the sapling it bends down until they are all within a few feet of the ground. At that point they all jump together, with precision. If one lingers, either because he is afraid, or more likely because he is "brave," it is not something he will do again, because he gets flung back up and may very well be injured. Even if he survives with nothing worse than a minor bruise, he receives no credit for his performance, because again he has spoiled the joint effort to "dance" (their term: *bina*) life's ballet of perfect coordination.

Little that the child does in the *bopi* is not full of value in his later adult life. While he is learning the fun and beauty of working and playing *with* others, not *against* them, he is learning in a positive way, by prescription rather than proscription, the essence of cooperative, communal life, to which competition is the antithesis. With cooperativeness in action comes community of spirit, and with community of spirit the foundation for truly social behavior are secured. But now how does he learn, as he must, to deal with the negative side, the inevitable exception that he himself will often enough make in his life, in pursuit of his own individual ends without due regard for the good of others? He does not know it, but he has already learned the two most important techniques used by adult Mbuti in averting conflicts and resolving them, if they cannot be averted, without violence. He began to learn one such technique as soon as he learned to crawl, and tested out the relative safety of different territories; even while exploring his mother's body he learned that some places are safer than others, some more comfortable, some more rewarding. Within the *endu* the same lesson was expanded. When born yet again into the *apa* world it was made very clear that if he got into trouble in one territory he could get out of it by moving to another. Then he found that what so demonstrably applied to geographical territories, *mother, endu,* and *apa,* also applied to kinship territories.

If in trouble with *ema* or *eba,* he could seek refuge with *tata,* and from this it was self-evident that the same applied to the *age* categories he learned. By simple movement either within any of these categories or between them, refuge can always be found. Those basic womb-like qualities of protection, comfort, and the satisfaction of all needs, including affection, are always to be found somewhere, so in a very real sense the Mbuti child *is* always in the middle of his sphere/womb, for his sustenance moves wherever he moves, provided only he does not move too fast.

In later life the child will find that mobility is one of his prime techniques for avoiding a dispute or for resolving one, for once he moves elsewhere, his sphere moves with him and the dispute is discarded. But what if neither he nor his opponent chooses to move, what technique is available then? It too has been learned in infancy. That first chortle of joy given by the newborn infant when he realizes that his new world, after all, is just as secure as his old one, is perhaps his first lesson in conflict resolution. His chortles quickly become laughter, and this laughter becomes his prime weapon against conflict and aggression and violence. Having learned to laugh with joy at birth the Mbuti learns to use both the joy and the laughter in more of his *bopi* pastimes, pastimes that are lessons in nonviolent conflict resolution.

The child, united with other children by the bond of age, retains all his trust and confidence in his kinship and territorial bondings; they have been well explored and tested, and while there is more to learn, he can safely take those bondings for granted, return to them at will (perhaps for refuge from his age-mates) and meanwhile, in the seclusion of the *bopi* not only explore this new form of bonding, but explore the shared experience of all these other categories and their infinitely complex inter-relationships. The category of sex is already beginning to creep in, as the child grows slightly older and is more in the company of youths when in the main camp. So when is a mother a woman and when is a father a mother? And what does it mean when someone you address as *ema*, or mother, is addressed by another as *miki*, or child? And why sometimes are personal names used, not these so widely inclusive terms that seem to link every person in the camp to everyone else? And how do you reconcile actions that are appropriate to territorial behavior with those appropriate to kinship or age behavior: which has priority of loyalty?

Here is a whole new realm for exploration, and the appropriate tool, the mind, is ready to undertake the task. At first the exploration is through imitation. What has been largely unconscious imitation now becomes conscious, and in the *bopi* children explore every possibility. They do not merely confine themselves, dutifully, to building miniature *endu* and "playing house," nor does imitating adult activities such as the hunt or the gathering of nuts and roots and berries, or the making of bark-cloth, or even copulation, interest them for long. These are mere techniques, the basics of which are quickly learned and the refinements of which can be mastered only as the body grows in size and strength. More fascinating, as pastimes, are imitations of how the wide diversity of territorial, kinship, age, and sex roles are played. Each child explores, through imitation, each role he has become aware of: young or old, male or female, good-tempered or bad, happy or sad. Together the children explore situations involving all of these. Little wonder that the *bopi* is full of such loud shrieks of laughter that sometimes an irate adult will come in, his or her afternoon nap disturbed; try and catch a child to slap him, failing, resort to even louder shouting and noise-making. And of course once that adult leaves, every last child rushes to the center of the *bopi* and soon there is a whole swarm of miniature irate adults shouting and yelling at each other, trying to catch and slap each other. And if the adult is stupid enough to stay too long, and sees himself being ridiculed in this way what happens? Physically he is no match for this bunch of young demons, so either he has to retreat and be subject to even more ridicule when the children return to the *apa,* where they will enact the whole scene so that adults can join in the ridicule of their fellow, or else, if he has sense, he will join in with the children and share their joy and laughter in his own self-ridicule.

But not for a moment did the children think that they had the right to disturb someone else's sleep, any more than that person had the right to disturb their play. Each had a valid grievance, and each made his point. No matter how the adult behaves, whether he joins in the fun or stalks off back to his *endu* in a huff, once he has gone the children will quieten down. They have had yet another lesson, in the value of *ekimi,* calm or quiet, over *akami,* disturbance or noise. These are the two words most frequently heard when Mbuti are using speech rather than ridicule in an attempt to resolve a dispute.

The children in the *bopi,* especially the older ones, when tired of physical pastimes, have many verbal pastimes. Many of these involve jokes—ways of exploring alternative modes of behavior, discovering those that are proper and work, and those that are improper and do not work. But often they involve the rational and verbal use of concepts such as *ekimi* and *akami* in the settlement of conflict situations. It may start through imitation of a real dispute the children witnessed in the main camp, perhaps the night before. They all take roles and imitate the adults. It is almost a form of judgment, for if the adults talked their way out of the dispute, the children, having performed their imitation once, are likely to drop it. If the children detect any room for improvement, however, they will explore that, and if the adult argument was inept and everyone went to sleep that night in a bad temper, then the children try and show that they can do better, and if they find they cannot, then they revert to ridicule which they play out until they are all rolling on the ground in near-hysterics. That happens to be the way many of the most potentially violent and dangerous disputes are settled in adult life.

Laughter, jokes, and ridicule are vital elements in Mbuti life, and I believe that together they constitute a major factor in developing the affective characteristics of the adults and in minimizing the disaffective. It is when the child is in the *bopi* that he acquires his first nickname, and it is likely to contain an element of playful ridicule. It may be the opposite of what a child would think appropriate. A boy or girl who shows a tendency to be proud of physical strength may be nicknamed "the weak one"; the one who seemingly has everything going for him is likely to be called "the poor one." Or the nickname may suggest a hidden quality—many of the animal nicknames are of this nature, indicating that the child has a hidden quality of trickiness, slowness, noisiness, grace, wisdom, and so forth. There is much experimentation before a child is finally fitted with an appropriate nickname by other children, but not without some influence on his own part, by his reactions if nothing else.

The experimentation is an educational pastime in itself, and teaches the child much about the virtue of non-aggressivity, and it is a healthy reminder to all children in the *bopi* of the same virtue. It may start when a relative newcomer to the *bopi* takes an active part in the ridicule of an adult or elder, as just described. He may display some latent talent here, say for eloquence. He may then be dubbed "dumb." More likely, being so young he will behave clumsily, or even stupidly, and then someone might call out and address him as "graceful dancer" or "clever elder." Others may take the

cue and try alternatives, and all will watch to see how the youngster reacts, then try a whole new series of names. But there is no
victimization and no hostility, it is all done with laughter, each
laughing at the name-caller's inventiveness or own stupidity or
clumsiness. If the name-caller himself displays anything of the
clumsiness, say, he is attributing to the youngster being named, the
latter then has an opportunity to join with the others who will
change the direction of attack, the caller becoming the called.

If any child teases another to the point of bringing him to tears
(a more likely reaction at this age than anger, among the Mbuti) a
new pastime will be improvised that demands that the tearful child
play the role of a joyful hero or heroine, and from this pastime the
offending name-caller will be absolutely excluded. A lesson in the
power of ostracism, this is perhaps the name-caller's first taste of
an adult Mbuti sanction one step more powerful than ridicule. He
must then learn the path of re-entry into the society from which he
has just excluded himself, waiting a judicious time until the others
have become so engrossed in their new pastime, or the succeeding
one, that what happened before has become irrelevant: after all it
belonged to a different time/space sphere. Then without much, if
any, effort he finds himself reincorporated. All that is required is
that he forget the incident just as the others have done and move
with them, a little more slowly, into the new center of life. The
cruelty that can arise so easily from ridicule is absent, because
cruelty is in the mental attitude of the performer, not in the act of
ridicule itself. At this stage the children are far too occupied with
appropriate use of action and speech to be bothered with concepts
such as cruelty or, indeed, kindness. But in the search for the effective modes of behavior and language, they discover, naturally, that
what is most effective also generally happens to be affective.

Yet another lesson is learned through nicknaming. Sometimes
the Mbuti relationship with the village world is brought into play,
and the vilagers themselves may be the object of ridicule in the use
of village nicknames, or the child's recent visit to the village and
relationship with the villagers may be the object. But in the use of
village names, especially the popular Ngwana names, of Arab origin, there is generally a clear sex distinction. This of course may be
reversed, when such a name is applied to an Mbuti child, that be-

ing a way of ridiculing either the villagers or the child or both. But what it does, in addition, is to bring to the attention of the children the fact that their own personal names are applied *without* distinction of sex. Here is another small intellectual problem the child has to face.

He has observed that certain groups are separated according to age, and that each age group has certain activities proper to itself. Indeed even as children in the *bopi* it is for them to light the hunting fire before the hunt goes out, as a ritual gesture of placation (the explanation of which, among the children, is in itself yet another lesson in the value of non-aggressivity!). This even gives them a measure of social control, for if they choose not to light the fire, the adults cannot go hunting. That means they go hungry, whereas the children are free to eat readily available foods forbidden to the adults, so the children do NOT go hungry. They do not exploit the situation unjustly, however, for they have already learned in the process of growing up that the initial dependence upon a series of mothers has developed into a relationship of interdependence of groups which they have learned to define clearly by kinship, territory, and age. Now they learn about the sexual differential. Already in the *bopi* they will be aware of the nature of sexual relationships between boys and girls and will have imitated and ridiculed an extraordinary number of variations on this theme, working their way through every kind of interhuman relationship (including, for this purpose, villagers as humans), and will have made good headway into the variations involving animals, animals and humans, birds and humans, birds and animals, showing minimal interest in the vegetable world. It would be wrong to pass this off as good, bawdy fun. Of course it is that, and their considerable ability and expertise in this area is much in demand, not only for entertainment of youths and adults in the main camp, but also, on rather rare but important occasions, in the jural process where an offender who has chosen to remain isolated in his own sphere must be subject to a form of ridicule that will either bring him back into the all-embracing sphere of the *apa* or drive him off to join another. It is usually the job of youths to take such jural action, but in the same way that children are recognized to have a ritual power (as over the hunting fire), so *their* ridicule is considered the most

powerful of all—perhaps even having the possible effect of trans-
ference, or what is often called "sympathetic magic." For the Mbuti
that is a matter of discussion and disagreement, however, and there
is certainly no intent that the sexual inadequacy or impotency being
mimed by the children be conveyed in a physical sense to the
offender.

It is almost impossible not to appear to digress, but here there is
such a multiplicity of educational events taking place, even within
one seemingly simple action, without any specified sequence, that
it is difficult to follow any one through to its conclusion before being led to another. We had started with nicknaming and ridicule,
between and within the age groups and in touching on the issue of
gender we moved into the area of sex. This was correct, for it is sex
and sexual relationships that are important to the Mbuti both as a
potential source of aggressivity and (perhaps we might say therefore?) as a principle of social organization. Their own naming
system and kinship terminology teach them at an early age that
gender is relatively unimportant. A boy and a girl may well go by
the same name. When that happens, indeed, they are taught that
they share a certain identity, and are under special obligations to
each other, for those obligations hold regardless of apparently contradictory obligations to the well-established spheres of territory,
kinship, and age. The contradiction is usually resolved by recognizing the nature and appropriate sphere of the context. But the
system of "kinship" terminology (in fact it is generational, having
little to do with descent) while also making it clear that no distinc-
tions of gender are made in the terms of address applied to children, siblings, or grandparents makes it very clear that the distinction *is* made at the parental level. In the eyes of the child, on first
contact and conscious awareness of the system as such, this applies
to the adult age level. He thus learns that gender is important to
adults and to the husband/wife relationships, thus to the *apa* and
endu but not to the *bopi*. He is then distinguishing between gender
and sex, and will soon learn that one of the major sources of *akami*
(noise of dispute) in the *apa* is indeed sex. Lack of gender in such
contexts (for all adults, to each other, are *apua'i*) provides a useful
counter-measure, and is integrative rather than disintegrative.

So much for the innocence of childhood. Our Mbuti boy is

barely four years old, and he already has all this under his belt, and a measure of social responsibility and control to boot. In the sense of being harmless, an old usage of the word, or not tainted by sin, pure, the Mbuti child might be considered innocent. But in the sense of being without guile, or even without knowledge of or contact with "wrong," the Mbuti child is far from innocent. However, the fact that he *is* placed in contact, as through ridicule, as through his jural role, is in itself a measure of his purity or lack of taint. The child has learned some of the "rights" and "wrongs" of Mbuti life, but has not learned the concept of evil, or conscious malevolence. In the welter of alternative and sometimes conflicting loyalties that he is faced with, it would be unreasonable for him to blame anyone for being "wrong" thinking. However clearly defined, the context of any given act or relationship seldom totally excludes all but one manner of bonding or grouping. Conflict is inherent in and an integral part of the system. The objective of any jural action, then, is never penal, but restorative: this means the restoration of the individual/group to the center of the most encompassing sphere of all, and that is *nduṛa,* or forest.

The child will learn more about this at a rational, intellectual level, in his next stage of life, as a youth. Already, however, the child has touched the essence of this even greater sphere, in his progress from one womb to yet another. After all, he is not merely expected just to light a fire before the hunters set out. Nor is he aware only that for some obscure reason if he does not light the fire the hunters do not set out, and do not simply light the hunting fire themselves. He is aware that the fire has to be lit by him and other children *because* they are children, at the foot of a certain kind of tree, on the trail or in the direction that the hunters have decided to take, so that they will pass it. It must be kindled in a special way, using special leaves, so that smoke will be given off. The smoke drifts up through the leafy canopy, disappearing into the depths of the forest. It also swathes the hunters as they pass by it. If it is rising too abruptly to cross the path, the hunters casually reach out their hands as they pass, and bring the smoke to them, as though washing themselves with it. Mothers with infants at their breasts anoint their suckling baby as well as themselves. It may be done quietly, or the words Mother Forest, Father Forest, may be sung or shouted with joy. There is plainly more here than smoke, more than the fire that makes the smoke, and more than the wood that makes the fire—there is the forest that is the source of all these things.

That is how adult Mbuti elaborate when discussing among themselves, or with an inquiring youth, the stories the oldest Mbuti tell the youngest Mbuti—for the elders, like the children, if not absolutely pure are among the purest. Purity is a condition proper, they say, to the other world, but held to its greatest extent possible among mortals by those closest to death, the infants and the aged. These stories involve another problem the children in the *bopi* will have become aware of, namely, that all living things, even trees, seem to die. Yet just as the forest continues, however, life springing from the old, so does humanity. But whereas you can see a firm, green young shoot coming out of the body of a dead, fallen tree, who has seen a child born from an old dead woman or a calf from a dead elephant? Mbuti tell the story of the origin of death in a number of ways, all centering on the concept of what we might call original sin. In some cases it is said to have come about because of disagreement between a father and a son, as in the legend of the bird with a beautiful song, a bird that sang only for the son, making the father jealous; so that the father tried to kill the bird, and in killing the bird killed himself, and killed the song, forever (the principle of age at work): or of how man stole fire from woman (the principle of sex?): or of how a couple went to a forbidden place (territory?): or of how a young Mbuti girl was abandoned by her family, living on by herself (as a bird) but bringing death to all others (kinship at work?). But the story most often told to the children and amongst the children is of how Mbuti were immortal until one killed his brother antelope, since when all Mbuti have been condemned to die, just as they brought death to the antelope. And they will continue to die until they can learn not to kill.[3]

That is lesson enough in nonviolence, but to these verbal lessons add all the other lessons that fill the preceding pages, add those many others known but similar enough to bear being omitted in this discussion (for some see *J.R.A.I.* and "Zaïre," note 3); and all those I most certainly simply never became aware of, since I was not born an Mbuti, alas, and did not grow up amongst them; and that will only begin to approximate to the number of lessons in nonviolence from which Mbuti children can draw, every day of their lives, to learn both the positive values of cooperation and interpendence (who would want to be *in*dependent in such a society!) and the equally positive value of avoiding conflict, aggressivity, and violence.

But it is time for our child to grow up and face the realities of adult life, and the unavoidability of conflict, and the probability of that conflict arising in the area of sex. As he grows from the age of four to eight or thereabouts (for age to the Mbuti is a matter of personality, skill, and size, amongst other things, not of mere years) he joins in the *bopi* pastimes with increasingly active intelligence. His power of reasons develops. He has been with his mother, since infancy, both on the hunt and while she has been off with other women gathering. Even when being carried it is on the hip, not on the back, so he has ready access to the breast and a full view of the adult world as seen by his mother. It is the same, of course, for a girl child. Both have learned more than the rudiments of adult economic activity, and they have been increasingly aware that certain activities lie more within the sphere of men, and others more within the sphere of women though none are totally exclusive.

During his second four years, the child moves from physical exploration, adding to it and overlaying it with intellectual exploration. He begins to indulge in story-telling, perhaps in imitation of a great story-teller among the adults. But the stories are his own. He draws from his own experience, merely following the model of the adult story-teller who draws on the day's activities, comparing them with other days, other peoples, other activities; comparing the human world with the animal world, the Forest with the nonforest, and occasionally passing indirect judgments in terms of *ekimi* and *akami*. The bulk of the child's attention is focused on *bopi* activities, therefore confined primarily to his own age group, which indeed is to become one of his major spheres throughout life. But from a child's point of view he also investigates the world of youths, adults, and elders, pooling his observations and ideas with his age-mates.

As he grows older the major change in his physical pastimes is a simple one. He becomes increasingly conscious of that fourth sphere, and that fourth principle of social organization, sex. Through increasing association with youths he will have acquired a different perspective on sexual activity, and as he grows he will carry his explorations into that realm, with girls in the *bopi*. But a rather beautiful thing happens. He does not exclude the boys, nor does his girl friend exclude the girls . . . whatever awareness there is of this new emotion is shared, as everything should be, between age-mates. They explore each others' bodies without discrimination, and will even imitate the act of copulation with equal lack of discrimination, in the form of dance. The following opinion is of necessity speculative, but since I was for about a year classified by the Mbuti as a child, which included being toilet trained and occasionally confined to the *bopi* (on the pretext of being needed there as a guard) and in most other ways treated as a child, and since for two years I was classified as a youth and lived with the youths as such, I have certain personal experience. It certainly cannot claim to be that of a true Mbuti, but I suspect it is somewhat comparable to that of the oddball Mbuti that can be found in every camp, and into whose role of clown, or buffoon, I eventually fell. But I would say that at the *bopi* stage the children hold nothing back from each other, and if they had the physical love to give, which perhaps rather fortunately they do not, they would give it. From every sense at my command, physical, rational, and intuitive, I could detect no discrimination in the emotion of love along lines of sex. We were all *apua'i*, without regard for sex or gender.

However, around the age of eight or nine, perhaps as late as eleven, and in my case at the age of thirty, boy children enter the *nkumbi*[4] (see p. 213) and emerge a mere three months later as adults in village eyes (for it is a village ritual) but as youths in Mbuti eyes. The Mbuti have no formal initiation of boys, nor is there any evidence that they ever had one. There might possibly have been greater recognition given to a child who catches and kills his first game—for that is both a dangerous act, compounding his original sin, and a necessary act, for by such acts alone can he survive in this world. But for a number of complex reasons described elsewhere, and to be elaborated on by a colleague (Joseph A. Towles), who as anthropologist playing the role of villager was able to penetrate the *nkumbi* far more deeply than I was permitted to do, the Mbuti find it useful to enter the village ritual. It is of paramount importance in bringing about effective relationships between the two potentially hostile groups. Within the forest world of the Mbuti it is merely an easy way of marking the rather uncertain transition of a boy from childhood to youth. For the girls there is no such problem, their transition is clearly defined by the first flow of menstrual blood, an event acclaimed with joy by all, for now that girl has the power to become a mother.[5] At that point she will become an adult, and her mate will become her husband, and an adult also.

Following the *nkumbi,* however, there are still six or seven or maybe more years to go in the realm of youth. The village ritual, with its explicit sex instruction and moral teaching and consecration of the individual to the way of the ancestors and to the society at large, has nothing to teach the Mbuti about forest life. What remains to be learned he will learn, with his age-mates, in this next stage of life facing him. Territory, kinship, and age have all been well explored. That exploration will continue, but the main sphere explored during youth is that of sex, and while that is being explored the rational ability is further developed and refined, and the youth finds himself (and herself) in a jural rather than ritual role, in the pastime of developing interdependence. During youth, also, the Mbuti becomes more fully cognizant of that ultimate all-embracing sphere, *nduɽa,* and finds that his lingering purity (he may not kill an antelope until late in youth) sometimes places him in a role that is ritual as well as jural. At this stage we should refine our earlier classification of the role of children as *spiritual* rather than ritual, though from the children's point of view I feel it is seen more as ritual, and only dimly sensed as spiritual, which is why I used it at that stage in this discussion.

The youth, in so far as he is less pure, or more contaminated, is such NOT because of his increasingly physical concern with sex, but because of his increasing proximity to the daily act of sacrilege, the hunt. If anything, his sexual activity would be a purifying element. I mentioned that in the *bopi* there was no sexual discrimination in the sharing of love among the children, to their fullest capacity. I maintain that this is the same during youth, yet not once did I come across a case of homosexual intercourse, although the existence of names for both male and female homosexuality suggest that it may exist. I came across one case of bestiality (a male youth and a female goat), which was openly acknowledged and respected to the extent that neither boy nor goat suffered any disability except that they were confined to the village. The grounds for exclusion from the forest were not uncleanliness or impurity, there was no taint of immorality, merely the practical observation that the boy's "wife" did not know how to hunt and would quickly die if she came with him back to the forest. The boy, torn between two loyalties, finally chose the forest, pensioned his goat-wife off by presenting her to a villager whom he knew would cherish her and keep her well and alive, since the villager thought he was acquiring enormous control over the forest, the goat being well impregnated with the sperm of the forest people. That boy then married an Mbuti girl with no difficulty, he was back in the center of the forest sphere and the goat was no longer part of the "here and now." I mention the incident because it says a great deal about the Mbuti concept of love, even when carried into the physical act of sex. Even when so carried, the two things remain distinct. It might well be for similar pragmatic reasons that there is no recorded instance of male or female homosexuality; one's "wife" or "husband" simply would not know how to gather or hunt.

By this time girls have spent increasing attention to women's activities, following them on the hunt and on their private gathering expeditions, and the boys similarly have increasingly been following the men, learning the finer points of hunting and other primarily male activities. Homosexuality is not the point, however, any more than bestiality. The point is that even when boys and girls discover the ecstasy of sex, and for whatever reason confine it to a heterosexual relationship, they continue to love each other regardless of shared sexuality and even carry something of the physical act into their relationships, as though almost regretful of being separated by it. I cannot speak for the girls, though I have seen and heard enough similar behavior amongst them to convince me there is not likely to be much difference, but the male youths delight in bodily contact throughout youth. It becomes interspersed with more frequent formal spacing as serious heterosexual courtship begins, but it continues even into early married adult life. Male youths tend to sleep together, either in the open around a fire, or in a hut built by one of them and used by all. They sleep in a glorious bundle of young life, full of warmth and full of love. There is little sexual fondling, and what there is is due more in the form of a joke than to give any sexual pleasure. However, there is no doubt that the close hugging is more than for mere warmth, necessary though that is on any night in the rain forest. And there is no doubt that a measure of physical sexual relief, or satisfaction, is achieved in this way, with or without ejaculation. An occasional muttered comment about ejaculation may be made by an individual to himself, much as I might mutter if my shoelace broke while walking along a crowded street. Messy or bothersome to the individual, but of little or no significance to anyone else. What is significant is that the growing separation of the sexes for the physical act of copulation, augmented by the growing division of the sexes by the allocation of labor, is in a very real sense being countered, and love is being snared, to the point that even if intercourse were to take place I doubt that it would add anything to the intensity of the relationship, except possibly for that one brief moment. The sacrifice of that moment, somehow, seems to make the relationship all the stronger. Before looking at the final stage of transition from youth to adulthood, which is also a transition from unconscious, or perhaps better nonrational non-aggressivity to conscious, rational non-aggressivity, a brief summary of the lessons learned and the symbols implanted will be helpful.

Values

By entry to youth (between the ages of eight or nine and eleven) the Mbuti child has learned the major values that militate against aggressivity and violence. The following are the most important.

security: The Mbuti themselves consider that their individual life stories begin with conception and their formation as a fetus in the womb of their mother. Judging by what seems to be a high incidence of trouble-free pregnancy and childbirth, accomplished with ease and resulting in a healthy child as well as a healthy mother,

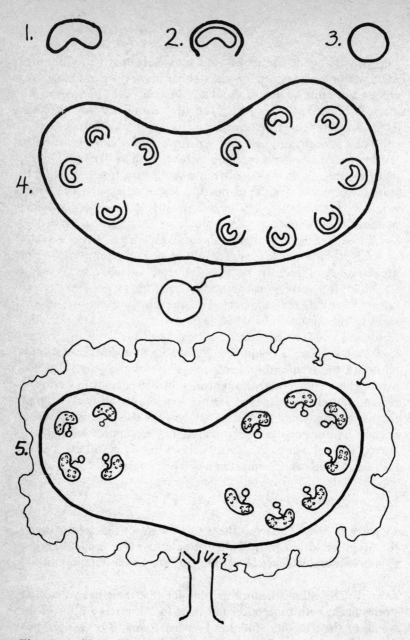

Figure 3. The major spheres of Mbuti experience: (1) womb; (2) household; (3) playground; (4) camp; (5) forest.

such experience of life as the child may have, in the womb, should be one of total security. From the moment of birth onwards everything is done to enable that sense of security to be transferred in steadily widening and inclusive circles from the sphere that is limited to the mother's body to the *endu* (leaf hut), to other *endu,* to the *bopi* (playground), to the *apa* (camp), and finally to the most inclusive sphere of all, *ndura* (the forest). The last may be taken to include, by opposition, the nonforest world of the village, for opposition is precisely the mechanism that provides the Mbuti with this ultimate security, safe within their sacred world against the profane. This process of increasing inclusion is the same process by which other values are gradually instilled, though from the point of view of the infant and the child each successive stage may seem more separate than inclusive, since he tends temporarily to abandon the one sphere once he has become secure in it, and experiment with the next. It is probably only in youth that the integrated nature of his total experience becomes apparent to him.

dependence: The steps are similar. His initial dependence on his mother is shown to have validity in relationship with ever expanding circles of other "kin," ultimately including every Mbuti in the camp, regardless of age or sex. But he also learns the value of dependence, just as he did that of security, with reference to territory (*endu, bopi, apa,* and *ndura*), and with reference to the four age grades.

interdependence is the next value learned, and again he sees this value as having applicability in all the areas in which conflict is likely to arise: kinship, territory, age, and sex. As a child he does not associate interdependence with conflict; that understanding comes with youth. But he quickly moves from the security of dependence in these areas to the even greater security of interdependence, where he gets his first real taste of responsibility and power.

coordination: This value was first learned as he coordinated the movements of his various limbs and then coordinated his overall movement with that of his mother. But he also learned coordination in and between the age groups.

cooperation: As the power of reason develops, so is the value of coordination, now well learned, transcended by an intellectual attitude that accompanies the necessity for cooperation demanded by the increasingly complex activities within the *endu, bopi,* and *apa.* Even the ultimate cooperative relationship between Mbuti and their prime (*ndura*) sphere has been amply learned, first while accompanying the hunt on his mother's side and later by setting off on foot with the men, if a boy, or with the women, if a girl. It is at this stage that this, and by inclusion the other values already learned, are extended to the fourth area of potential conflict, the differentiation between the sexes.

ekimi/akami: still, until youth, primarily at a physical rather than rational level, the child has been introduced to the positive value of *ekimi,* or quiet, as against that of *akami,* or disturbance. He has learned to associate *akami* with hunger, since noise, ill temper, lack of the proper manifestation of the other values (the lack of any of these values is described as *akami*), generally leads to an unsuccessful hunt. He has equally learned that the proper manifestation of the values learned so far results in *ekimi,* a word he now begins to use in other contexts much as we would use the word "happiness." He finds that one of the most common occasions on which the word *akami* is used is in reference not to noise on the hunt, which is unusual, but for verbal disputes in the camp. He also learns to differentiate between "good" sound, such as song, and "bad" sound, such as an argument, though in our sense the song may be a great deal noisier than the argument. Similarly he learns that *suso* (wind) is generally classified as *ekimi* unless it is *kuko* (wind that does damage) in which case it is *akami.* His starting point with this value is sound, which applies to both *ekimi* and *akami,* but he quickly learns, well before entering youth, that it is not sound itself that results in one value or the other, but the *effect* of that sound.

Techniques of Learning

The overall technique by which all this is learned in itself contributes to the enormous confidence with which an Mbuti faces his

total world by the time he reaches youth, which becomes a time
of testing that confidence, each youth consciously challenging himself and putting his confidence to the test. The overall technique
involves allowing the child, from infancy onwards, the safe but
adventurous exploration of each successive sphere, at the child's
own pace, while developing (through good use) his sensory and
motor abilities, his as yet nonrational sensitivity to the totality (in-
tuition?) while consciously dealing with one segment of experience after the other. Thus the ground is laid, by youth, for his rational, intellectual integration of the totality of his experience and
confidence. The various techniques we have looked at include:

endu: suckling, rocking, listening, smelling, tasting; his mother, his
father, their bed, the floor and walls of the hut.

apa: physical exploration is continued so that all the various *endu*
are included, though as yet the child has little experience of the
apa as a single unit.

bopi: the techniques here include firstly pastimes that develop muscular strength and coordination, and although played out in company of others, they are solitary explorations. They then develop
into more complex pastimes that require cooperation of increasing
numbers of children, such as climbing and bending the sapling to
the ground: imitation of adult economic activities (hunting, gathering, making bark-cloth); imitation of adult domestic activities
(house building, cooking, eating, sleeping, quarreling); imitation
of the political activities of youth (ridicule of each other, of youths,
adults and elders; ridicule of villagers). Here the pastimes demand
intellectual, rational content as well as physical, especially in the
ridicule of adult disputes which calls for considerable improvisa-
tion and exploration of the value system. Then there is, finally,
limited imitation of the ritual role of the elders, in which they perceive some similarity to their own role as lighters of the hunting
fire. But the children also imitate the role of elders as story-tellers,
partly by repeating the stories, and partly by improvising similar
stories of their own. Here their intellect and power of reason are
being developed in such a way as to reinforce the values learned,

and to prepare the way for their entry into youth and the integrated world of the *apa*. Through their physical exploration of space after space the children have come in physical contact with the major elements that will form such an important part of their later world of symbols. It may or may not be stretching things a little to link the warmth of the womb to that of the mother's body and both consequently to fire; however, I have heard Mbuti in apparently casual conversation liken the womb to a fire. But the child undeniably forms close associations with the hearth of his *endu*, that of other *endu*, that of the *bopi*, that of the *hunt*, and that which, even before he takes part in it as a youth, he will have seen in the center of the *apa*, the *kumamolimo*: the hearth (literally: vagina) of the *molimo*, a hearth lit only at times of major crisis. Similarly his contact with air might be said to have begun with the first breath he drew, before the cutting of the umbilical cord, and continued through learning to play various kinds of whistles and flutes, learning to blow a fire into life (fans are never used), learning to sing, to learning to blow the breath of life through the sacred *molimo* trumpet so that the hot coals at the far end throw fiery sparks out into the forest. Earth similarly has been a constant in his life, from his first explorations of the ground within the *endu*, *apa*, and *bopi*, the trees that grow out of it, to the earth that again, as a child, he may have been or will shortly see rubbed into the *molimo* trumpet or scattered over the *molimo* hearth when, finally, it is extinguished. And water—his first contact with water was special—the water of the forest vine. Even splashing about in the forest streams was special, because that was when he began to look at reflections and when elders might tell stories of the other world. As children they are warned away from that special part of the stream where the *molimo* trumpet is kept during the *molimo* festival, warned simply by a special barricade of forest vines. And if they have not yet seen it, by peeping out from the inside of their huts at nighttime, they will soon as youths see the *molimo* trumpet be given water to drink. Their contact with the supreme symbol, the forest itself, has been far from restricted to the mere climbing of trees—in the same way that they have come to recognize their interdependence with all other Mbuti so have they come to realize their interdependence with the natural world of which they are an integral part. While in the womb the boy's mother talked to him of the forest, and sang and shouted the praise of the forest, and ever since emerging into the *endu, bopi,* and *apa* worlds he has heard similar protestations of confidence and belonging, and himself has learned to call the forest mother or father as he leaves the camp for one of his many adventures of exploration.

At entry to youth this educative process is continued, all the values that so effectively militate against aggressivity are strengthened by further activities, which are extended to include that area of potential conflict with which the child has had least contact, sex. At the same time youths now develop an intellectual ability to integrate the *values,* just as they can now rationally integrate their various spheres and realms of activity. In the course of this they become involved in a number of institutionalized forms of behavior that bring them into both physical and intellectual contact with the underlying, omnipresent value of non-aggressivity.

For instance, while as children being carried on their mothers' sides or trotting along beside one or another parent they were indirectly aware of the separation and physical opposition of the sexes on the hunt, it was indirect because it was to large extent involuntary and insignificant. Now that as youths they take an increasing part in the hunt, and have their special place in it, the division, and opposition, of the sexes is very real. It has its own powerful logic as a division of labor, but its ritualization in various institutionalized forms raises it to another level. The hunting song in which the youths play a major part reproduces the physical opposition of men at their nets to women driving game towards the nets, with youths in an approximately medial position on each side (see Fig. 4). While it might be difficult to demonstrate that this song is a ritual rather than another educational, value-reinforcing pastime, there are other undeniably ritual activities that involve similar antiphonal singing techniques and which are even more directly manifestations of the need to avert conflict between the sexes. Appropriately these are activities in which both adults and youths participate, not elders or children. It is expected that the conflict will arise within the age grade of adulthood, to some extent it is their role to manifest such conflict, and it is the role of youth to resolve such conflict if they cannot avert it.

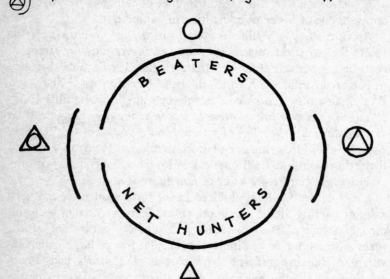

○ = women, who are the beaters

△ = men, who are the net hunters

△
△ } = youths, who catch game escaping the adult opposition

Figure 4. THE HUNT: showing opposition of women to men. Youths occupy a medial position and catch game that escapes the adult opposition.

One such activity is the tug of war. This is usually initiated by adults, but is generally not very successful or prolonged unless youths join in. It most often occurs during the honey season, which is a time of general relaxation, involving the fission of the hunting band into small groups that roam the territory in search of honey, with no communal hunting to bind the band together as a corporate unit. While this season may serve an ecological function, effectively putting an end to the hunt for up to two months, it undoubtedly also serves the political function of allowing unresolved disputes and potential disputes and lines of conflict to be brought into the open. The tug of war expresses the major line of potential conflict, between male and female. Men take a vine rope on one side, women pull on the opposite side. They sing in antiphony. However, if one side or the other were to win that would resolve nothing, so when the men seem to be winning one of them will abandon his side of the tug and join the women, pulling up his bark-cloth and adjusting it in the fashion of women, shouting encouragement to them in a falsetto, ridiculing womanhood by the very exaggeration of his mime. Then when the women begin to win, one of them adjusts her bark clothing, letting it down, and strides over to the men's side and joins their shouting in a deep bass voice, similarly gently mocking manhood. Each person crossing over tries to outdo the ridicule of the last, causing more and more laughter, until when the contestants are laughing so hard they cannot sing or pull any more, they let go of the vine rope and fall to the ground in near hysteria. Although both youths and adults cross sides, it is primarily the youths who really enact the ridicule. In this way the ridicule is performed without hostility, rather with a sense of at least partial identification and empathy. It is in this way that the violence and aggressivity of either sex "winning" is avoided, and the stupidity of competitiveness demonstrated.

The honey season is considered a time for relaxation and enjoyment of the pleasures of life, of which honey is one of the main symbols. Sexual activity among the youths is heightened. But the association of the individual quest for pleasure, however legitimate, with conflict is brought to the fore in the honeybee dance. Again, both adults and youths participate. The males form a single-file line, armed with bows and arrows, and with fire which they have to "steal" from the various *endu* hearths. Here is the first representation (in this particular dance) of the male/female conflict: fire is controlled by women, who are responsible for carrying fire with them on the hunt or whenever they accompany the men on any journey, and above all when moving from one camp site to another, so that the *endu* hearth never dies. The Mbuti know but eschew two traditional village techniques for making fire, and use matches (if provided) *only* for "profane" acts such as lighting cigarettes.

The men then, have to "steal" fire from the hearths to carry it with them, as they do on the real honey gathering expeditions, to

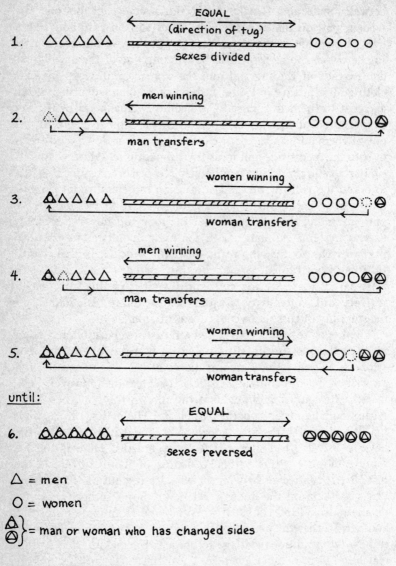

Figure 5. TUG OF WAR

smoke out the bees and enable them to "steal" (again recognizing the aggressive nature of the act, comparable to stealing the life of the game they hunt for meat) the honey, and the larvae of future life which Mbuti consume with the honey. As the men dance around the *apa,* looking upwards as if looking and listening for bees, the women form another line and follow the men, dancing behind them, or parallel with them, sometimes in front, even dancing in and out of the men's line as though invisible. Then the women change direction and dance towards the men. They also are carrying burning firebrands, but unlike the men, every woman and girl has a live brand in her left hand, whereas only two or three men may have brands with them, sheathed in phrynium leaves. As the men approach the women, who have slowed down, the women break ranks and attack the men, beating their glowing firebrands over the heads of the men, covering them with sparks and hot coals that "burn like the sting of bees." The men are routed, and re-form and start all over again, looking for the nonstinging kind of bee. Unlike the tug of war, this dance has a rather more definite conclusion in that the men never succeed in their attempt to "steal" honey. One or other of the women (not a girl) may end the dance by dancing into her hut and coming out with a leaf cup of honey or a piece of honeycomb, and offer this to the men, who accept it and consume it, sharing some with the women (bees).

Hoop dancing and rope skipping are two activities particularly common during the honey season, and in certain forms restricted to older girls. Girls also spend a great deal of time, in this season, decorating their bodies with the juice of the gardenia fruit, and demonstrating their nubility by playing with the small gardenia fruits, rolling them from their shoulders onto their upstanding breasts, from which they toss them up to the air and catch them and throw them back onto their shoulders again. The camp clown, a male, will frequently demonstrate that this is one thing a boy can NOT do; but the boys have pastimes of their own such as playing a "game" with beans, seeds, or small stones, according to rules by which both sides "win." This is a variant of a favorite village gambling game, and an important way in which both Mbuti and villagers socialize when Mbuti are in the village. Boys also decorate themselves during this season, with leaves and orchids and fresh cut bark clothes. These are often preliminaries to the great joint pre-marital festival, the *elima,* which ideally but not necessarily takes place during the honey season. It involves all the adult male and female youths from the *apa* as it is constituted at the moment, a few only of the elders in specific roles such as the "mother" of the *elima* (either an old widow or a younger barren woman) and a "father" of the *elima,* a less formal role generally taken by a widower or a cripple (both the "mother" and the "father" thus being in a sense sexless); the other mothers in the camp act as guards of the *bamelima,* the girls who are living in the *elima* hut. Finally, male youths form other hunting territories, near or far, visit the camp in order to participate in the festival. Adult males, children and elders (other than the "mother" or "father" of the *elima*) are excluded except as spectators.

As with other social institutions, the *elima* can be looked at from a number of different points of view. It is occasioned by the dramatic and unmistakable entry of any girl in the *apa* into womanhood, marked by the appearance of the first menstrual blood. Unlike many societies, African and other, this is widely publicized and acclaimed with joy and exuberance, for it means that a mother has been "born." A camp may wait until another girl similarly "sees the blood" for the first time, so that the two girls can combine their *elima* festivals. A girl from another camp may be brought by her parents, under the pretext simply of joining the camp during its monthly shift from one site to another, but really so that she can join the *elima.* This is most likely if the girls are friends. The girls invite other friends to join them in the *elima* house, where they live with the *ema'abamelima* (mother of the girls of the *elima*). Effectively, then, the older youths of the camp are strictly segregated at this time into male and female, and even the younger youths follow suit, separating themselves in activities they would normally pursue together.

While the *elima* is consciously thought of as a pre-marital festival, providing an opportunity for formal courtship and sexual experimentation, it can also be thought of as a joint male/female initiation that signals the approaching advance of adults into elderhood, another impending area of conflict, of possible aggressivity if not violence. The Mbuti themselves refer to this transition period as one of *akami* for the individual concerned, whereas the transitions from childhood to youth and youth to adulthood are *ekimi*. The *elima* may be used by adults on the verge of elderhood to temporarily play the role of clown. They do this, if male, by classifying themselves one generation down, as youths, fighting their way with male youths toward the *elima* house, even into it for a brief moment perhaps. Older women more rarely opt for such a medial role; if widowed the transition into elderhood is smoother than for the men, and even if not widowed they are not barred from food-gathering in elderhood to the same extent that male elders are barred from hunting. But older adult women who feel ambivalent about the approaching change of status take advantage of the *elima* by sitting with the young girls when they emerge from the *elima* house. In this way transitional adults, by allying themselves with the lower generation temporarily, automatically identify themselves with the superior generation by the principle of alternate generation alliance, which operates strongly in Mbuti society.

The main feature of the *elima* that concerns us here is the ritual conflict between male and female youths, manifest in the battle waged with sticks, large nuts and seeds, small burning embers or even logs thrown by the women, and smaller seeds or pieces of tough skin fired from the bow by the male youths, and long supple sapling whips used by the *bamelima* girls. In order to gain access to the *elima* house and thus acquire the right to sleep with one of the girls, a male youth or medial male adult has to fight his way through the barrage of fire set up by the adult women. Once inside, or even outside, they may be met by the girls themselves, armed with their whips. The same whips are used by girls in their frequent forays into the camp, and even into neighboring territories, to beat boys (and medial adults) as an invitation to visit them in the *elima* house. There are obviously a number of complex lessons being learned here. Apart from the intense discussions the girls have with the mother of the *elima,* and the boys with the father, which provide them with an intellectual understanding of what they are being prepared for, the very physical violence they are met with in pursuit of their individual sexual desires is a dramatic ritualization of the inherent conflict between their individual and social selves, a conflict that is one of the keynotes of the adult life into which they are moving. The fact that they have already learned that adults are *expected* to be troublemakers, that it is even one of their allotted roles, that adulthood is a time of *akami,* now for the first time becomes part of their own personal experience. Yet all the familiar symbols of security are there; the mother and father, the *endu* (of the *bamelima*) with its own hearth; the firebrands they throw or have thrown at them; the very special leaves they sleep on when they gain admittance, which leaves have to be ritually disposed of afterwards; the young saplings with which they whip or are whipped; and the songs they are expected to sing in clear antiphony, distinct from all other song in form and style. Water is used in the final ritual washing of both boys and girls, when the *elima* ends.

Youths learn, through the *elima,* that the pursuit of individual desires, although not wrong in itself, is likely to lead to *akami,* and if they wish to pursue such desires they had better temper them in such a way that they are acceptable to the rest of the society. The adult women are perfectly capable of preventing even the strongest and most aggressive youth from entering the *elima* house if they so wish; they may beat him with sticks or even with thorns, or may simply pick him up bodily and throw him in the nearest stream or river. The *elima,* which lasts a month, is obviously a disruptive time, and when it is over there are many disgruntled adults and a general time of *akami.* The very youths who were the unwitting cause of *akami* are then called upon to play what is perhaps their most important role, a role that prepares them admirably for their own inevitably disputatious adulthood. In this role they are the bearers of the *molimo madé,* the lesser *molimo.* The word *molimo,* which has to do with "leopardness," is perhaps best translated as the soul or spiritual essence of the forest. Its visible and audible symbol is a long trumpet, traditionally made from a special tree which, when cut young, can be hollowed out with a tough abrasive vine. It is usually six to ten feet in length. Elders control the *molimo mangbo,* the great *molimo,* which is used on occasions of major crisis such as death or prolonged and serious bad hunting; the *molimo madé* is brought into action to "quieten" a "noisy" camp. Thus it is youth who sit in judgment and primarily on adults; youth which is called upon to rectify the harm done by the adulthood into which they will shortly pass. While the *molimo mangbo* (by youths again, but under the direction of elders) is made to sound like a leopard, and to sing like Mbuti (both symbols of *ekimi*) and is given water to drink, rubbed with earth, and made to produce fire as well as song by the breath of life, the *molimo madé* of youth is made to sound like an angry elephant, the destroyer of the forest; when it comes into camp instead of being fed with earth, fire, water, and air it is taken hold of by all the male youths and stampedes back and forth, destroying anything in its path, attacking all the *endu* in turn, perhaps but not necessarily paying rather more attention to the *endu* of the troublemakers who caused the *molimo madé* to be "awakened."

Nothing the adult or even the elders can do or say has any effect on the control of the youths over the *molimo madé*. It is youth that decides not only when the *akami* is serious enough to warrant such action, or whether they should merely resort to ridicule, but it is youth that affectively decides *what* constitutes *akami:* youth has the power of revising the values of society, of shaping the future. Youth's wealth of experience is now backed up by a well-developed intellect; youths hold long and serious discussions about adult behavior with reference to *akami* and *ekimi,* but as concepts rather than as rigid codes of behavior. Similarly, although adults have no control over sexual escapades of youth outside the institution of *elima,* the youths themselves, increasingly recognizing the potential of sex as a source of conflict, discuss among themselves their preferences as to when and where to have sexual intercourse with a girl. It must be a time and place of *ekimi* they say, and in their discussions they state their preferences in terms of proximity to water, so that they can look at it or listen to it; to earth in terms of the soft feel or sweet smell of the earth (or leaf mold) in this place as against that; to air in terms of the sound of a breeze rustling the leaves. When any pair of youths decide that they have experimented sufficiently to be able to bring this *ekimi* with them into adulthood, for without it the sexual act would be neither affective nor pleasurable, they get married. For the Mbuti this involves little formality. The male youth has to show his prowess as a hunter by catching and killing "large" game (large enough to feed a nuclear family), either on his own or by virtue of his position at the extremities of the semicircle of hunting nets; and the girl has to be willing to go with him and build a house for them to live in. Parents have little say, though they may quietly voice their opinion; elders only intervene if they feel the marriage is too "close," a concept that involves both kinship and territoriality.

Adulthood is entered without formality as soon as youths feel ready to undertake the responsibility of marriage. Once married the youths are classified as adults. The boy's mother gives him a hunting net, and as adults the young man and his bride set off for the daily hunt with the rest of the camp; there is no vertical hierarchy within the age grade. It is then that they begin to realize fully how full of conflict is adult life. Once a child is born the husband is expected to abstain from intercourse with his wife for three years. There is no openly stated prohibition against sleeping with other women, least of all unmarried girls, but to do so immediately places him in competition with other adult males or with youthful suitors. The adult male is also the killer of game, and so the one who perpetuates human (and animal) mortality. He has to rely on children to minimize this necessary act of violence and aggressivity, through the hunting fire. He has to rely on youths to restore *ekimi* when his unwise flirtations or jealousies cause *akami*. He has to accept that the youth of the day may redefine the concepts of *ekimi* and *akami* in ways not entirely agreeable to him. And when, usually in adulthood, he is faced with the death of his own parents the adult male has to rely on the power of the elders to invoke the *molimo mangbo* and restore *ekimi* even in the face of death. At the height of his sexual potency the adult male finds himself, socially, remarkably impotent. This is largely minimized by the values learned from childhood onwards, the value of dependence and interdependence. It is further offset by his all too recent experience as a youth, and the hostility that might result between these adjacent generations is lessened by their very proximity, and by the intensive cooperation demanded between them in hunting and gathering as in ritual/sacred song and dance.

It is the adults who are primarily involved in the most dangerous of all areas of conflict, that between the sedentary village farmers and the nomadic hunter/gatherers. Because of their economic role it is they who are expected to bring meat, mushrooms, saplings, and leaves for the house-building, and other forest products, to the village. The villagers misread this economic control of the adult Mbuti as indicative of political control, and conduct all their negotiations and disputes with Mbuti through the adults. This places adults, male and female, in a difficult position, since any attempt to implement the wishes of the villagers is likely to cause enormous dispute in the Mbuti forest camp, and failure to do so is going to create equal trouble in the village with which they have to deal if they are to succeed in keeping the villagers from coming into the forest and getting what they need for themselves. We cannot go into the village aspect of this conflict here, except perhaps just to draw attention again to the participation of Mbuti boys and their fathers in the village *nkumbi* initiation, by which the villagers believe they achieve ultimate supernatural control over the Mbuti, when political control through the Mbuti adults fails. Participation of Mbuti couples wishing to get married in village marriage ritual also serves the same end. But in the forest the adults are invariably blamed for the *akami* that results from even the most reasonable requests of the villagers. In the forest camp, then, it is usually the adults who in the guise of entertainment ridicule the villagers constantly, such as when recounting tales of their visit to the village: how they swindled the villagers or cheated them or stole from them, beat them at their own gambling games, and so forth. In such pantomimes the adults ridicule the villagers as clumsy, stupid, noisy, dirty, but also as dangerous, like the elephant.

The constant mobility of the Mbuti, who change camp sites almost every month, helps prevent conflict between Mbuti and villagers. The camps fluctuate in both size and composition as well as in location so that a villager never knows which Mbuti are where. This same process of fission and fusion is of course also a major element in conflict avoidance between Mbuti themselves, allowing potential disputants to separate themselves into different camps, temporarily, before the dispute flares up into major proportions. (See Fig. 6.)

More than any of the above, however, as a factor in controlling aggressivity, violence, and conflict in adult life, is the demonstrably positive value of *ekimi* that the adult has perceived at every stage of his life and which he still perceives and strives for, even in the

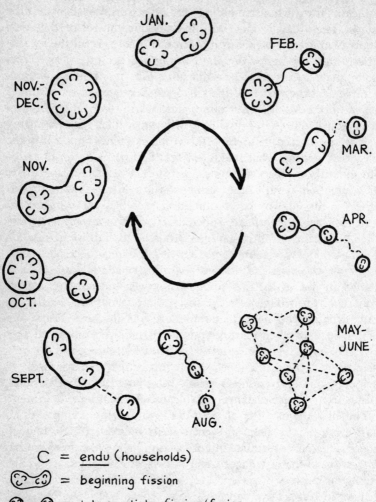

Figure 6.   Idealized series of camp changes showing process of fission and fusion utilized for conflict avoidance.

pursuit of individual satisfaction. The *molimo* festival is demanding and exhausting. While stressing *ekimi* it almost inevitably creates *akami*. The *molimo* is always accompanied, then, by rituals that reverse *akami*. The *molimo madé* is one, the other is focused on sex. As the prime noise-makers it is not surprising that it is the adults, male and female, that are expected to perform *ekokomea*, the most formal of all the various rituals of reversal and/or rebellion. Like other rituals *ekokomea* demonstrates, rather as a controlled experiment does, the danger of alternative modes of behavior and thought. Here again we see that underlying the diversity of ways of actively expressing and expelling aggressivity there is a constant focus on purity, or health, without which the ritual dramas would be empty and ineffective. In *ekokomea* the sex norms are all cast aside, reversed and ridiculed. Alternative modes of behavior are experimented with and tested by mime and ridicule. In particular both as individuals and as groups women and men are able to ridicule the opposite sex, most often in terms of sexual behavior and cleanliness. As with the tug-of-war, each individual act of ridicule adds to the general hilarity and detracts from the underlying latent aggressivity, until the ridicule goes so far beyond the realm of reason that aggressivity itself becomes unthinkable. The *ekokomea* group then collapses in hysterics, rolling on the ground, eyes streaming with tears, gasping for breath; and when they recover men and women alike resume their normal roles as though nothing has happened, other than a general improvement in their good spirits.

The *molimo mangbo,* however, is the greatest of all purificatory rites or festivals among the Mbuti, serving as a dynamic reminder to all, of any age or sex, of the value of *ekimi,* and of the vital necessity for cooperation in order to achieve *ekimi.* It is here that the Mbuti see themselves as being united together in the center of the most inclusive of all wombs, that of the forest. It requires cooperation on this scale to restore *ekimi* in the face of that supreme *akami* of death. The very nature of the ritual cooperation required represents the mutually complementary roles of all four age levels in Mbuti society, and in just the same way that life (and *ekimi*) would be impossible without this daily interaction and interdependence between children, youths, adults, and elders, so would the *molimo mangbo,* and the reversal of *akami,* be impossible without the cooperation of the same groups. The *molimo mangbo* integrates the age groups, the sexes, and it unites all the individual *endu* (however disunited in terms of kinship) in terms of common territoriality. Finally, the *molimo mangbo* expresses the greatest opposition of all, that between the forest and nonforest. In this one ritual every major potential source of conflict is expressed. Thus there are three periodic, constantly repetitive situations that demand the ritualization of conflict and expulsion of aggressivity. The annual honey season, during which the territorial band breaks down to its minimal segments; the *elima,* whenever a girl in the band has her first menstrual period; and the *molimo mangbo* which takes place whenever any adult or elder (sometimes a youth) dies. It is not impossible to have all three at the same time, though generally an *elima* will be delayed if there is a death *molimo.*

In the *molimo mangbo* the role of children, and some younger youths, is to "steal" (again) the food and fire from each *endu* hearth for the central *molimo* hearth, the *kumamolimo.* That they have to mime the act of stealing focuses attention on the inherent conflict between the individual and the social good; and it is at the adult level that this conflict is most likely to be manifest. As in the *molimo madé* the youths are the bearers of the *molimo* trumpet, and it is one of them that sings into the trumpet, giving the song of the men a special power as they repeat it and echo it on into the forest, so that *ndura* will hear. But instead of the trumpeting of an elephant, they make the *molimo* reproduce the soft growls and coughs of a leopard, the symbol of death itself, but of the kind of death that leads to life, not the kind of death brought by the elephant. While the elders initiate the *molimo mangbo,* determining both its moment of beginning and its moment of ending, it is the youths who decide if and when the *molimo* trumpet itself shall enter the camp and feed at the *kumamolimo.* This is consistent with their jural role. If they decide that adults, elders, and children, male and female, are not cooperating and giving their all to the festival, if they judge that there is *akami* in the camp, then that night when they take the trumpet out of its stream, bathe it, and give it water, earth, and fire to eat and drink, and invest it with their own breath of life, they approach the camp but do not enter.

And instead of sounding like the leopard, the reconciler of death, it will sound like the elephant, and early in the morning it is the *molimo madé* that might enter the camp, not the *molimo mangbo*. Once again the youths, about to enter that disputatious and noisy time of life, adulthood, are given the responsibility of restoring *ekimi*.

The adult males, who represent the first male hunter to bring death and *akami* to mankind, are the ones who suffer the most discomfort during the long and tiring festival. Even their singing, which is the loudest, does not have the necessary quality to bring the *molimo* into camp. It has to be transformed by the trumpet and transposed by the voice of youth into a sound of pure *ekimi* that the forest will surely hear. Some laxity is allowed the elders, youths, females, and children; but if an adult male as much as nods during the long nights of *molimo* singing he is threatened with death. The intensity of his singing, equally, must be greater than that of any of the others. And finally the adult male has to suffer the indignity, toward the end of the festival, of having his role usurped by the women, who come in and take over the men's song, tieing the men all up with nooses made from the *nkusa* vine from which hunting nets are made, so that as they say the women have tied up the song, and tied the hunt. Only when the men make an appropriate propitiatory gesture will the women release them, and allow the *molimo* to continue. Even then, one old woman will in a gesture of supreme control slowly and deliberately trample right through the *molimo* fire, scattering the logs and embers to all sides, threatening to extinguish life forever. Each time the men rebuild the fire and "rekindle" the smoldering embers with a dance in imitation of the act of copulation, the old woman dances through again, scattering it, to say that as the giver of life, she also has the ultimate power of bringing death, through the negation of her life-giving power. After the female elder has repeated this for perhaps two or even three nights, the *molimo* comes to an end; with the very last embers of the hearth being carefully extinguished by a male elder; the *molimo* trumpet being triumphantly carried back to the depths of the forest by youths. Only at this point are the adults allowed to wash and cleanse themselves of the taint of death, and resume normal daily activities.

It will be seen that both male and female adults have been effectively educated from infancy onward to avoid conflict, avert it, divert it, or, when it erupts despite all precautions, to resolve it with a minimum of aggressivity, mental or physical. Adulthood offers the most opportunities for *akami,* and the lessons and habits acquired in infancy, childhood, and youth are not enough in themselves to avert *akami* at all times. However, adulthood is marked by a different phenomenon, that of sexual differentiation at a level not previously known. Until entry to adulthood the only age level to which the terms of address distinguish sex as well as age, is adulthood itself. To infants, children, and youths alike, all adults are separated into *ema* or *eba,* whereas amongst themselves, within their own age group, they are all *apua'i* regardless of sex. Or if addressed by someone older they are *miki,* regardless of sex. Now, as adults, however, while addressing each other as *apua'i* they find, for the first time, that when addressed they are separated into male and female. Further, although the *elima* prepared the way for a new distinction in behavior and role, clearly giving the initiative to the female, the adult male still seems to find it difficult, at times, to reconcile himself to female dominance. He sees himself as the hunter, but then he could not hunt without a wife, and although hunting is more exciting than being a beater or a gatherer, he knows that the bulk of his diet comes from the foods gathered by the women. And while his wife shares almost every aspect of his social life, he can never share her role as a mother, except in the strictest classificatory sense. And once his wife gives birth, she seems to remove herself still further from him by refusing to have intercourse with him for three years. Open and devoted affection persists throughout all this, but in any one hunting camp tensions are always rising to the surface along these lines.

It is almost as though at this point the woman (the mother) becomes sacred and the male (the bringer of death) profane. The obligatory reluctance of the woman to contribute to the *kumamolimo,* her power to tie up (women often use the word "to silence") the song and the hunt, her power over the fire of life, all this is consistent with her role as life-giver, as the bringer of *ekimi.* Similarly the adult male is consistent as the bringer of *akami,* and it is just as vital that he play that role as it is that the female plays hers. Tendencies to aggressivity among the males, however, are curbed throughout adulthood not only by the various rituals in which male and female must cooperate, or reverse their roles, nor even by the necessary cooperation and interdependence required by hunting and gathering, but also by their proximity at one end of adulthood to youth, and at the other end to elderhood. The young husband, newly a father, and already deprived of the right to sleep with his wife, may spend much of his time with youths whose company he has just left. He may even take part in the *molimo madé,* and so he is still to some extent acting out a jural role as well as his adult economic role, however unofficially. Even when he is too old to continue this association with youth, it is still recent enough for him to be influenced by it, and for him to be ready to accept the judgment of the *molimo madé* and the will of youth.

At the other end, when his wife has ceased to give birth to children, he is close to elderhood, and so he is that much closer to purity. The transition from adulthood to elderhood is a gradual one; for those who find it difficult a way out may be found by playing the role of clown. Others, probably most, tend to slip more easily into elderhood by embracing it at just the moment they finally let go of their last contact with youth. In this way they move from contact with a jural role to contact with the role that elders play as meditors. Thus adulthood, for the male, is in itself a medial position, marked by ambivalence. The alliance between the alternate generations of youth and elderhood is a major asset in the prevention of aggressivity during adulthood.

Once the transition to elderhood is over, the danger of aggressivity is reduced to practically nil. The elders, who are addressed as *tata* even by their adult children, are again not differentiated by sex —the sexes are joined once more. Further, because of their proximity to death they are increasingly imbued with spiritual power, and associated with *ekimi.* Their role as arbitrators is informal, by virtue of their age they merely have a wider range of experience from which to cite precedent. Or they may, wordlessly, insert themselves physically between two disputants, making the argument or fight that much more difficult to continue. But whereas in the control of aggressivity the youth, with the *molimo madé,* is dealing with the sphere of the "here and now," and appealing by argument to reason, the elder is introducing an element of the "other" sphere, the "other-than-here-and-now," and is invoking spirit, not reason, through the *molimo mangbo*. If youth has power, elderhood has authority. At both levels, other than in the context of the *elima,* there is no sexual differentiation, and in this respect the two are allied to childhood, and all three differentiated from sexually differentiated adulthood.

Almost by definition aggressivity and violence are virtually impossible in Mbuti society until adulthood; its manifestation then is restricted primarily to manifestation by adult men, and this is controlled by the powerful jural and spiritual institutions adjacent to adulthood, from one of which the adult has just passed, and into the other of which he is about to emerge; a juxtaposition that in itself is an effective measure of control. Throughout this dangerous state of life the adult woman stands firm as the symbol of *ekimi,* however closely allied to adult male *akami.* The frequent ritual manifestations of her ultimate control cannot help but serve as a reminder of the ultimate security offered by the most inclusive womb/sphere of all, the forest. It is little wonder that when Mbuti die, they do so without fear, and it is only right that the songs that mark such a death are songs of the same joy in which life itself was conceived. It is the same joy with which the infant is born into the *endu,* the child into the *bopi,* and the youth into the *apa;* for all come from and return to *ndura.* For the Mbuti this joy, which accompanies him throughout life, from sphere to sphere, is *ekimi,* the antithesis of *akami.* At the very least the Mbuti experience teaches that aggressivity is politically inexpedient; *ekimi* simply is not compatible with the supreme *akami* of violence.

NOTES

1. Colin M. Turnbull, *The Forest People.* New York: Simon & Schuster, 1961; Colin M. Turnbull, *Wayward Servants.* New York: Natural History Press, 1965; Colin M. Turnbull, "The Mbuti Pygmies: An Ethnographic Survey," *Anthropological Papers of the American Museum of Natural History,* 50:3 (1965).
2. Ashley Montagu, *Prenatal Influences.* Springfield, Ill.: C. C. Thomas, 1962.

3. P. E. Joset, "Notes ethnographiques sur les Babira-Babombi," *Bull. Assoc. Ancienne Ethnog.* Belgique: Univ. Colon, 1 (1947):9-24; P. E. Joset, "Buda Efeba: contes et légendes Pygmées," *Zaïre,* 2:1 (1948):25-56 and 2:2 (1948):137-57; Colin M. Turnbull, "Legends of the BaMbuti," *J.R.A.I.* 89:1 (1959):45-60.
4. Colin M. Turnbull, "Initiation among the BaMbuti Pygmies of the Central Ituri," *J.R.A.I.,* 87:2 (1957):191-216; Colin M. Turnbull, *Wayward Servants.* New York: Natural History Press, 1965.
5. A girl's early menstrual cycles are usually anovulatory, so that usually she does *not* yet have the power to become a mother. See Ashley Montagu, *The Reproductive Development of the Female.* New York: Julian Press, 1957.

Tahitian Gentleness and Redundant Controls

I.

Anthropology has been constructed out of contrasts, contrasts in the behavior of members of exotic communities with, for the most part, American and European observers' sense of the ordinary.[1]

One of the kinds of behaviors that contrasted with our sense of the normal has to do with aggression. Western observers often found their "natives" either wildly aggressive or idyllically more gentle than they expected people to be. Out of such unexamined, naive senses of differences, methodologically and theoretically purified, anthropology has grown. These are, as Gregory Bateson has called them in relation to units of meaning, "the differences that make a difference."

Even when one does get some grasp of reliable and intuitively meaningful behavioral contrasts, one gets into difficulty, and this is particularly true in psychological anthropology, with questions of interpretation. Here, among other difficulties, seductions of ideology and theoretical allegiance enter. If one wishes to believe that all human beings are "basically aggressive" or "basically loving" it is not difficult to manipulate one's analysis of the data to make everything come out satisfactorily. What is primarily at issue is the considerable difficulty in going from surface behavior to some sort of nontendentious concept of underlying tendency or structure. One cannot discard these underlying structures. In relation to aggression, we all know from personal experience that there is, for example, some sort of difference between "gentle people" and "people who act gently in certain situations." We assume that gentle acts have different meanings—different kinds of underlying structures.

It seems clear from the anthropological literature that there are groups in the world who at least act considerably more gently (or less gently) than others. Tahiti is a case in point. From shortly after the time of the discovery of Tahiti all successive observers reiterated impressions of gentleness. "The people in general are of the common size of Europeans . . . their gait easy and genteel and their countenance free, open, and lively, never sullied by a sullen or suspicious look—their motions are vigorous, active and graceful and their behavior to strangers is such as declare at first sight their humane disposition, which is as candid as their countenances seem to indicate, and their courteous, affable and friendly behavior to each other shows that they have no tincture of barbarity, cruelty, suspicion or revenge. They are ever of an even unruffled temper, slow to anger and are soon appeased and as they have no suspicion so they ought not to be suspected, and an hour's acquaintance is sufficient to repose an entire confidence in them" (Morrison [1784], 1935:170). "In short their character is as amiable as that of any nation that ever came unimproved out of the hands of nature" (J. Forster, 1778:231). "The character of the Tahitians . . . their gentleness, their generosity, their affection and friendship, their tenderness, their pity" (G. Forster, 1777: Vol. II, 133). The Tahitians "are, generally speaking, careful not to give offense to each other. . . . There are . . . few domestic broils; and were fifty natives taken promiscuously from any town or village, to be placed in a neighborhood or house—where *they* would disagree once, fifty Englishmen, selected in the same way, and placed under similar circumstances, would quarrel perhaps twenty times. They do not appear to delight in provoking one another, but are far more accustomed to jesting, mirth, and humor, than irritating or reproachful language" (Ellis, 1830: Vol. II, 24). "They certainly live amongst each other in more harmony than is usual amongst Europeans. During the whole time I was amongst them, I never saw such a thing as battle; and though they are excellent wrestlers, and in their contests give each other many a hard fall, the contest is no sooner concluded, than they are as good friends as ever. Their frequent wars must be imputed to the ambitions of their chiefs; and were it not for the restless disposition of these men, I am persuaded that war would be almost unknown among them. . . . Their dispositions are gentle to an extreme. [With two exceptions] I never saw an Otaheitan out of temper the whole time I was in Otaheite" (Turnbull, 1812: p. 339 and p. 372). And so forth.

There were some reports of violence and heavy drinking in the second decade of the 19th century when the Tahitians were undergoing enormous stress during a period of transition from the traditional society and culture to a new set of patterns under the impact of Western contact, particularly Protestant missionary influence. But this time of disturbance was soon over, with the digestion and domestication of the new cultural influences, and Tahitian gentleness re-established itself.

Tahiti in the early 1960's when I began my field work there seemed in regard to gentleness little different than the reports of the late 18th and early 19th century had suggested. Available statistics on crime and suicide, impressions of administrators, and my own observations during a period of more than two years in a rural village and a small enclave in urban Papeete indicated in comparison with Western experience and in comparison with reports of many other non-Western societies an extreme lack of angry, hostile, destructive behavior.

But what *kind* of gentleness was involved? Why and in what way were people acting gently? In what ways did the aggression and hostility that they did manifest show itself? To attempt to explore such questions one can no longer use relatively unambiguous and quantifiable evidence such as murder, suicide, mayhem, physical fights, and other clearly hostile behaviors, but one must look to subtle expressive clues, necessarily based on more or less overt assumptions about human personality organization and interpersonal processes.

The detailed behavioral observations and psychological interviewing that I did in the two communities showed very little indication of expression of hostility at the *visceral-autonomic* level (anxiety, indications of psycho-physiologic stress), nor at the *vol-*

untary muscular level (muscular strain, headaches, back aches, tense posture, and movements); nor were there more purely *psychological* signs of problems about poorly controlled hostility (hypochondriasis, fear of death, self-punitive depression, conscious fantasies with overtly destructive themes). That is, whatever hostility people had to deal with, was not a *problem*—it expressed itself neither in strongly disruptive interpersonal action nor in discomforting symptoms at any of the three levels of personal organization where one might expect it to show itself—visceral–autonomic, voluntary muscular, or symbolic, an analysis of expression at these different levels being one key to the specific structure of the personal control and integration of hostility. This does not mean that there were not indications of hostility and its controls—the socialization practices I will discuss are indications of this. Hostility had to be trained for, frustrations diminished, controls of potentially escalating destructive processes had to be established—and some rigidities and projections gave clues as to how this was done. But this was done in such a way that hostility as pathology, as a disrupting force in personal or interpersonal organization was kept to a minimum, and this in a graceful way, with minimum costs. Elaborate secondary controls (i.e., severe social sanctions such as prison, or severe personal self-control) were not required.

The lack of hostility as a problem has[2] something to do with the cultural and physical environment in which people operate, and something to do with their socialization. The traditional Tahitian environment is complexly nonfrustrating. It minimizes externally induced irritation. The village adaptation to its surroundings is successful; people do not have difficult problems in providing a varied and bounteous supply of food and other needs, and the traditional arrangements for land ownership, distribution of goods, and for maintaining the general social organization of the village work well.

Not only are the technological and social arrangements mediating between the village and its environment adequate, but there are also a series of cultural understandings which, operating both through the perspectives individuals bring to their social and physical environment and through their effects on the other people with whom each individual has to deal, operate to reduce the "frustration significance" of that environment. For example, it is shared common sense that individuals have very limited control over nature and over the behavior of others; that, in fact, if an individual strives too much, tries to force reality into new patterns, that reality (God, nature, others) will inevitably react back and destroy the offender. On the other hand, if one does not strive and force things, then reality will inevitably take care of the individual. People learn to be passive optimists. This common sense, generated by the conditions of socialization, was reinforced by legends, healing practices of spirit doctors, and generally expressed conscious values. A universe so defined is *cognitively* less frustrating than those cultures which define realities in which almost anything is possible to individuals.[3]

If we turn from the experienced situation in which hostility may or may not be generated, in itself a complex mix of objective and subjective aspects, to the problem of Tahitian cultural influence on "subjectivity," on culturally prevalent personal tendencies bearing on hostility or gentleness, we are involved with questions of socialization, of informal education, of cultural influence on the formation of personality and cognition.

The striking thing about such influences in the two Tahitian communities that I studied was that those influences bearing on hostility/gentleness were pervasive and multiple.

Some of these influences are the following:

(1) A number of aspects of community life, including the prevalent institution of adoption which allows mothers to give away babies whom they are not ready for, the fact that patterns of marriage tend to produce relatively comfortable and anxiety-free relationships compared to many other cultures, plus a set of parental orientations about an infant's relative strength and ability to grow because of its own internal integrity, tend to produce anxiety-free, warm early relationships between the infant and the mother. Their sense of the child's self-development, autonomy, and limited sensitivity to pressures from others, at this and later stages, diminishes the parents' ambition about him. They feel they must take adequate care of the child—not to do so is a matter of severe community shaming—but this care is not considered particularly difficult. Such factors, presumably, foster in the child a core sense of the elemen-

tary adequacy and safety of the world, a sense of basic trust. He (or she) will, presumably, be able to tolerate later culturally produced frustrations more easily because of this. Young infants are the center of attention, cherished, fussed over, gratified, protected.

(2) As the gratified, relatively anxiety-free child gets older, between the ages of three through five, he is taught in various forcibly presented ways that he must accept definite limitations. There is a dramatic and marked diminution of indulgence by his caretakers, and he is pushed from the center of the household stage. This is a time of life when expectably another child may enter the household, but it occurs generally even to children who are the last born.

The child going through the period of his parent's withdrawal of indulgence typically goes through a brief period of rage and temper tantrums and begins to look sullen and depressed. At this time he is encouraged to enter the company of other children. He soon recovers and is in active and happy interaction with his peers. (This peer play in itself is markedly lacking in fights and confrontations.) I assume that the satisfaction of the first period makes the period of disindulgence by his household less traumatic by far than would have been the case if his core orientations were anxious and insecure.

(3) As the child leaves the infant stage he encounters a situation which becomes most marked about the time of his disindulgence and that is that he is managed, controlled, socialized, educated, not primarily by a single adult or a pair of adults but by a whole network of classificatory siblings and parents. The effects of having socialization messages passed on through such a diffuse network are complex, but for the question of aggression one of the major implications seems to be a sense that social frustrations are not caused by one or two specific individuals against whom one can rebel, or with whom one can deal by one or another strategy of seduction, rebellion, or evasion but rather by a whole system against which one is powerless to deal by any external, struggling activity. One gets a sense of resignation. The system has its rules to which one must adapt.

It is important to note again that a frustration which is considered to be somehow arbitrary is capable of evoking much more aggression than frustration considered to be in the nature of things. We do not usually get angry because we cannot walk through walls but must seek a relatively distant door. The frustrations of the "inevitable" are most generally not met with rage. We recognize Dylan Thomas',

> Do not go gentle into that good night.
> Rage, rage against the dying of the light.

as a wistful, childlike, immature (and thus poorly socialized) residue of innocent hope.

(4) There are cultural forms directed against aggression, in the general sense of "aggression" as the changing of the given structure of things, the given situation. The training against general aggression is subtle. Not only is the child taught through the structure of the socialization system that it is difficult to resist or change social reality, but there are a number of other significant institutional patterns which also convey this message. For example, the very prevalent custom of adoption—more than half of the homes in the rural community are involved in adoption—seems to have the purport and meaning that the society as a whole has dominance over individual relationships and, thus, individual striving. Furthermore, the main perceived symbolic message of the required ritual for adolescent males of dorsal incision of the foreskin of the penis is that adult masculine sexuality is dangerous, but that these dangers can be healed and reintegrated with the help of socially mediated resources of nature. Masculinity, striving, and aggression are dangerous, but cooperation with nature will be successful.

In a more direct way general aggressive behavior is suppressed, in that the kinds of behaviors which socializers pay attention to and punish are precisely those which disrupt the peaceful order of things. "Aggression" is that which activates the family training system, which brings about punishment. Achievement is not rewarded, risk is not encouraged, but making a disturbance is punished.

(5) In regard to socialization patterns *specifically* directed to hostile behavior there is a clear, dependably repeated set of reactions to children. Small children are permitted and in fact encouraged to exhibit brief, explosive aggressive behavior in response

to clear frustration and annoyance. However, prolonged sulking, vengeful continuing hostility, and hostility thought to be unjustified are discouraged in various ways. One of the most common is the use of vague threats. "You will get beat up." "Something will happen to you." Then, at a later period, when a child has an accident or is hurt, caretakers will say, "It serves you right. This is what you deserve." Timidity is encouraged and cultivated. People are pleased when their children become socially timid. Retaliations from socializers or nature are promised, which will come inevitably and at some unexpected future time to those who are too hostile or vengeful or proud or cocky or ambitious, who are not humble, cooperative, and gentle. Such vague threats, enlisting nature, irresistible, coming from anywhere, also avoid the outcome for learning produced by being beaten by others for aggression, which, as has been frequently pointed out, leads to the child's learning aggression as a coping mechanism by modeling on or identifying with the behavior of the punishers. And as an accident will always occur to a child, the threat is always confirmed.

(6) There is great cultural clarity about the nature of hostile aggression. There is a large vocabulary bearing on nuances of hostile action, clear cultural doctrine about which behavioral states are expression of hostility (e.g., suicide), and a great deal of cultural doctrine about the effects of hostility and what to do about it. It is felt that intense or continued hostility is dangerous to the body, that it should be expressed verbally to the person who is its object in order that dangerous chronic long-term feelings of hostility and chronic social effects should not be maintained. It is also felt that severe and chronic hostility is very dangerous because it can lead to magic consequences, the activation of protective ancestral spirits, which will often cause, in a complicated doctrine of retaliation, the death of the angry person himself. Compared to many other emotional areas in the traditional culture, such as loneliness and deprivation, the vocabulary and doctrine concerning anger is enormously developed. It is "hypercognated," and this very clarity is one factor in its control.

(7) Doctrine about anger states that anything more than a transient verbal expression of anger is wrong, that it is an indication of a lack of self-control and of competence. That is, it is a

matter for shame. People who find themselves with hostile feelings in spite of the various compelling controls will not express them if they have a wish to be regarded as a competent citizen and to avoid feelings of shame which are, for various reasons, particularly disturbing to traditionally oriented Tahitians.

Note that it has been necessary to include a number of influences which are not in any *direct* way directed to the socialization of hostile aggression. It is an unjustified simplification to think that effective training for any trait is only that which the socializers themselves (or a naive behavioristic theory of learning) take to be directed to the production of a trait. In fact, those training behaviors directed narrowly to the production of a trait very often have unintended outcomes. The child learns something else than the socializer (or experimenter) intends.

Let us summarize the presumed effects of these disparate influences. There is a calm, non-anxious, core sense that the world is basically dependable and non-threatening. But there is also a strong sense that the gratification of one's desires must be limited. This frustration is in the nature of things, and thus unavoidable. But if one *does* try to violate limits, there will be automatic retaliation, punishment, rebalancing. However, acceptance of limits, cooperation with nature and the group, will work, one will be supported dependably within these limits. If one becomes angry, cultural forms provide clear definitions of what is going on, and what one should do about it. Anger is felt as disruptive to the self and to relationships. It should be expressed verbally with a discussion of its interpersonal causes, in the hope that chronic effects will not result. Anger which is not so handled, and mastered, is considered to represent a regressive lack of control, and if other people become aware of an individual's failure in mastering it, this is a cause for shame.

For an individual on whom these various socialization influences have acted, in whom the whole set of effects has been produced, there is a pervasive, redundant set of controls tending toward gentle behavior. He will not get angry often, when he does he will be uncomfortable about it, fearful about it, and will resolve it as quickly as possible.

II.

The conception of a series of rather different kinds of influences all shaping Tahitian behavior toward gentleness has various implications.

(1) "Gentleness" is a behavior which from the point of view of psychological organization is a *surface* behavior. Its underlying structure may be of varying kinds.

(2) Those behaviors which a given culture emphasizes, which are salient, controlled by dominant values, necessary for its particular socio-environmental adaptations—are *necessarily produced and controlled by a redundant set of influences*. All stable systems use redundant sets of controls to maintain essential variables. (The control of oxygen levels in animal physiology is an example.) Gentleness is a salient adaptive behavior in traditional Tahitian society, as competitiveness was in the changing European society after the industrial revolution. If a behavior is relatively indifferent to a society the extent of redundant control should be less. This is in part by definition as the judgment as to importance of a behavior is in itself based on the extent of the control systems which maintain it.

(3) Among those societies which emphasize a particular trait such as gentleness, what will characterize them is most likely to be not a particular child-rearing technique which will produce a resulting underlying structure which in turn will explain the trait— but rather a particular *pattern of controls* for that trait. One would expect the Tahitian pattern of controls for gentleness to differ from that of other gentle groups in its overall patterning, even though some elements of control may be the same.

(4) The pattern of control is redundant in that various kinds of controls bearing on different psychological sub-systems have a similar import for action, although they have different forms. This is different from the idea expressed in early configurational theories of culture that many cultural areas have the same shape—child rearing, myths, adult relational patterns—with redundantly configurational force acting to shape behavior.

(5) The controls are not only redundant but to some degree hierarchical. That is, from the point of view of the individual those controls which are learned or "internalized" earlier in his or her life are more pervasive and forceful than those learned later. They are "ego syntonic" and "natural." They may also be more generalized, relevant to a wider variety of behavior systems than later ones. To the degree that an earlier established behavioral control doesn't operate, then a later control will be "activated." Thus if the common sense assumptions about the resistance of the social and physical environment to aggression do not hold, an individual contemplating or beginning aggressive action will feel shame for his "deviance," and the feelings of shame will control his action.

(6) If a given culture is characterized by a hierarchy of redundant behavioral controls for each socially important trait (and thus by a cluster of redundant controls for the full set of important cultural traits) then there is a limited, culturally specific set of *personality types* in regard to a particular behavior (or cluster of behaviors) within a given culture. Each type is determined by the specific way in which selected controls from the cultural set combine to produce an individual's behavior in relation to, say, gentleness or aggression. That is, not all controls are learned by all individuals. An only child in a small household would not be affected by being socialized through a diffuse network. A favorite child may not experience the distancing from indulgence that most children go through. A child of a temperamentally more choleric parent may be hit more than he is threatened in punishment and may tend to learn aggression by identification. Such children will be non-aggressive (assuming that the entire control system doesn't fail) in different ways, which should be open to empirical study. They will behave differently. They will be personality subtypes within the general and culturally specific pattern of redundant control of the culture. But they will be limited and characterized by options within that culturally determined control set.

(7) I have argued that Tahitian gentleness does not suggest through symptoms in the autonomic-visceral, voluntary muscular, or symbolic psychological systems that it is tenuously controlled, a matter of "forces" in obvious struggle with each other. This observation is crucial for what is usually involved in the slippery

question of "are human beings basically aggressive or basically gentle?" The question is ideologically stated: When people act gently is it because they are suppressing biological aggression with social help? Or (if one's ideology is contrary) when people act aggressively are they stirred to it by social pathologies and frustrations? As the capability for aggression is always humanly present, as are a multitude of other capabilities, the significant question about non-aggression seems to me to be, is it built into the systematics of people (in particular cultures, or learning environments) as a relatively cost-free integrated aspect of their personalities, or as costly, conflicted, stressful types of control? These later systems may be referred to as "basically aggressive"; the first can be so called only for the purposes of saving some simplistic biological theory of human nature. The Tahitians have potentialities for hostile aggression. They have learned to construct themselves so that they are not "basically aggressive." They do not generally have to *suppress* hostility in themselves, they are structured to minimize the problem.

III.

"Why are Tahitians gentle?" If a complex and subtle set of controls exists to produce gentleness this leads to a next question. How does a group as part of their culture arrive at the subtle techniques which will produce a given kind of behavior? This would not be a problem if the behavior was adaptationally trivial—for techniques and resulting behavior would have originated as a circular, interdependent package because of historical factors. But suppose that gentleness, aggressiveness, bravery, competitiveness, independence, and so on, are behavioral traits which are specifically necessary for technological and social adaptations to various kinds of environments. One can speculate on the sequence going from childhood experience through learning to resultant behavior. But the part of the adaptive cycle going from those parts of an environmental situation which are compelling, which must be adapted to, to the production of one of the possible sets of behaviors which are adaptive in that environment is not a simple one. For ultimately the question of "Why are Tahitians gentle?" is answered in that gentleness for these island horticulturalists and fishermen is one of a series of traits—those which have to do with adaptation to a sufficient, dependable, steady-state, delicate ecology—which are highly successful in their particular Polynesian environment.[4] How did the Tahitians develop the mechanisms for insuring the psychological stability of these behaviors? It is one thing to sense the desirability of a trait, to value it—but something rather more difficult to produce it.

If it is so that mechanisms for the production of an adaptive trait are complex, subtle, pervasive, redundant, and hierarchical, we are faced with the interesting question bearing on the feedback loops from situations to cultural adaptations, how do these mechanisms develop in the history of a culture?

NOTES

1. Ethnographic detail and the other behaviors which form a context for gentleness are reported in *Tahitians*. The material on aggression and socialization is presented in this paper in a partial and summary form for the purposes of the argument.
2. The ethnographic present as of the early 1960's is used in this paper. The two communities which I studied have changed greatly since then.
3. For an example of the complex ways in which culturally shaped learning may produce cognitive assumptions in middle-class American culture, see Levy, 1975.
4. The picture is complicated by intermediate social and political adaptations. The Tahitian adaptation represents a successful adaptation to the environment following the destruction of the old genealogically based system of Chiefs.

BIBLIOGRAPHY

Ellis, William 1830 *Polynesian Researches*. London: Fisher, Son, and Jackson.
Forster, George 1777 *A Voyage Round the World . . . in the Years 1772, 1773, 1774, 1775*. 2 vols. London: B. White.

Forster, John 1778 *Observations Made During a Voyage Round the World.* London: G. Robinson.

Levy, Robert I. 1973 *Tahitians: Mind and Experience in the Society Islands.* Chicago: University of Chicago Press.

——— 1975 "A Conjunctive Pattern in Middle Class Informal and Formal Education." *Ethos,* 3:269–79.

Morrison, James 1935 *The Journal of James Morrison.* London: Golden Cockerel Press.

Turnbull, John 1812 *A Voyage Round the World in the Years 1800, 1801, 1802, 1803 and 1804.* London: A. Maxwell.